Harrison Birtwistle

Jonathan Cross is a Lecturer in Mus
He has written and lectured extens
century music, and is author of *The S*
is also Associate Editor of *Music An*

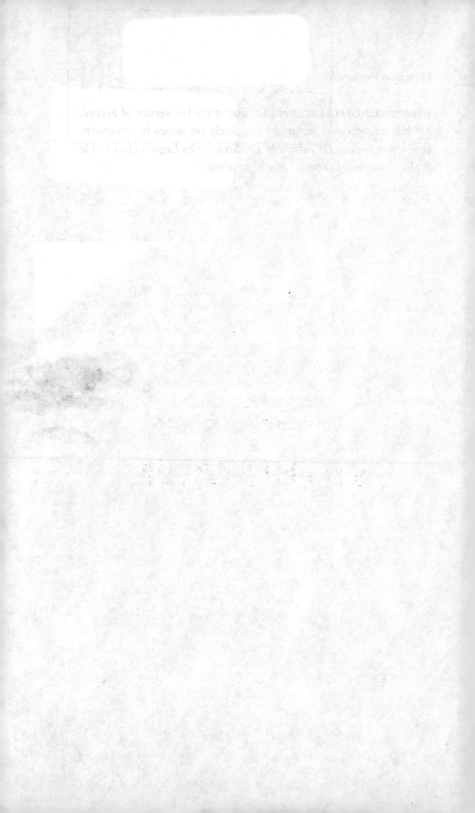

Harrison Birtwistle

MAN, MIND, MUSIC

Jonathan Cross

faber and faber

First published in 2000
by Faber and Faber Limited
3 Queen Square London WC1N 3AU

Typeset by Faber and Faber Ltd
Printed in England by Clays Ltd, St Ives plc

A CIP record for this book
is available from the British Library

ISBN 0-571-19345-5

10 9 8 7 6 5 4 3 2 1

To my mother and father

Contents

Prologue – Preface and Acknowledgements

The work of Harrison Birtwistle occupies a significant place in twentieth-century Western art and is arguably among the most exciting, original and challenging music ever to have been produced by a British composer. The origins of his thinking are clearly rooted in early European modernism – in the music of Debussy, Stravinsky, Varèse and Webern, and in the painting and ideas of Cézanne, Klee and Picasso – while his work stands alongside and shares aspects of the aesthetics of, among others, Berio, Boulez, Messiaen and Stockhausen. The ability of his music to speak powerfully to performers and public alike lies partly in its obsessiveness, in its ongoing exploration of the basic and primeval aspects of music and the human psyche. It has often been commented that Birtwistle is a single-minded composer who, in some senses, writes the same piece over and over again: even he has implied as much in his comment that 'Pieces don't really start: they're part of a continuous process'.[1] Meirion Bowen's description of him, after Isaiah Berlin, as the hedgehog who 'knows one big thing'[2] remains pertinent. What this 'one big thing' is, however, is difficult to define, but it seems in essence to be something tragic, and involves an instinctive understanding – in Nietzsche's terms[3] – of the primordial impulses of Dionysus which he attempts to contain (sometimes barely: witness the furore over the première of *Panic* in 1995) within the rational forms of Apollo.

Birtwistle is, appropriately, a man of few words. His music suggests and attempts to articulate those truths which language is incapable of expressing. Like Stravinsky, like Cézanne, Birtwistle's art is generally concerned with the universal rather than the particular, with the collective rather than the individual, with landscape rather than portrait. Hence his preoccupation with myth and ritual, with formal theatre and stylized drama, with contexts that can give shape to these deep feelings and ideas. And hence his obsession with simple musical structures – such as verse-refrain forms – and with the very basics of musical language – pulse, melody, repetition, variation. Every one of Birtwistle's works, from the largest-scale 'opera' such as *The Mask of Orpheus* to the smallest-scale study such as *Hoquetus Petrus*, explores these musical fundamentals, these universal human truths.

In this book I do *not* attempt to catalogue Harrison Birtwistle's complete life and works to date. Rather, my principal aim is to uncover the sources and functions of the composer's aesthetic, to present a critical account of his musical, dramatic and philosophical development and preoccupations, and to examine his major works for concert hall and opera house in these contexts. Birtwistle has often likened his musical processes to viewing a three-dimensional object from many different angles; likewise, I structure this book by topics rather than works, attempting to come to an understanding of the mind of the composer through an examination of his output in a variety of ways and from many different perspectives. But I also adopt a literary conceit which I hope Birtwistle himself will enjoy. The formal structures of Attic tragedy have been a continuing source of fascination for the composer, and many of his works – and by no means only his stage works – have taken on the characteristics of ancient Greek theatre. In a book concerned with the tragic nature of this composer's art, in a book whose various episodes seem continually and inevitably to go over the same ground from new perspectives, it seemed to me utterly appropriate that my ideas too should be shaped according to some abstract notion of Greek tragedy. Thus, the *parados*, the first entry of the chorus, sets the scene for the unfolding of the drama, and provides a context within which the narrative can be interpreted; various *episodes* follow, which reveal different but related aspects of the protagonist's character; at the centre-point of the drama stands the *stasimon*, the still centre around which all the other ideas turn, being the moment of *anagnorisis* or self-recognition; and the closing *exodos* ties together the strands of the narrative and looks forward to the future. So, echoing Choregos, the Greek chorus leader, at the start of *Punch and Judy*, I entreat the reader 'please to enjoy our littel play'. . .

Though only one name is credited as author on the cover of this book, there has been a vast, hidden support team working away behind the scenes. I can here do little more than list these individuals' names, but this does scant justice to the fact that, without their many and varied contributions, this book would never have been written at all. To all who helped me find materials, commented on drafts, criticized, supported, encouraged and cajoled, I owe an immense debt of gratitude: Michael Durnin and, especially, Belinda Matthews at Faber and Faber, David Allenby at Boosey & Hawkes, Miranda Jackson at Universal Edition, Craig Ayrey, Margaret and John Cross, Tim Cross, Emma Dillon, John Pickard, Jim Samson, Jane and Peter Slade, Arnold Whittall, Anna Williams and, of course, Emma, Alice and Rebecca. I am very grateful to Richard Huw Cole for his expert setting of many of the music examples. And I should also like to thank Harry himself – the alpha and omega of this project – for his immense generosity, personal and creative. His music has been an inspiration to generations; if I have only one hope for this book, then it is that it will engage further generations of the musically curious and enthuse them to discover such deep pleasure as I continue to find in the extraordinarily passionate and beautiful music of Harrison Birtwistle.

J.C.

BRADFORD-ON-AVON

MARCH 1999

The publishers are grateful to Boosey & Hawkes and Universal Edition for permission to reproduce music examples from the works listed below. All works are by Harrison Birtwistle unless otherwise stated.

1.1 *Four Songs of Autumn* © 1988 by Universal Edition (London) Ltd.
1.2 *Agon* by Igor Stravinsky © 1957 by Hawkes & Son (London) Ltd.
1.3 *Punch and Judy* © 1968 by Universal Edition (London) Ltd.
1.4 *Refrains and Choruses* © 1961 by Universal Edition (London) Ltd.
1.5 *Secret Theatre* © 1991 by Universal Edition (London) Ltd.
1.6 *Melencolia I* © 1977 by Universal Edition (London) Ltd.
1.7 *Refrains and Choruses* ©1961 by Universal Edition (London) Ltd.
2.1a/b *Verses for Ensembles* © 1969 by Universal Edition (London) Ltd.
2.2 *Secret Theatre* © 1991 by Universal Edition (London) Ltd.
3.1–3 *The Second Mrs Kong* © 1994 by Universal Edition (London) Ltd.
3.4 *The Mask of Orpheus* © 1986 by Universal Edition (London) Ltd.
3.5 *Panic* © 1996 by Boosey & Hawkes Music Publishers Ltd.
3.7 *The Mask of Orpheus* © 1986 by Universal Edition (London) Ltd.
4.1 *Down by the Greenwood Side* © 1969 by Universal Edition (London) Ltd.
4.2, 5.1, 5.2 *Verses for Ensembles* © 1969 by Universal Edition (London) Ltd.
5.3 *Antiphonies* © 1992 by Universal Edition (London) Ltd.
5.4 *The World is Discovered* © 1963 by Universal Edition (London) Ltd.
5.5 *Pulse Shadows (Frieze 1)* by Harrison Birtwistle/Paul Celan/Michael Hamburger © 1998 by Boosey & Hawkes Music Publishers Ltd. and Universal Edition (London) Ltd.
6.1 *Pulse Sampler* © 1981 by Universal Edition (London) Ltd.
6.2–3 *For O, for O, the Hobby-Horse is Forgot* © 1976 by Universal Edition (London) Ltd.
6.4–6 *Silbury Air* © 1979 by Universal Edition (London) Ltd.
6.7 *9 Settings of Celan (White and Light)* by Harrison Birtwistle/Paul Celan/Michael Hamburger © 1997 by Boosey & Hawkes Music Publishers Ltd. and Universal Edition (London) Ltd.
7.1 *Melencolia I* © 1977 by Universal Edition (London) Ltd.
7.2 *The Cry of Anubis* © 1996 by Boosey & Hawkes Music Publishers Ltd.
7.3 *Endless Parade* © 1987 by Universal Edition (London) Ltd.
7.4 *The Triumph of Time* © 1974 by Universal Edition (London) Ltd.
7.5a/b *Gawain* © 1990 by Universal Edition (London) Ltd.
7.6 *Duets for Storab* © 1983 by Universal Edition (London) Ltd.
7.7 *Symphonies of Wind Instruments* (1947 version) by Igor Stravinsky

© 1926 by Hawkes & Son (London) Ltd. Revised version © 1948, 1952 by Hawkes & Son (London) Ltd. U.S. copyright renewed

7.8a/b *Monody for Corpus Christi* © 1961 by Universal Edition (London) Ltd.

8.1 *Three Niedecker Verses, Number II* by Harrison Birtwistle/Lorine Niedecker © 1999 by Boosey & Hawkes Music Publishers Ltd. 'Mr Friend Tree' by Lorine Niedecker used by permission of the literary executor, Mr Cid Corman

Harrison Birtwistle

1 *Parados* – Origins, Contexts, Models

Northern Light

Birtwistle was born in the north of England, in the industrial Lancashire town of Accrington. This may seem a relatively insignificant fact of biography, but it throws interesting light on much of his later work. Anyone who hears Birtwistle talk even today will recognize immediately that he has lost little of his soft but gruff Lancastrian accent. Despite his many international successes, despite his prolonged periods of residence in the south of England, the United States, Scotland and France, despite even his espousal of a certain cosmopolitanism (he owns a modishly furnished flat in London's Docklands with commanding views of the River Thames), he seems to retain some of the manners and attitude of a working-class northerner. It is as if his roots are still firmly planted in his native region's soil, from which he continues to draw nourishment.

This manifests itself in part in the genres and subject matter Birtwistle has chosen to work with throughout his creative life. It is perhaps most obvious in the 1984 opera *Yan Tan Tethera*, which draws on a folk tale concerned with the rivalry between a northern and a southern shepherd, Alan and Caleb Raven. The libretto was provided by the Yorkshire-born poet Tony Harrison, with whom Birtwistle had collaborated on an earlier project at the National Theatre, *Bow Down* (based on versions of the northern/Scandinavian ballad of 'The Two Sisters'), as well as on the much-acclaimed *Oresteia* project in Harrison's dialect translation. *Yan Tan Tethera* employs an ancient northern dialect for its obsessive rituals of sheep-counting: yan, tan, tethera, methera, pimp . . . (1, 2, 3, 4, 5 . . .). Alan is reminded of his geographical and spiritual alienation (a northern shepherd in the south) each time he hears a mysterious piper playing a 'Northern air'. He sings:

I know there's a piper but don't know where
the tune always comes from behind me.
When I hear that piper play
I think of the north, and I don't want to stay,
Though my flock's growing bigger each day.

In order to resist the lure of the piper's tune, Alan also sings the 'Northern Shepherd's charm':

Yan, Tan, Tethera,
1–2–3
Sweet Trinity
Keep
Us and our sheep.

From this, it begins to become apparent how important a sense of place is to Birtwistle. Specific locations form the starting-points for a number of his works, such as the story of his witnessing a carnival in the medieval Italian walled town of Lucca which generated his trumpet concerto, *Endless Parade*, or the mysterious prehistoric Silbury Hill in Wiltshire which inspired *Silbury Air*. In *Yan Tan Tethera*, another Wiltshire hill even has its own music, while the Knight's Green Chapel in *Gawain* is resonant with mystical significance ('a place more like a hill than a house, more like a cave than a hill, more like a tomb than a cave'). But perhaps more important for him is a general notion of landscape, and in particular the English landscape. Landscapes, real or imaginary, are ubiquitous in Birtwistle's work. They are to be encountered in the Klee-like imaginary landscapes of *Silbury Air* and *An Imaginary Landscape*, in the geological strata of *Earth Dances*, in the reinterpretation of Arcadian landscapes in *Nenia: the Death of Orpheus*, *The Fields of Sorrow* and *The Mask of Orpheus*. Elsewhere, landscape acts as a background context defined in terms of omnipresent seasonal cycles, such as in *Down by the Greenwood Side*, *The Triumph of Time* and *Gawain*. Niklaus Pevsner has argued that such concerns are in general characteristic of English art and architecture: 'always line, not body'.[1] Hence the preference in England for the landscape garden. On William Blake, for example, Pevsner comments that '. . . his figures are not primarily representations of bodies, but part of an overall calligraphy . . . In other cases, where energy rather than abandon is intended, he forces figures into an imposed abstract geometry.' The English, concludes Pevsner, 'are not a sculptural nation' (he quotes Alexander Pope: 'A tree is a nobler object than a prince in his coronation robes').[2] These descriptions would also seem to apply to Birtwistle, a composer usually more concerned – even in his operas – with landscape/context than with figures/characters, more concerned with line and geometry than with representation. Whether or not his music is identifiably 'English' (and whether or not this is even a valid issue), there is no denying that his preference for British folk subject matter, his predilection for the pastoral, his exploration of the linear and the lyrical, locate him clearly within an English tradition. Despite his modernism and his full absorption of twentieth-century avant-garde ideas and techniques, it is still possible to see Birtwistle as having emerged from that English musical tradition of the late-nineteenth and early twentieth centuries represented by Elgar, Holst, Vaughan Williams, and even Britten and Tippett.

Birtwistle's (mostly no longer extant) pre-college pieces he has himself described as 'sub Vaughan Williams'.[3] A sense of landscape, a sense of place, is undeniable in the music of Vaughan Williams's *Hugh the Drover*, the 'Pastoral' Symphony and *Sinfonia Antartica*, and in Holst's *Egdon Heath*. And it could be argued that Birtwistle also shares with these English predecessors the expression of some sort of collective 'folk' (via an essentially lyrical modality), rather than identifying with any particular individual. This also implies a certain distance from the ideas and materials being represented, something which Pevsner explained in relation to English Gothicism as 'an expression of the narrative as against the purely aesthetic interest . . . [I]t can also be seen as a sign of detachment, as against passionate single-mindedness.'[4] The narrative line is key to Birtwistle, though rarely is it expressed simply, singly or unequivocally.

The 'detachment' of which Pevsner wrote manifests itself in Birtwistle's music in various ways. It is, in large part, an obvious consequence of Birtwistle's deep debt to Stravinsky, whose music's objectivity – its playfulness, its sense of irony and critical distance from the musical materials, its positive celebration of collective ritual – has proved provocative and creatively fruitful for so many composers in the twentieth century. Stravinsky's balancing of the 'natural' and the 'artificial' – if you like, the tempering of the passionate with the objective, the complement of the Dionysian and the Apollonian – is, as Daniel Albright has argued, at the heart of Stravinsky's aesthetic, and is most clearly symbolized by the opposition between the live (chromatic) and mechanical (diatonic) birds in *The Nightingale*:

> This, I think, is what Stravinsky's music is 'about': the deep equivalence of the natural and the artificial. At the center of his dramatic imagination is the desire to juxtapose in a single work two competing systems – one which seems natural, tasteful, approved alike by man and God, the other of which seems artificial, abhorrent, devilish – and to subvert these distinctions as best he can.[5]

The incorporation of the natural and the mechanical in the work of Stravinsky's major successors, such as Messiaen's use of 'natural' bird-song within the context of highly repetitive, artificial block structures (*Chronochromie*, *Couleurs de la cité céleste*, etc.), manifests itself in Birtwistle's notion of the 'mechanical pastoral' – the subtitle of *Yan Tan Tethera*. *Carmen Arcadiae Mechanicae Perpetuum*, which preceded the opera by six years, is based on the imaginary song of a mechanical bird (the subject of Klee's 1922 painting *The Twittering Machine*) and is a perfect example of mechanical pastoral as well as a clear indicator of the importance of both Stravinsky and Messiaen as models for Birtwistle.

Unlike Holst and Vaughan Williams, examples of pure or simple pastoral are infrequent in Birtwistle. The idea of a mechanical pastoral suggests that the 'rural' ('natural') is somehow tempered by the 'urban' ('manufactured') and vice versa. This usefully takes us back to Birtwistle's Lancashire upbringing. His father was a farmer and his childhood home was a smallholding on the edge of Accrington, at the point where the black industrial town met the moorland. Looking back, Birtwistle describes it as 'paradise', a kind of Arcadia; it still lives with him. D. H. Lawrence's descriptions of the coal towns of Nottinghamshire are perhaps not so dissimilar from Birtwistle's early experiences of industrial landscapes: '... all over the countryside were these same pits ... the few colliers and the donkeys burrowing down like ants into the earth, making queer mounds and little black places among the corn-fields and the meadows'.[6] Accrington was not a coal- but a mill-town; nonetheless, the young Harry grew up with the co-existence of industry and countryside, of factory chimneys and sheep, of workers' terraces and farmhouses. And a concern for *rus in urbe* is, according to Pevsner, 'eminently English',[7] and is entirely characteristic of Birtwistle. *Panic*, for instance, is a Dionysian celebration of the nature god Pan for the decidedly urban soloists of saxophone and drum kit plus orchestra of wind and percussion (no strings). His two works for brass band, *Grimethorpe Aria* and *Salford Toccata*, demonstrate a sympathy for and affinity with the sounds of industrial northern working-class music-making, though again this musical world is tempered by its opposite. In the case of *Grimethorpe Aria* (commissioned by his fellow Manchester student, Elgar Howarth, for the Grimethorpe Colliery Band), an elegiac, endless melody – the eponymous aria – sings its way through the piece, while the rest of the band punctuates, supports, interrupts and occasionally overwhelms it. The relative (quasi-modal) simplicity of the song has an almost folk-like freedom which contrasts with the ensemble's 'hard-edged' sounds and stronger rhythmic organization: as clear a musical representation as one could wish of *rus in urbe*.

Birtwistle began principally as a clarinettist, not a composer. At the age of seven, with the local bandmaster as teacher, he took clarinet lessons, soon joining the Accrington military band, and later playing for local drama society and pantomime performances. So it was that his formative musical experiences were more of (amateur) working-class music-making than, necessarily, of (professional) middle-class concert halls. These industrial sounds – of wind, brass and percussion (he has a self-confessed discomfort with writing for strings) – have dominated his sonic imagination ever since. The majority of his works feature solo or prominent woodwind or brass instruments – from *Nomos* (for orchestra with amplified solo flute, clarinet, horn and bassoon) to *The Cry of Anubis* (tuba concerto), from *Verses* (clarinet and piano) to the Clarinet Quintet – while the sounds of the wind band are evident in the scoring of such works as *Verses for Ensembles* and *Panic*. The vast orchestra for *The Mask of Orpheus* contains no strings and the sound of a pair of tubas dominates *Gawain*. It would, of course, be all too easy to make some direct causal connection between Birtwistle's scorings and his early musical experiences; it is more likely that this upbringing fostered a certain predilection for these sounds which then led him in the direction of those modernist composers who shared his sonic preferences: Stravinsky, Varèse, Messiaen. Wind writing *in extremis* is clearly characteristic of some of the most striking works of Stravinsky and Varèse (from the famous high bassoon opening of *The Rite of Spring* to the squealing E♭ clarinet of *Octandre*), while those works which have made the deepest impression on Birtwistle are scored for 'wind band': Stravinsky's *Symphonies of Wind Instruments* and *Symphony of Psalms*, Messiaen's *Couleurs de la cité céleste* and *Et expecto resurrectionem mortuorum*.

As a child, Birtwistle would have had little experience of musical modernism. He claims to have had a recording of one immensely influential work, *The Rite of Spring*,[8] but otherwise performances of contemporary music outside London were few and far between. Access to published scores was equally difficult. Another key work for Birtwistle was Messiaen's *Turangalîla-Symphonie* (itself modelled in part on *The Rite of Spring*)[9] which he discovered in 1954 while still a student at Manchester:

> I went to London with Sandy [Alexander] Goehr to hear his father do Turangalîla Symphony . . . As we got there [to stage

> level] they were doing the movement that begins with pure percussion. That was an absolute magical moment for me. At that point, there was a one-to-one relationship with what I had imagined, and saw it was possible.[10]

The movement he is referring to is the 'Développement de l'amour'. What is fascinating here is his creative *mis*-hearing of Messiaen: the movement does *not* begin with *pure* percussion, but *only* the percussion has remained imprinted on Birtwistle's memory. He is a blinkered, single-minded composer; he only hears what he wants to hear, in the way he wants to hear it. And, in many senses, such 'mishearing' is indicative in general of his approach to composition. As with Stravinsky, repetition is at the heart of Birtwistle's music, and yet things rarely repeat exactly: 'There are things that keep repeating, but if you listen to them or look at them closely, they're not repeating.'[11] Birtwistle relies creatively on his 'flawed' memory when reworking already given musical situations: 'I decide what the order is, through my ears, through my intuition . . .'[12]

> If I arrive at a context where a procedure is required, I will always invent or re-invent a procedure. I will never look back to see how I did it before. That would be too academic. I think that's what's wrong with some of Messiaen's music. He finds a way of doing something and repeats it verbatim. So, apart from very rare exceptions, I either create something new or call on memory in order to make every situation unique.[13]

The Manchester Generation

It was as a clarinettist that Birtwistle won a scholarship to the Royal Manchester College of Music (now the Royal Northern College of Music) in 1952, studying with Frederick Thurston (clarinet) and Richard Hall (composition). Although he has stated that 'I think what I'd always wanted to do, right from the beginning, was write music',[14] nonetheless he was known primarily as a clarinettist throughout his time at Manchester. Goehr confirms the fact that Birtwistle was hardly composing, though (forty years on) he claims even then to have recognized Birtwistle's potential and originality.[15] Hardly any music survives before his first acknowledged work, *Refrains and Choruses* (1957): we often hear the (apocryphal) story of the symbolic selling of his clarinets the moment he heard this work had been selected by the Society for Promotion of New Music for performance at the 1959 Cheltenham Festival.

One short piece which does survive, and which recently came to public light in a recording by Stephen Pruslin,[16] dates from *c.*1950. The *Oockooing Bird* for piano, a copy of which – in the composer's hand – is now in Pruslin's possession, is a fascinating gem of juvenilia because so many of the composer's later preoccupations already seem to be present here in embryonic form. Its title refers to an imaginary bird of the composer's invention and whose presence foreshadows those many mythical people and creatures who populate the later works, from Father Christmas to King Kong, from the twittering birds of *Carmen Arcadiae Mechanicae Perpetuum* to the singing sheep of *Yan Tan Tethera*. Here, the bird's song is expressed by the falling fourths and thirds of the piano melody, and is placed in the simplest ritualized context of a kind of verse structure built from a varied ostinato pattern. Its essentially mixolydian modality (though chromaticisms do intrude in the later stages of the piece) and insistent parallel thirds invoke, among others, Debussy, while its closing chorale-like texture strangely parallels the endings of so many of Stravinsky's works (without sounding at all like Stravinsky). The piece's extraordinary poise, its confident control of very limited musical materials and its sense of dramatic pacing suggest a compositional imagination rare in one so young and reveal those features which have made Birtwistle's later music so distinctive. And it is interesting that the composer is still quite proud of this piece, of its symmetries, of (prophetically) the way it views the same limited material from changing perspectives. One other striking feature of this music is its neo-medievalism, again a prominent feature of much of the later music, and an interest that was also to be shared at Manchester by Peter Maxwell Davies and Alexander

Goehr. While the young Birtwistle was not consciously invoking medieval precedents, its modality and its essential structural simplicity have remained features of even Birtwistle's most complex orchestral works; the fascination with medieval music later manifested itself in, for example, arrangements of Machaut (*Hoquetus David*, *Machaut à ma manière*), the use of hoquet technique (most explicitly in *Hoquetus Petrus*), the exploration of a renewed kind of 'cantus firmus' technique (he literally employs the term 'cantus' for the omnipresent line of *Secret Theatre*) and even, as Michael Hall has extensively demonstrated,[17] another *ars nova* technique of isorhythm (also found in, for example, Maxwell Davies and Messiaen). Furthermore, central to Birtwistle's modernist aesthetic are such features as anti-narrative, ritual and ceremony, ostinato, drone, the processional, new kinds of (timeless or non-directed) time, even a certain naïve boldness or simplicity, all of which echo the medieval. This medieval fascination is not, among modernists, uniquely Birtwistle's,[18] but what is of particular interest here is how early this manifested itself in Birtwistle's music and how persistent a feature it has remained (however heavily disguised).

The Royal Manchester College has come to be identified with the renewal of British music in the 1950s and beyond, and in particular with its harbouring of a generation of composers and performers who excitedly embraced modernism and the avant-garde – the so-called 'Manchester School'.They were groundbreakers in many ways. For a start, as state-funded grammar-school boys their backgrounds were very different from the privileged upbringings of previous generations of London-based composers. They breathed a different air; they were less constrained by convention. It was almost by chance that Birtwistle, Maxwell Davies and Goehr, the pianist John Ogdon (in 1962 the first British winner of the Tchaikovsky Prize) and the trumpeter and conductor Elgar Howarth were studying in the same place at the same time. As northerners by birth, Manchester was perhaps the obvious point of gravitation for four of these. For Goehr, son of the émigré German conductor and Schoenberg pupil, Walter

Goehr, it was a definite choice to study at this provincial college, principally because of its professor of composition, Richard Hall. According to Goehr, Hall 'wasn't a firebrand . . . He was of a speculative turn of mind, very different from the kind of people who normally taught music in colleges or universities. The alternative would have been Lennox Berkeley (at the Royal Academy in London). Hall was a different kind of man.'[19] Berkeley had studied in Paris with Nadia Boulanger and his many distinguished pupils included David Bedford, Richard Rodney Bennett, Brian Ferneyhough, Nicholas Maw and John Tavener. Nonetheless, his Roussel-like neoclassicism stood in stark contrast to what Goehr dubs 'a certain Central European feeling' about Manchester. There was a 'Busoni tradition' there, Hall's classes being 'anti-Stravinskian, anti-Nadia Boulanger';[20] this was clearly far more in tune with Goehr's own Teutonic background.

But what of Birtwistle, who had never left Lancashire? What did he learn from his years in Manchester? Thirty years later, he claimed he did not know what his lessons with Richard Hall had meant: 'I didn't know how to identify the music I wrote with what I was being taught.'[21] What he was being taught by Hall was a kind of serial technique – Goehr claims they were being prepared to understand principles such as hexachordal twelve-tone systems. But it was principally through Goehr, the group's intellectual leader, that together these musicians 'discovered', among other things, the music of the Second Viennese School and the latest continental developments. 'I think I moved the dominant influence in the Hall class away from Busoni and towards Schoenberg', writes Goehr.[22] It was, for example, at a Manchester performance of Berg's Four Pieces for Clarinet and Piano, Op. 5 given by Birtwistle and Goehr that they first met Maxwell Davies. Until this time, many key works of early musical modernism were simply inaccessible to British music students, and in any case a deeply rooted attitude prevailed that such music was either unimportant or corruptive. The story is often told of the refusal of the Royal College of Music to buy a score of *Pierrot lunaire* for Benjamin Britten and of the refusal of Sir Hugh Allen (the college's principal) to allow him to study in Vienna with Berg. Britten later recalled: 'There was at that time [the 1930s] an almost moral prejudice against serial music – which makes one laugh today! [1963]'[23]

In order more fully to explore the works of the continental avant-garde as well as to play their own compositions, in 1953 these young musicians formed the New Music Manchester group. Their one-and-only London concert was organized in 1955 by William Glock, music critic, founder of the Bryanston (later the Dartington International) Summer School and, from 1959, influential trailblazer of modernism as Controller of Music at the BBC. The programme included Goehr's *Songs of Babel*, Piano Sonata and Fantasias for Clarinet and Piano, Maxwell Davies's Sonata for Trumpet and Piano, plus works by Elizabeth Lutyens and Hall. Birtwistle played, but none of his music was performed. After this, the composers intermittently cooperated on other projects as outlets for their own music – for example, all three helped establish the short-lived Wardour Castle Summer Schools in 1964, and Birtwistle and Maxwell Davies set up the Pierrot Players in 1967. But since the reconstitution of the Pierrot Players as The Fires of London in 1970, the three have worked independently and have moved in very different musical directions. What they shared in the 1950s was a virtually unique curiosity and enthusiasm for the brave new world of the post-World War II continental avant-garde. It is an interesting fact that this was the first generation of composers who chose to proceed to institutions beyond Britain to further their studies (Goehr to Paris, Maxwell Davies to Rome and then Princeton, Birtwistle to Princeton and Colorado). And while the music of Stravinsky and the Second Viennese School was certainly known in London (Schoenberg, Webern and Stravinsky, as well as Strauss, had all conducted their own works with the BBC Symphony Orchestra in its early days), very few British composers had taken it seriously. Those who did, such as Frank Bridge and Elizabeth Lutyens, were shamefully marginalized. The shared engagement by the 'Manchester School' with both pre- and post-war modernism was unprecedented. It changed the face of British music for good.

Birtwistle's Modernism

From the (unconscious) Debussy-like concerns of his early piano pieces and his knowledge of *The Rite of Spring*, from his discoveries in Manchester of Viennese modernism and the contemporary avant-garde, from his self-acknowledged debt to, among others, Webern, Varèse and Stravinsky, Picasso and Klee, it should by now be clear that Birtwistle's art is firmly rooted in early European modernism. The primitivism of his music, its formality, its concern with ritualized, anti-narrative structures and with myth, its interest in rhythm and in constructing new kinds of temporality are all clear indicators of his engagement with that modernist tradition. He is still single-mindedly ploughing his own modernist furrow, re-evaluating, reinterpreting and renewing that legacy for the *post*modern age. *How* he has worked both with and against the work of his modernist forebears is the principal subject of the remainder of this chapter.

Three Portraits

FORMAL LANDSCAPES: CÉZANNE

Presented recently by his interlocutor with a list of his 'favourite' painters – Piero della Francesca, Bruegel, Vermeer, Cézanne, Picasso, Bacon, Klee, Rothko – Birtwistle commented that he responded to these artists in particular because

> . . . I think that there's a formality; also, they all use the subject matter to express paint and painting, rather than the other way round. It's something you wouldn't get in Rembrandt for instance. I've never consciously formulated it, but I'm absolutely fascinated by it, and I'm much more interested in it than a lot of things in music.[24]

This analysis of the spirit of these painters – and which applies particularly to the modernists among them – could also stand for Birtwistle's own music and aligns him once again with that modernist thread associated with Stravinsky. It brings to mind, for example, Stravinsky's famous comment about *Oedipus Rex*: 'My audience is not indifferent to the fate of the person, but I think it far more concerned with the person of the fate, and the delineation of it which can be achieved uniquely in music.'[25] Birtwistle feels that, in Cézanne, the actual subject matter is almost an irrelevance;[26] it is the formal manner in which it is delineated that is of importance. And such formality manifests itself at every turn in his own work. This is not to say that his music is without passion or expression. Far from it: there are many highly expressive moments in his operas, from Judy's beautiful Passion Aria in *Punch and Judy* to the poignant final scene with Kong and Pearl in *The Second Mrs Kong*. But these moments are contained, framed, formalized, in a manner more akin to Baroque opera than to naturalistic nineteenth-century drama. Birtwistle has been drawn time and again to opera primarily because of the stylized formality of the genre: 'There are certain things you don't have to justify in an opera, and one of these is its formality . . . I am interested in exploring a different order of formality, a different ritual situation – possibly something to do with oriental theatre.'[27] This is as true of *Punch and Judy* as it is of *The Mask of Orpheus*. Hence Birtwistle's lifelong preoccupation with the function, significance and power of myth. It is the universal qualities of myths that appeal to him, their concern primarily with collective rather than individual experiences, even though those experiences may be focused on one individual such as Mr Punch or Orpheus. Rarely does Birtwistle concern himself with conventional kinds of operatic characterization and it is certainly difficult to identify directly with the characters one sees and hears on the stage. When Orpheus (represented in triplicate) dies many times and in different ways in *The Mask of Orpheus*, we do not weep because we are not looking at one man in a particular time and place, but at Everyman. Peter Zinovieff, the work's librettist, argues that Orpheus did not exist as an individual but is a collective inheritance. Thus, we are presented with multiple versions of the Orpheus legend in the one work. As with his favourite painters, so Birtwistle's favoured dramatic models are those which give a primacy to formality, to stylization, to ritual presentation: ancient Greek tragedy, Baroque opera, mystery plays, puppet theatre, Noh drama . . . and, more recently and perhaps surprisingly, film.

The importance of Cézanne as a leading figure in early modernism lies in part in his movement away from naturalism. Cézanne himself often commented on the autonomy of art – '*L'art est une harmonie parallèle à la nature*'[28] – a remark which obviously anticipates Stravinsky's famous (and misunderstood) comments on 'music about music':

> . . . music is, by its very nature, essentially powerless to *express* anything at all . . . (1935/1936)[29]

> *Pourquoi ne pas l'aimer [la musique] pour elle-même? Pourquoi ne pas l'aimer comme on aime un tableau, pour la belle peinture, le beau dessin, la belle composition? . . . Elle se suffit à elle-même* (1935)[30]

> . . . music is supra-personal and super-real and as such beyond verbal meanings and verbal descriptions . . . music expresses itself (1962)[31]

Cézanne's late paintings of Mont Sainte-Victoire in Provence, for example, illustrate this clearly. The traditional landscape subject matter with the ominous, mythical mountain in the background is transformed into something new in which form, shape, colour – the very formality of the painting – become its subject matter. It parallels the natural phenomena; it does not represent them directly. The abstract surfaces of these paintings make play of lines and colours, while also drawing attention to the balance between surface and depth. In Cézanne's words, 'Nature is not on the surface; it is in the depths. Colours are the surface expression of this depth.'[32] This also leads to a sense of timelessness to these paintings, both in the mythical permanence of the subject matter, and in the formalized, almost ritualized rhythmic way in which it is interpreted: 'His pictures aim . . . at creating a permanence in the sense of timelessness, but a timelessness that also embraces solidity and flux, order and flexibility.'[33]

Another notable feature of Cézanne's work is that he produced paintings in series. The same objects – fruit, pitchers, plates – frequently recur in his still lifes, while even within an individual picture the objects are seen from multiple viewpoints. In the Mont Sainte-Victoire paintings, he keeps returning to the same subject matter, to the same object, and viewing it in different ways, from different perspectives. In a sense, the artist's understanding of the whole can only be fully appreciated in the context of all the versions. Moreover, no one version has a greater authority or authenticity than any other, such relativism being another aspect of his modernity. There is not necessarily a direction or development through these different versions, reinforcing the modern sense of timelessness in his work. And this is a familiar motif in Birtwistle too: he often talks of his musical materials as 'objects', and the listener 'views' them from different angles. Speaking of the central brass ritornellos in *Verses for Ensembles*, he commented that he

> was interested in the notion that you could have a piece of music which only existed in the abstract. It's like looking at an object: every view is unique, but the object exists irrespective of the way it's viewed. So it's the notion that this piece of music exists, just like an object, and what you can do is perform certain facets of it, examine it in different ways.[34]

While obsessed with time, much of Birtwistle's music has a paradoxical timeless quality. Many of his works seem to have no real beginning or ending – it is as if only a portion of the whole work is witnessed – or else they are concerned with circular processes which are eternally present, such as the turning seasons or the movement of the tides. This is exceptionally clear in many of the 'processional' works of the 1970s such as *An Imaginary Landscape*, *The Triumph of Time* and *Melencolia I*. In *The Triumph of Time*, two particular musical objects are seen in new contexts or viewed from new perspectives as the piece unfolds (or, if you will, as the procession proceeds across the landscape): a three-note fragment (E♭–G–D) repeated seven times on amplified soprano saxophone, and a haunting cor anglais melody which occurs three times.

While in his own note on *Silbury Air* Birtwistle alludes to Paul Klee, the work also invites fascinating parallels with Cézanne. The ancient man-made Silbury Hill, while in no way as imposing as Mont Sainte-Victoire, intrudes on its surrounding landscape in not dissimilar ways and its brooding physical presence has a strange effect on anyone who stands near it. The site has a mythical intensity, resonating as it does with forgotten prehistoric burial rituals. As the clouds move over the Wiltshire plains, the light on the hill is always changing; one sees it from ever new perspectives. Yet the mysterious power of the mound also comes from a sense of a timelessness – it is a feature that seems to have been there for ever, and will for ever remain there. The hill itself is, of course, not literally represented in Birtwistle's piece. But just as the surfaces of Cézanne's paintings concern themselves with line, form and colour, the changing (spatial) relationships between static elements, so Birtwistle's work is constructed from fixed musical ideas whose (temporal) relationships are constantly being re-evaluated. In terms which could almost as easily be applied to Cézanne, the composer has commented that 'I have often alluded to my music of landscape presenting musical ideas through the juxtaposition and repetition of "static blocks" or, preferable in my terminology, objects. These objects themselves being subjected to a vigorous invented logic via modes of juxtaposition, modes of repetition, modes of change.'[35] One aspect of the 'vigorous invented logic' by which Cézanne orders his surface is what has been described as 'colour modulation'. The following account of his *Still Life with Compotier* (1882) is revealing:

> While the color formulas in the painting are derived from careful and logical plotting by locality and spatial symmetry, the over-arching compositional plan is just as apparent. The limited repertory of colored patterns . . . results in

> the creation of a subtle rhythm of chromatic repetitions and counterrepetitions throughout the painting.[36]

And the same could be written of *Silbury Air*. The 'invented logic' here is the 'pulse labyrinth' which prefaces the score and ensures – to a degree – the smooth transition from one tempo to another, or the coherent superimposition of different tempi in the piece ('metric modulation', to appropriate Elliott Carter's term). The result is highly ritualized music where the same actions (objects) are constantly being repeated yet are never quite the same. Something which is highly organized temporally gives the impression of being time*less*, unending, eternal. The final four harp chords, like those which also punctuate the endings of *Tragoedia* and *Melencolia I*, call an artificial halt to a ceremony which could otherwise continue *ad infinitum*. The formality that Birtwistle admires in Cézanne – and, no doubt, in Dürer too, from whose 1514 engraving *Melencolia I* takes its name – is here in this music; the resulting musical ritual invites parallels with the object in nature (Silbury Hill) without ever attempting to represent it directly.

TAKING A LINE FOR A WALK: KLEE

Paul Klee, like Birtwistle, was something of an individualist, and he never formally aligned himself with any particular group or style: 'Klee, more than any other artist of our century, was consciously detached from the mainstream of modern art and its theoretical assumptions'.[37] From his published notes and writings, it is clear that Klee was essentially concerned with the two poles of his art: expression and structure – that is, with a 'spiritual reality' beyond the canvas achieved through a clear and exact understanding of line, tone and colour, of 'points, and linear, plane and spatial energies'.[38] Furthermore, Klee – himself an accomplished musician and sometime professional violinist – thought of his art in musical terms. In his theoretical writings he reveals a constant concern for movement in his work, for a sense of a picture's 'dynamic'. The very first illustration in the *Pedagogical Sketchbook*, for instance, shows a line as something active, 'moving freely . . . the mobility agent is a point, shifting its position forward.'[39] Evidence that he considered painting a *temporal* art can be found throughout his writings: 'space is also a temporal concept'; and an understanding of movement and rhythm is thus central to Klee.

This fascinating fusion of musical and visual ideas is, no doubt, one reason why Birtwistle is attracted to the work of Klee. Hall goes so far as to describe the *Pedagogical Sketchbook* as Birtwistle's 'musical bible'.[40] The correspondences between composer and artist are striking; to highlight these parallels is to make clear not only the sources of much of the composer's thinking (as well as offering a context for the interpretation of the music) but also serves further to identify the nature of Birtwistle's modernism. These parallels also draw attention to Birtwistle's similarities with other modernist composers. Varèse, for example, was similarly interested in the visual arts (as has been documented by Jonathan Bernard)[41] and given his avowed propensity for geometrical structures, particularly influenced by the thinking of the Cubists, it is also very likely that he would have come into Klee's sphere of influence (they were virtual contemporaries and moved in the same artistic circles). Varèse's rhetoric of sound masses, spatial planes, moving figures, colour zones and a primary concern for rhythm is close to the language of Klee, and clearly resonates very powerfully in Birtwistle's creative imagination.

The central concern of Klee's *Pedagogical Sketchbook*, first published in 1925, is form and the way in which form is derived from nature. From this statement alone it can be seen why Birtwistle is drawn to Klee. Klee's art, like Cézanne's, is not abstract in that it parallels nature, but it is not representational (in a naturalistic sense) either. It is the formality of Klee's surfaces that fascinate Birtwistle, a formality which points to a deeper expressivity. The first part of the *Sketchbook* deals initially with the ways in which a static dot or point can be transformed into something dynamic, something linear. A line can simply be a line, it needs no necessary direction or intention, but it is always in motion, always dynamic: 'A walk for a walk's sake.' This line can be accompanied by various forms which reflect its essential motion, which are given meaning or motivation by it, and yet which remain relatively independent. These can take the shape of complementary ideas, secondary lines or even by the line circumscribing itself.

Following Klee's lead, it is possible to argue that the motivated, non-directional line lies at the centre of Birtwistle's structural thinking. His lines often begin with a 'point' and extend in time to provide a formal context for other complementary kinds of musical activity. Take, for example, the frequent starting-point of much of his music: the note E. This initial idea is 'taken on a walk . . . shifting its position forward' and becomes a musical line. The *Four Songs of Autumn* offer a particularly pertinent example. Aside from the two notes at the beginning and the three at the end (a cadential frame), E is a constant presence. The initial point is introduced in the cello and extended in time to become a line, shifting its plane for each of the four songs (it moves up, an octave at a time, through the instruments of the quartet); there is also a sense of progression in that the higher the E moves, the more regular its rhythmic organization becomes, from no rhythm at all (a sustained pitch in song 1) to highly regular repetitions in song 4. Yet, despite this progress (a 'motivated' line), the line is nonetheless 'non-directional' in that its duration is potentially infinite; its actual 'length' is determined not by itself but by other factors, i.e. the structure of the vocal line. This offers – in Klee's terms – 'complementary forms'. In song 3, for example, it can be seen (Ex. 1.1) that the soprano's line is organized symmetrically around E (though an E an octave higher than that sounding in violin 2): thus, there are two complementary lines, organized according to similar principles but operating in different ways.[42]

It is also appropriate to consider Birtwistle's 'processionals' of the 1970s in terms of 'taking a line for a walk'. The composer's account of *The Triumph of Time* confirms this, and parallels Klee: '. . . parts of a procession must already have gone by, others are surely to come: a procession made up of a (necessarily) linked chain of material objects which have no necessary connection

Ex. 1.1. *Four Songs of Autumn*, song 3 (opening).

with each other . . .'[43] The line here is motivated yet non-goal-oriented; as the audience, we glimpse only part of a potentially endless line. The emergence of the explicit 'cantus' in the 1980s, the 'endless melody' of *Secret Theatre*, only serves to confirm the centrality of such linear thinking, reinforced by Birtwistle's comments on the fundamental melodic line at the heart of *Gawain*.

Next in the *Pedagogical Sketchbook* Klee discusses what he calls two-dimensional planes which are brought into being by the simultaneous movement of lines. Equivalents are to be found in Birtwistle. The kind of musical layer found in *The Fields of Sorrow*, for example, is made initially not of one strand centred on E, but of a block of sound starting simultaneously with four different Es – firstly on the pianos, later taken up by the choir, soprano soloists and vibraphone. The 'field' or 'plane' thus defined is further articulated by linear movements within it, often symmetrical motion either side of the pivotal Es. The same idea is to be found at the end of the work, now centred on D. The use of 'pitch wedges' is another instance of this kind of 'activation of planes'. Beginning from a single point, a wedge shape gradually emerges, filling out its musical space symmetrically to provide a musical layer around which other musical ideas can operate. The earliest example is to be found in his first published work, *Refrains and Choruses*. In the fourth section of this work (beginning at bar 89) the process begins to unfold from (again) the note E, proceeding symmetrically, and coming to end at the section's climax at bar 122, as follows:

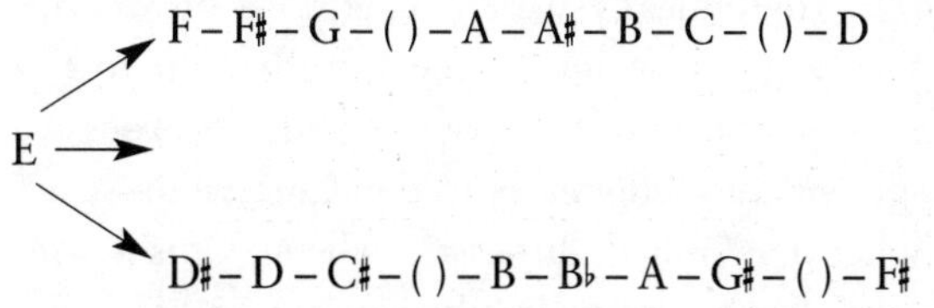

F – F♯ – G – ( ) – A – A♯ – B – C – ( ) – D
E →
D♯ – D – C♯ – ( ) – B – B♭ – A – G♯ – ( ) – F♯

The E remains an ever-present line while the wedge opens out from it, occasionally being interrupted by a vertical sonority in all five voices. But this apparently straightforward symmetry is only one aspect of the music in these bars; other ideas seem to proliferate outwards from it (the 'line accompanied by complementary forms') and become more elaborate, eventually obscuring the original line almost completely in a welter of free counterpoint. The general course of this section thus mirrors the wedge's opening out from its centre, in that it proceeds from a simple, quiet beginning on a single note, building in complexity and dynamic to a climax when the music is most active and registrally at its widest. The line has been taken for a walk. The result is decidedly modern and typical of Birtwistle in that the context (process) is fixed and coherent even if its realization is free; related (complementary) ideas (objects) are superimposed on and interact with, but are never subsumed into, the originary line.

Klee next proceeds in the *Pedagogical Sketchbook* to examine structure which he argues is articulated by means of repetition – what he terms 'structural rhythm'. In its simplest form, such rhythmic articulation is achieved by the repetition of the same unit; on a larger scale, more complex units are built up, also of repetitions, which are themselves repeated.

It is a truism to state that Birtwistle's music depends on repetition. Formally ordered repetition is central to his most obvious modernist models – Varèse, Stravinsky, Messiaen – as well as to the work of Cézanne and Picasso. Birtwistle's procedures clearly owe far more to a Stravinskian model of repetition/variation and associated forms (especially verse-refrain structures) than they do to a progressive Schoenbergian model of *developing* variation. The intricate, rhythmically varied repetitions of Stravinsky's melodies, such as at the opening of the 'Introduction' to *The Rite of Spring* or in the 'Danse sacrale', or elsewhere its obsessive repetition of fragments, pre-eminently in the 'Cortège du sage', are models for what one finds in Birtwistle. The result is a non-developmental, non-directed music in which notions of ritual are central. Hence Birtwistle's sympathies with Varèse and Messiaen. In Birtwistle as in Klee, repetition is employed at all levels of structure, from the repetition of the smallest units to form a regular pulse, through repeating devices or 'mechanisms', to the large-scale repetition of whole passages. Overt regular pulsation is to be found in many works of the later 1970s and 1980s, as evidenced by their very titles: *Chronometer*, *Pulse Field (Frames, Pulses and Interruptions)* and *Pulse Sampler*. The fascinating aspect of *Chronometer*, his only exclusively electronic piece (created in collaboration with his *Orpheus* librettist, Peter Zinovieff), is how the regular pulsation of the sounds of different clocks – juxtaposed, superimposed, transformed in various ways – produces something which is far from regular and predictable. And this preoccupation continues: in 1997 he stated: 'I'm very interested in pulse – more and more. I'm thinking about it a lot at the moment.'[44] One obvious result of that thinking has been another extraordinary set of 'clock' pieces, or musical timepieces as he calls them, *Harrison's Clocks* for piano solo. The punning title refers to the five maritime chronometers built by the eighteenth-century clockmaker, John Harrison, in his quest after a solution to the so-called 'longitude problem'.[45] The 'tick-tock' of different clocks is heard in each of Birtwistle's pieces and at many different levels, usually audibly represented as repeated, alternating pairs of notes or chords. No. 5 is the most obsessive, in keeping perhaps with Harrison's last watch, 'H-5', 'a thing of beauty in its simplicity'.[46] It is a frantic *moto perpetuo* (marked 'quaver = 288 or maybe less') in which pulsating, oscillating semiquaver pairs are mechanically maintained throughout the movement (with just one triplet hiccup in bar 105) and only disrupted in the closing 26 bars as the clockwork mechanism audibly begins to run down. The pieces as a whole experiment with a wide range of kinds of repetition: for example, the regular recurrence of the same cadential (framing) two-bar flourish which opens each piece and punctuates the course of No. 4, or its variant which separates the 'verses' of No. 1; the precisely measured exact repetitions of the closing bars of No. 1; the subtly varied *Rite of Spring*-like grace-note groups which open and predominate in No. 3; the repeating blocks of No. 4; and the repeated notes or pairs everywhere. Each piece is remarkably consistent; furthermore, because each separate piece is concerned with similar, carefully contained processes, each sounds like a variant of the others. Thus one gets the impression not only of cogs turning within cogs inside each piece (especially in No. 3) but also of each piece operating as a cog in relation to all the others. In other words, a series of verses.

On a much larger scale, too, repetition generates entire structures. This is at its most obvious in Birtwistle's most formalized pieces from the 1960s and 1970s, though it is perhaps less apparent in many more recent works, even those of the largest proportions (*Earth Dances*, *Antiphonies*, *Exody*), where through-composition would appear to be more significant. The repeating cycles of both *Punch and Judy* and *The Mask of Orpheus* are a fundamental aspect both of the works' structures and of their ritual dimensions. Both are, in some senses, violent works, but that violence remains on a stylized level, a ritualized violence, because of the way in which it is contained by the formality of the repetitions (*The Rite of Spring* provides an obvious model for this). Once again, the formality Birtwistle admires in Cézanne, Picasso and Klee is evident in his own work: he uses his subject matter to express the musical structure and not the other way round. Hence, indeed, the 'irrelevance' of the actual subject matter (*The Mask of Orpheus* began life as 'Faust'); it is arguably the way in which the narrative unfolds that is most important, not the narrative in itself. In the 1960s Birtwistle took this position to an extreme in stating, polemically, that he could rewrite many of the works of this time with entirely different notes and it would leave the substance of the music unchanged.[47] *Punch and Judy*, to a libretto by Stephen Pruslin, is the largest-scale work of the 1960s to demonstrate structural repetition at every level. At the highest level are the 'Melodramas' whose substance, while never repeated exactly, nonetheless remains constant, and the pattern of their regular recurrence articulates the music's structure (in Klee's words, 'divisional articulation . . . purely repetitive and therefore structural'). Within these 'Melodramas' there are repeated sequences of 'Murder Ensembles' and 'Quests for Pretty Polly', which in turn are built from smaller, separate musico-dramatic units and which are themselves repeated: 'Proclamation', 'Passion Chorale', 'Travel Music', 'Weather Report', and so on. Even within these units, repetition can play a structural role, whether the simple strophic organization of 'Punch's Lullaby' or the more mechanical repetitions which form the backbone of the 'Morals'. *Punch and Judy* is built from more than a hundred self-contained numbers and so invites comparison with other stylized kinds of music theatre, most obviously Baroque opera. *The Mask of Orpheus* is similarly divided into 126 discrete events – always grouped in threes – with such formal titles as 'Song of Magic', 'Poem of Reminiscence', 'Orphic Hymn' and 'Hysterical Aria'. Furthermore, each is given a conventional operatic designation (usually recitative or aria) which defines its 'ritual situation', its musical and dramatic personality. As in *Punch and Judy*, when an event is repeated, it is usually transformed in some way, the same object being viewed from a different angle. However, Birtwistle is also quick to point out the differences between the two works: 'I wanted to invent a formalism which does not rely on tradition in the way that *Punch and Judy* [did] . . . In *The Mask of Orpheus*, I didn't want to hark back any more; I wanted to create a formal world that was utterly new.'[48] In both works, formalized repetitions generate structure and articulate the subject matter, not the other way round; thus, the repetitions themselves become the principal focus of the ritual. This is most apparent in Act 3 of *Orpheus* where any sense of conventional narrative is lost (partly through the use of an invented 'Orphic' language) and the work's identity becomes embodied in the movement of the tides, the repeated sequences of death, the constant varied return to the same musical and symbolic objects.

One further example from *Orpheus* is appropriate here. The central act, concerned with Orpheus's descent into and return from the underworld, is dominated by the allegorical device of the 'arches': 'an imaginary architectural fantasy', 'a visionary architectural structure with practical applications'.[49] There are seventeen arches, each of which represents a different attribute of Orpheus's world: countryside, crowds, evening, contrast, dying, and so on. The arches also correspond with the seventeen verses of Orpheus's second 'Song of Magic', each verse of which is itself made up of a dream (aria), a fantasy (recitative), a nightmare (speech) and a sudden awakening in varying (precisely specified) proportions. Yet it is never intended that this structure is seen: it serves both to symbolize and give order to Orpheus's dream of his descent and return. Like the allegorical title taken from Bruegel that Birtwistle gave to *The Triumph of Time* (completed just before he began serious work on *Orpheus*), the arches are an allegory of time where the river flows through the seventh arch from the past to the present, while the future is contained in the water flowing across the arches from the dead to the living. Within the context of this imaginary structure, Orpheus dreams of his journey to find Eurydice, the people he encounters on the way (reworkings of the music and characters he had met in Act 1), his turning only to lose Eurydice once again, and his death. The parallels with Klee's notion of a structural rhythmic concept built by means of repetition should be clear. It is also perhaps worth noting that Klee himself painted a series of arches which he called the *Revolution of the Viaducts*.

One of the most sharply defined examples of structural repetition can be witnessed in *Verses for Ensembles*. While it is possible to discuss this extraordinary work from a number of different perspectives (its theatre, its formal parallels with Greek drama, its ritual character and instrumental role play, its symmetry, its block structure, etc.), in a sense all these features depend on repetition, which here operates on many levels. One kind of repetition is extremely rare in Birtwistle: *exact* repetition. But here, the entire passage between figs. 18 and 30 – itself built from repeated, juxtaposed blocks of music – is repeated note-for-note between figs. 58 and 70. These are the structural pillars around which the entire piece is constructed – in Klee's terms, 'the most primitive structural rhythm based on a repetition of the same unit from left to right.' Between these pillars is a section of music built of varied repetitions, but now taking the form of Birtwistle's favoured verse-refrain pattern. The horn line remains fixed (an elaborate kind of ground or chaconne) while, in turn, each of the high woodwind instruments weaves a free verse around it, related yet independent, and decorated by percussion (a 'line on a walk . . . accompanied by complementary forms'). The refrain which punctuates this recurring cycle of verses is the brass ritornello discussed by Birtwistle above, a musical object which is always the same yet always different. The object on the page (the printed score – see Ex. 4.2) remains identical on every repetition; however, in performance the players are given choices as to the 'routes' they take, and as to whether they play loud or soft, legato or staccato, muted or unmuted. Birtwistle: 'What I find interesting are those situations where I create the multiple object but others select what facet is to be looked at.'[50] Compare this with Klee: 'The eye must "graze" over the surface, grasping sharply portion after portion, to convey them to the brain which collects and stores the impressions.' It is only by viewing the object from many angles that the whole can be comprehended.

For Klee, as for Cézanne, the relationship between the painted surface and nature is crucial. Klee's credo is summed up in one short sentence: 'Art does not reproduce the visible; it renders it visible'. He continues: 'In this way we learn to look beyond the surface and get to the roots of things.'[51] Nature is ritualized; Klee creates, one might say, a rite of spring. After the discussion of geometry, the *Pedagogical Sketchbook* goes on to examine the structure of natural objects. In nature as in geometry Klee makes a distinction between structural and individual units. He comes to the conclusion that there is a 'hierarchy of function' between units that is of primary significance; any object in itself is relatively insignificant: 'One bone alone achieves nothing'. Klee's studies of and writings on nature were extensive; natural objects frequently occur in his paintings and drawings (human figures, fish, birds, plants, etc.). Yet he never uses natural objects naturalistically; they exist as familiar images on the surface of the work intended to draw the viewer into the deeper spiritual reality of a picture:

> His forms are derived from nature, inspired by observation of shape and cyclic change but their appearance only

> matters in so far as it symbolizes an inner actuality that receives meaning from its relationship to the cosmos.[52]

And the same could be written of Birtwistle who has incorporated ideas derived from observations of natural processes into his music without in any way attempting to represent such ideas literally. His landscapes, like Klee's, are imaginary, his pastorals mechanical. The parallel formalism of painter and composer can easily be seen by comparing *Earth Dances*, where the composer's understanding of the stratification of the elements of the earth's crust gives the substance of the work's structure (a fusion, in Klee's terms, of 'cosmic' – earth – and 'cultural' – dance – rhythms), and Klee's 1930 pastel, *Individualized Measurement of the Strata*. According to Norbert Lynton, what matters in Klee's picture 'is the subtlety and rareness of these particular colour confrontations and the effectiveness of the rhythmic grouping and different shapes and sizes of colour areas.'[53] The precise distinction of twelve horizontal strata (subdivided by five verticals) is achieved through colour. In *Earth Dances*, there are, according to the composer, six separate strata characterized by their 'intervallic hierarchy', as well as their register, and distinguished by their rhythms.[54] In practice, the six strata are rarely explicitly present simultaneously but periodically come to the surface – 'layers are overlaid like geological strata which one after another erupt and push their way towards the light. It is as though an earthquake were in progress.'[55] It is through these continually shifting relationships between strata that it might be said that the 'earth dances', just as the surface of Klee's picture is rhythmically animated by its colour distribution.

The second principal section of the *Pedagogical Sketchbook* deals with dimension and perspective. Klee does not hold a unitary understanding of perspective. He is concerned with a *shifting* viewpoint – indeed, a distinctly modernist viewpoint. Birtwistle, like the Cubists, has an ongoing interest in viewing the same object from many angles: the viewpoint shifts. This is central to their shared modernism, as it is to the aesthetic of Stravinsky and

Varèse. A related concern of Klee's is that of balance. He introduces two kinds: first, 'symmetrical balance as restoration' where, for example, if a scale's balance is disturbed, it is corrected through a counterweight, a counter-effect; second, 'non-symmetrical balance' where an object which is 'too heavy' can have its balance restored by adding more 'light' to compensate. What is crucial is the establishment of an equilibrium from these unequal elements – balance, proportion, equilibrium, harmony. Balance and symmetry are crucial to Birtwistle's work. Hall has explored symmetry in his work quite extensively, though, as already seen, exact symmetries are comparatively rare and, when they occur, are fairly obvious, such as the use of 'pitch wedges', or the 'pillars' of *Verses for Ensembles*. Such obvious symmetries, like Birtwistle's use of random number charts as a means of producing pitch material, lie on the surface; as Stephen Walsh has commented:

> . . . it seems that random numbers and mechanical schemes do not have a great bearing on the essentials of Birtwistle's music (otherwise it would hardly impress us as an integrated body of work) but they do valuably generate 'situations' within which he can work, and they do trivial work for him.[56]

The notion of a non-symmetrical balance, however, would appear to be generally more useful in understanding Birtwistle's structures. There are many examples of works with a symmetrical 'background' but whose realization in the music is compromised or even contradicted as a result of the exigencies of the surface workings of material – even while being contained by the background model. He has himself given good reason why he permits such contradictions. For example, the overall structure of *Tragoedia* is based on the formal categories of Greek tragedy, the essence of which is 'bilateral symmetry in which concentric layers are grouped outward from a central static pillar'.[57] Yet in practice the structure is not exactly symmetrical: that would be too predictable. What matters to Birtwistle is the way a work evolves *against* the expectations set up by the use of a symmetrical model.

Changes have to be made. 'The non-literal symmetry that results from all these changes is crucial, since an exact mirror symmetry, even though motivated earlier in the work, would limit the form unnecessarily to one dimension as the work drew to its close.'[58] It is the tension between model and realization that, in part, gives the work its dynamism. This balance of progress (non-symmetry) and stasis (symmetry) – which manifests itself variously as line and circle, recitative and aria, horizontal and vertical, and in the case of *Melencolia I* literally as 'stasis in progress' – is a fundamental aspect of Birtwistle's modernity and, indeed, of his musical identity as a whole. Such a balancing of opposites without the one collapsing into the other – thesis and antithesis without the unifying synthesis, that is, negative dialectics – is at the heart of what Max Paddison, after Adorno, has defined as the 'dilemma of modernism':

> the predicament faced by the artist caught between, on the one hand, the traditional demands of the art work for unity and integration (the harmonious relationship between part and whole) and, on the other hand, the loss of faith in any overarching unity on both individual and social levels in the face of the evident fragmentation of modern existence.[59]

The negation of traditional kinds of synthesis while preserving aspects of connectedness is thus central to an understanding of Adorno's negative dialectics, of modernism, and of much modern art from Cézanne to Bacon, from Stravinsky to Birtwistle.

In a sense, the short third section of the *Pedagogical Sketchbook* continues this theme, giving insight into Klee's *spiritual* dynamism: 'there are regions with different laws and new symbols, signifying freer movement and dynamic position'. Birtwistle tends not to discuss such matters; he relies on his intuition without analysing it. He has described this as the 'magic' of his music, 'meaning the element of surprise and transfiguration that perturbs the regular processes of his scores and provides their fascination'.[60] Klee talks of 'loose' and 'rigid' continuity, the tension between the regular and the irregular, between natural, immutable laws (such as the force of gravity) and human will (the desire to escape from that gravitational pull). In Birtwistle, too, a similar tension can be found between the inevitability of regular and symmetrical schemes and structures, and the disruptive will of the composer who works against such schemes while never fully escaping their influence. In Birtwistle's music there is always a dynamic tension between the regular and the irregular, the predictable and the unpredictable. His account of *Silbury Air* makes this point: the labyrinth is fixed, the composer's journey through it is whimsical. 'I do make "form schemes" (for pitches, rhythms . . . everything), but once started, the piece seems to establish a life of its own, which is more interesting than the original sketches.'[61]

Whether, in the light of this detailed examination of the *Pedagogical Sketchbook*, it can be argued that Birtwistle's compositional practices and aesthetic have been derived directly from Klee is impossible to sustain. While it is evident that Birtwistle thinks about music in visual terms, to make precise one-to-one correspondences between an early twentieth-century painter and a late twentieth-century composer would be misleading. Nonetheless, it is certainly true that Birtwistle's 'way of thinking' parallels that of Klee in fascinating ways and that to have some insight into Klee's use of line, colour, form, rhythm, nature, and so on, provides a useful context for interpreting Birtwistle's music as well as helping to articulate the nature of Birtwistle's modernism. Whether a bible (containing the sacred modernist texts) or merely a *vade mecum* (a handbook to which he turns for guidance or confirmation of current practice), what Birtwistle's interest in Klee's *Pedagogical Sketchbook* (and the notebooks) reveals is how his concerns for repetitive ritual, formalized reading of nature, balance of opposites, of symmetries, of simultaneities, are rooted in early European modernism and are as evident in the bold formalism of his music of the 1960s and the 'mechanical pastoral' of the 1970s and 1980s, as they are in the large structures of some of the most recent works. Birtwistle remains a committed modernist and it is in that context that it is most fruitful to interpret his music.

MULTIPLE PERSPECTIVES: PICASSO

One other modernist painter is highly significant in relation to Birtwistle: Pablo Picasso. Birtwistle owns a signed Picasso print whose composition he regards unequivocally as 'perfect'. He has spoken (albeit in a rather vague way) of the omnipresent cyclic processes in his own music as a 'sort of musical Cubism'[62] and which he also finds in, for example, Stockhausen's *Zeitmasse*. This, of course, reinforces an understanding of Birtwistle's modernism (Cézanne was an important precursor of Cubism, and Picasso was a significant influence on Klee), but it also resonates outwards to other influential modernists such that it is impossible to say whether Birtwistle's Cubist tendencies stem directly from his love of Braque and Picasso, or via Stravinsky. The influence of Cubism is hard to escape – John Golding has declared that it 'remains the pivotal movement in the art of the first half of the century.'[63] Birtwistle shares this view and equates the importance of Cubism for all subsequent artists with the importance of serialism for all subsequent composers. Glenn Watkins's fascinating account of Stravinsky's association with Cubist artists, and his accord with and participation in Cubism, is instructive.[64] Attempts to relate Stravinsky's music to its contemporary Cubist art date back to the time of the premières of the works (such as *The Rite of Spring*) themselves, while more recently even the sceptical Richard Taruskin has acknowledged the appropriateness of Cubist analogies: 'As Cubism purports to represent multiple perspectives on a two-dimensional plane, Stravinsky's music often suggests multiple layers of a single unordered moment in time, presented in an arbitrary, nonsignificant sequence.'[65] Perhaps the most obvious correspondence is between the rhythmic interaction of independent planes in analytical Cubism, and Stravinsky's music built from musical blocks – preeminently the *Symphonies of Wind Instruments*.[66] This latter work has had a deep impact on Birtwistle:

> I think that the *Symphonies of Wind Instruments* is one of the great masterpieces of this century . . . and certainly one

> of the most original, in that it's to do with the juxtaposition of material without any sense of development . . . If someone said to me, what's the biggest influence on your life as a composer, I would say this piece.[67]

As already mentioned, Varèse, too, was strongly influenced by the Cubists; his account of interpenetrating planes and masses, devoid of any conventional counterpoint, is clearly closely related not only to the structure of analytical Cubist works of intersecting planes and facets, but also to an understanding of Stravinsky's music made of juxtaposed static blocks: '. . . the movement of sound-masses, of shifting planes . . . Certain transmutations taking place on certain planes will seem to be projected on to other planes, moving at different speeds and at different angles.'[68] Varèse's term for his musical blocks was 'zones of intensities', which were 'differentiated by various timbres or colors and different loudnesses . . . The role of color or timbre would be completely changed from being incidental, anecdotal, sensual or picturesque; it would become an agent of delineation.'[69]

That aspect of Cubist practice which seems to have been most suggestive for Birtwistle is its ability to examine an object from multiple viewpoints. At an abstract level, it corresponds in interesting ways with serial practice where an 'object' (the row) can be observed in many different ways, even sounding in different ways simultaneously, and yet that 'object' fundamentally remains 'the same'. Birtwistle is not a serialist, but the concerns of serialism have nonetheless left their mark on his music. Other kinds of 'multiple perspectives' are important to Birtwistle and their origins can also be identified in Stravinsky's 'Cubist' practices. The first of the *Three Pieces for String Quartet* is a fascinating example of a movement built from independent yet complementary ostinatos. Each component moves at its own speed, each retains a fixed identity, yet its relationship to the others is continually changing. It is very much akin to Cubist attempts at representing the three-dimensionality of objects in two dimensions. And it is a recurrent theme of this book that such procedures are to be found everywhere in Birtwistle. We have already encountered perhaps his most extreme Cubist instance: the brass ritornellos from *Verses for Ensembles*.

Picasso's work, like that of Cézanne and Klee, strikes an effective balance between the representational and the anti-naturalistic. Familiar objects and landscapes are fractured; we, the viewers, are made to look at the natural world in new ways, and in new formal contexts. This is true of Birtwistle too. His music is never utterly 'abstract'. It engages with the world about us; it engages with the past. But it does not represent these objects and ideas directly: it reinterprets them in fresh ways by inventing new contexts for them. This is the enduring primeval power of a work such as *Earth Dances*. Golding writes that Cubism 'had fearlessly confronted and produced a new kind of reality. It had evolved a completely original, anti-naturalistic kind of figuration, which had at the same time stripped bare the mechanics of pictorial creation, and had in the process gone a long way towards destroying artificial barriers between abstraction and representation.'[70] In this light, it should hardly surprise us that Picasso's thinking has offered an enduring model for Birtwistle's art.

Musical Mentors

STRAVINSKY

The wider significance for Birtwistle of Stravinsky (and of Stravinsky's modernism) cannot be underestimated. The structural importance of rhythm in Stravinsky, the construction of new kinds of musical time, structures built both from the opposition of blocks and of the simultaneous layering of opposed materials (two different kinds of stratification), repetition and variation, verse-refrain structures, modality (especially melodically), ritual and role play, the suggestive richness of folk art . . . all these key and influential facets of Stravinsky's modernism are central to an understanding of Birtwistle's modernism too. A number of sources have already been identified: the primordial rhythmic energy of

The Rite of Spring, the block forms of the *Symphonies of Wind Instruments*, the instrumental role play of the *Three Pieces for String Quartet*; also one could select the formalized ritual of the *Symphony of Psalms* and *Canticum Sacrum*, the rough, folk theatre of *Renard* and *The Soldier's Tale*, the melodic directness and sheer sense of fun of the *Octet*. One work has been widely discussed and acknowledged by the composer as of particular influence: *Agon*. Birtwistle undertook a detailed analysis of *Agon* as part of the classes he attended while at Princeton as a Harkness Fellow. The results of this intimate encounter can be heard everywhere in his music. But why this work in particular? Birtwistle is not the only composer to have been fascinated by it; Boulez and Tippett, to name but two very different composers, have drawn much from the work's sound and structure. It is fascinating, for example, that Tippett's encounter with *Agon* in 1958 coincided with his work on his 'block' opera, *King Priam*; it was 'germane' to *Priam*, Tippett writes, not least because of the instrumental possibilities it suggested.[71] At the time, *Agon*'s bold audacity, its precision, virtuosity and energy, suggested that Stravinsky had in later life found a new musical direction, a new, much more rarefied kind of neoclassicism, an even more refined stylization of past forms and traditions. Furthermore, its adoption of certain aspects of serialism indicated an accommodation between what had formerly been perceived as irreconcilable poles: Stravinskian neoclassicism and Schoenbergian/Webernian dodecaphony. What *Agon* suggests is that Stravinsky's approach to serialism is hardly radically different from procedures found in earlier works; it merely rationalizes his approach to, for example, the characteristic cycling of a limited number of pitches in nearly all his melodies. The varied repetitions of a given object which the serial method makes possible coincides with Stravinskian practice; his interpretation of the method exploits its circularity, rather than being a tool for development and a force for unity, as it was for Schoenberg. Stephen Walsh effectively summarizes Stravinsky's approach to serialism:

> His serial treatments typically make capital out of the fact

> that twelve-note rows are in essence repetitive . . . By nearly always preferring bold linear forms, Stravinsky throws this property of serialism into relief, making us at least subconscious of the fact that the various twelve-note forms are no more than different routes through the whole field, like so many changes in a peal of bells.[72]

This account immediately suggests other later developments. The process music of Steve Reich, for instance, owes much to Stravinsky. Berio's 'serial' practices, too, are closer to Stravinsky than to Schoenberg: the cycling of the basic seven-note set of *O King* (1968) is in some senses characteristic of late Stravinskian practice, while echoes of *Agon*'s concern for sonority can also clearly be heard.

Agon will have appealed to Birtwistle initially, no doubt, because of its formalism. The fact that its title and subject matter allude explicitly to an ancient Greek ceremony or 'contest' was in tune with even his earliest compositional exercises. A ritual is enacted which depends on more-or-less explicit rules, in which dancers and musicians interact in a formal and preordained manner, in which the geometry of its organization is of as great a significance as its expressive content. Another feature of *Agon*'s structure which would have appealed to Birtwistle (and which reinforces the sense of its ritualized formality) is its parallels with the *Symphonies of Wind Instruments*, nowhere more apparent than in the block-like opposition of musical ideas in the opening '*Pas de quatre*'. This also acts as a frame (structural pillars – 'exodos/parados') in that it recurs virtually note-for-note as the coda at the very end of the work. The work as a whole, while being dependent in many ways on the number twelve – twelve dances, twelve dancers arranged in various combinations of 1, 2, 3 and 4, and of course twelve notes – is organized in the kinds of interlocking cycles that were to characterize Birtwistle's music of the 1960s (see Fig. 1.1). Comparison with the overall structures of *Tragoedia*, *Punch and Judy* and *Verses for Ensembles* is revealing (see Fig. 2.1). The sequence of French seventeenth-century dances ('*pas de trois*') in the centre of the work resembles (structurally speaking) the episodes at the centre of *Tragoedia*, while the '*pas de deux*' – the turning-point of the work – is a kind of 'stasimon' and is itself punctuated by a refrain, just as the central dances are punctuated by the prelude/interludes. Such interrupted continuities once again call to mind the 'stratification' and 'interlock' – to use Edward Cone's terms – of the *Symphonies of Wind Instruments*. The high degree of structural repetition suggests a strong constructivist/Cubist dimension to the work in which different but related facets of the whole are shown.

FIG. 1.1. Stravinsky's *Agon*: overall organization

pas de quatre	pas de quatre 2				
	pas de quatre 3	prelude	pas de trois 1	sarabande	
				gailliarde	
				coda	
		interlude	pas de trois 2	bransle simple	
				bransle gay	
				bransle double	
		interlude			pas de deux
			4 duos		
			4 trios		
coda					

Other aspects of *Agon* feature in Birtwistle's work: Stravinsky's attitude to instrumental usage (such as the prominent and significant role played by the harp and the striking spacing of chords) and his reinvention of an archaic past creating a music with a certain timeless quality (fruitfully compared with, say, *Punch and Judy* which – in Pruslin's words – was a 'source opera' which though written after all other operas, would give the illusion of having been written before them).[73] A closer examination of the prelude/interludes sequence reveals further, more detailed correspondences. The 'Cubism' of, say, the brass ritornelli in *Verses for Ensembles* is evident in *Agon* too. Each statement takes the same bipartite shape, the first part slightly longer than the second, and in a strict tempo relation of 3:2 (crotchet = 126:84). The second part is identical on each of the three playings; the first becomes more elaborate on each occasion through the accretion of new layers. There are essentially three components to the first part: (i) a rhythmic object (dyads) which seems to be reinterpreted from a number of angles (intervals expanded or inverted); (ii) a fanfare figure, characterized by scotch-snap rhythms, and which takes the reiterations of (i) as its starting point; and (iii) a rising diatonic semiquaver line. These three elements are layered simultaneously. In the first interlude (Ex. 1.2), elements (i) and (ii) from the prelude reappear in identical form while (iii) is accompanied by overlapped, augmented and rotated versions of itself, i.e. the simultaneous (Cubist) viewing of the same object from different perspectives. In the second interlude, element (i) is similarly additionally accompanied by varied forms of itself. Thus there is a kind of three-dimensional viewing of musical objects not only within a musical unit but across them too. This interpretation of events is further reinforced if one considers the musical material of the prelude/interludes to be a variant of that of the opening '*pas de quatre*' (which also employs reiterated pitches, fanfare figurations, rhythmicized dyads, scotch snaps): the framing role of the '*pas de quatre*' is reinterpreted as a punctuating role in the prelude/interludes.

A similar sequence from *Punch and Judy* will serve to illustrate this.[74] The singing of the 'Morals' by Choregos (the chorus figure

Ex. 1.2. Stravinsky, *Agon*, 'Interlude' (1) (opening).

and Punch's alter ego) is associated with Punch's cyclic 'Quest for Pretty Polly'. On the first two occasions (see Ex. 1.3), Punch's advances are rejected and Choregos comments:

> Weep, my Punch.
> Weep out your unfathomable, inexpressible sorrow.
> It is impossible, yet, restless, you try,
>   and torment yourself,
>   and are tearful.
> Weep, poor, pathetic Punch.

The mood of this number is appropriately melancholic, adopting the topic of the lament or 'commos' which, according to Aristotle, is so characteristic of certain tragedies. The music consists of a circular, repeating mechanism in the orchestra, and a contrasting linear, falling (weeping) vocal part. In both, symmetry plays a key constructive role. 'Moral 2' occurs in a similar position in the next 'Quest'. As with the *Agon* interludes, all the music of 'Moral 1' is present in the next element of the sequence, but with a new layer added also: a bassoon line which shares aspects of the music around it (D-centricity, symmetry, 'eleven-ness' – see below) but which nevertheless maintains its own distinct character. In other words, a new perspective on familiar material. It is interesting that just as Stravinsky played with twelves in *Agon*, here Birtwistle plays with elevens: different durations of eleven units in the orchestral 'mechanism'; a total content of eleven pitch classes in 'Moral 1' (the absent G♮ being the centre of symmetry of the vocal line); a bassoon wedge of eleven pitch classes in 'Moral 2' (symmetrical achievement of the final A♭ is avoided in order to allow circular repetition). A kaleidoscope of elevens. The next element in the sequence is labelled 'Morale' reflecting Pruslin's clever inversion of text and dramatic meaning: 'Leap, leap, proud, pellucid Punch'. Choregos's line remains, but now with a corresponding inversion, transposition, expansion and reordering of intervallic patterns in various ways and accompanied by a new horn line. Both horn and voice make a feature of scotch-snap rhythms (a coincidental link with *Agon*, perhaps, though trochaic

Ex. 1.3. *Punch and Judy*, 'Moral 1'.

rhythms – especially in an accompanimental context – are a consistent Birtwistle fingerprint from his earliest to his most recent works). The dramatic situation and the musical object are once again viewed from new angles. The final element in the sequence, 'Moral 3', involves a further rearrangement of the objects and combines aspects of the 'Morals' and the 'Morale'. There should be little doubt that *Agon* provided a rich model for much of Birtwistle's music of the 1960s.

The other important element of *Agon* for Birtwistle is its serialism. Birtwistle has never been a card-carrying orthodox serialist. His earliest serial experiments would have been made under the tutelage of Richard Hall at the Manchester College. Hall's method, according to fellow-pupil Goehr, was to give his students only the five notes of the pentatonic scale and to derive melodies, counterpoint and harmonic systems from this: 'it reproduces in an extremely simplified form some of the objective criteria of intervallic (or even twelve-tone) technique'.[75] Hall was also interested in applying mathematical principles to composition. It was Goehr who brought about a shift in interest in favour of Schoenberg and his ideas, as well as towards the work of such figures as Krenek and Hauer. As for Birtwistle, Goehr claims that he 'wasn't interested in academic technique, or any of the other things that were on offer at the College'.[76]

Nonetheless, serial thought has left its mark. His earliest published works evince the clearest traces of twelve-note practice. *Refrains and Choruses*, while being Varèse-like in so many ways, makes a feature of organizing the total chromatic in a variety of (fairly un-Schoenbergian) ways. One technique, the symmetrical pitch wedge, is not a row as such, but a systematic arrangement of the chromatic all the same. However, though this process forms the backbone to this section of the piece, it is not the entire story; the 'essence' of the music lies elsewhere, that is, in the material that proliferates outwards from the wedge. Birtwistle is never constrained by the system, by 'academic technique'; indeed, he seems to take a wicked and often witty pleasure in subverting such systems. More 'regular' twelve-note procedures can be observed towards the end of the piece. From bar 132, a twelve-note row is presented in symmetrical fashion, shared between pairs of voices ('chorus'), and its progress is punctuated by a fixed five-note chord ('refrain'); once the chromatic has been exposed, the two-part texture of the 'chorus' (including an informal kind of mirroring) continues while the row provides the source of the pitch material, though its ordering is not followed strictly. Finally, it contracts to a single clarinet voice (just as the vertical space occupied by the 'refrain' similarly contracts, even though its pitch classes remain fixed) and the row is retrograded though, once again, its ordering is freely interpreted (see Ex. 1.4).[77] Borrowing the terms Birtwistle coined for *Secret Theatre*, it might retrospectively be appropriate here to label the twelve-note chorus the cantus (essentially linear) and the five-note refrain the continuum (essentially vertical); both are concerned with cycling through a fixed pitch-class sequence, but with different results. What is typical of Birtwistle is his cavalier attitude to his 'row'. He is not bound by it; it merely generates material with which he can work, which he can accept, reject or subvert as he chooses.

Whether a direct model or not, the procedures found in some of Stravinsky's earliest serial compositions offer fascinating parallels. The eleven-note set of Stravinsky's *Cantata* or the eight-note set of his *Septet*, both dating from the early 1950s, suggest precedents for Birtwistle's use of segments rather than the entire chromatic. Walsh's comment on these works is also appropriate to Birtwistle: 'What is striking is how readily the old cellular technique marries with the new excitement of integrated counterpoint. It is as if the idea were already latent in every piece Stravinsky had written before, waiting only for the right electric charge to bring its particles into line.'[78] Aspects of serial thinking are certainly in tune with the way in which Birtwistle writes – the use of pitch collections (modes) to generate both horizontal and vertical ideas, symmetries, numerical ordering – but, like Stravinsky, he does not want to be slave to an inflexible method which smothers his own voice. Both composers wanted, to give just one instance, to retain the possibility of focused pitch centres which was denied

Ex. 1.4. *Refrains and Choruses*, bars 131–end.

within the Schoenberg–Webern camp. An eleven-note succession ('row'?) occurs earlier in *Refrains and Choruses*. At bar 73 a vertical five-note chromatic segment is presented, proliferating symmetrically out from the middle D that had formed the pitch centre of the preceding bars. Then the horn, acting here as 'protagonist' in Michael Hall's terms, presents melodic statements formed from an eleven-note row (missing note: A) and subsequent slightly varied repetition and retrogradation (bars 73–89). Interestingly, if the total pitch content of this entire horn line is arranged vertically, it can be seen that it is built symmetrically around the absent A as centre. Thus, both the initial chord (refrain/continuum) and the horn line (chorus/cantus) are, in different ways, concerned with the symmetrical organization of chromatic cells. Serial concerns thus manifest themselves not just in these various mirrorings but in the correspondences of horizontal and vertical, of melody and chords. The rest of the material in this passage is freely generated from the horn's 'row', which makes a prominent feature of overlapping forms of Birtwistle's favourite three-note collection: in its most basic configuration this consists of a semitone and a perfect fourth outlining a tritone (in Allen Forte's nomenclature,[79] this is set-class 3–5, an [0,1,6] collection, e.g. C–C♯–F♯). Once again, though not a strict serial procedure, the horizontal and the vertical are intervallically connected in a manner not dissimilar from that of the serialists.

DARMSTADT

The extant piece which seems most obviously indebted to avant-garde serial thought of the 1950s is *Précis* for solo piano, written in the summer of 1960 for John Ogdon to play at the Dartington Summer School. Its gestures of rapid activity followed by still, sustained notes, its comparative sparseness, its obvious symmetries, have much in common with Stockhausen's points and groups of the earlier 1950s, with the stylized 'moments' of *Klavierstück XI* (1956), and especially with the extraordinary sound-world of Boulez's Third Piano Sonata (1957–8). The contrasting 'points' and 'blocs' of Boulez's 'formant 3' are an obvious parallel and the 'new' aesthetic of the 'work in progress' Boulez adopted in this sonata (derived from, among other sources, Mallarmé's *Livre*) comes remarkably close to the ideas Birtwistle was to adopt over the coming decade. For example, 'formant 2' of the sonata, labelled 'tropes', consists of the sequence 'texte – parenthèse – glose – commentaire', ring-bound so that the actual order may be rotated in performance; each section is a 'trope' on every other. Birtwistle, too, has embraced – to a limited degree – aspects of freedom throughout his composing career: the alternative routes through instrumental lines in *Verses for Ensembles* and *Cantata*, the indeterminate relationship between the three melody instruments of *Dinah and Nick's Love Song*, the repeating mobiles of *The Fields of Sorrow*, the variable synchrony of *Silbury Air* and *Ritual Fragment*, the flexibility of number and order of movements in *Pulse Shadows*, the various mobile formal elements and non-synchronous relationship between oboe and piano in *An Interrupted Endless Melody*. Furthermore, the idea of the open-ended art work is one that is not alien to Birtwistle and certainly the kind of multiple views of the same object proposed here by Boulez and explored in many of his subsequent works, is one that parallels closely Birtwistle's aesthetic. In discussing his sonata, Boulez talks of infinitude, and employs the decidedly Birtwistle-like images of the 'labyrinth' and the 'expanding universe' (a temporal spiral).

As for *Précis*,[80] though it appears to adopt the rhetoric of Darmstadt, its substance is much more typical of what we have come to associate with Birtwistle. The symmetries are more immediately apparent: mirroring both about the horizontal axis in the musical ideas themselves, and about the vertical axis in the overall five-part ABCB'A' scheme. The twelve-note vocabulary is subverted to the composer's own purposes to reveal, by turns, a lyrical tendency (clearest in the final section), a concern throughout for the dramatic placement of resonant single pitches, and even a Stravinskian kind of role-play – a characteristic 'cadential' upward-rising arpeggio figure signals the transition between the first and second, and fourth and fifth sections (a procedure which uncannily re-emerges in the preludial flourishes of his next solo piano piece, written almost forty years later, *Harrison's Clocks*). In fact, the exact model for *Précis*, the composer admits, was provided not by any of the big names at Darmstadt, but 'second-hand' via *Quantitäten* by Bo Nilsson, a Darmstadt-based Swede strongly under the influence of Stockhausen, which Birtwistle discovered via Ogdon. The one Darmstadt work he readily acknowledges as being important to him at the time, and indeed still today, is Boulez's *Le marteau sans maître*. He first heard the work at a concert in London on 6 May 1957, a programme which also tellingly included Webern's Concerto Op. 24 and Stockhausen's *Zeitmasse*. He possesses a copy of the 'original' handwritten version of *Le marteau* published by Universal Edition which he argues is much 'simpler' than the later version. What he admires is the work's formality, the way it does not attempt to express the texts but finds frames for them, the way in which the settings and the instrumental commentaries are cyclically distributed across the whole, the way in which the ideas are revisited ('troped'). He is also fascinated by the instrumentation of *Le marteau* – how Boulez is able to make the voice connect 'seamlessly' with the untuned percussion – and by the fact that it is 'against orchestration'.[81] Its serial origins are, it would seem, incidental. He still talks frequently of works by Stockhausen of the 1950s and 1960s – *Zeitmasse*, *Gruppen*, *Momente* – as being defining statements in twentieth-century music and enjoys having this music programmed alongside his own. It is also not coincidental that these are some of the most ritualized works of the post-war years.

Brief mention might also be made here of other aspects of limited aleatoricism to be found in Birtwistle's approach to composition. One such is the use of random numbers. Another almost Cage-like example can be found in Birtwistle's description of a fascinating self-imposed restriction in the making of his Clarinet Quintet: 'I gave myself one condition: each [musical statement] had to be exactly as long as the paper I was using. It wasn't a question of writing until I came to the end of the sheet, then stopping; each had to fit the page exactly, each had to be complete.'[82] Like the use of random numbers, this restriction operates in the earlier stages of composition; the end result shows few traces of its origins. It is a stimulus to further (higher level) compositional decisions, not the composition itself (and thus clearly distinguishes itself from the Cagean 'anti-composerly' aesthetic).

The missing link between the freely treated dodecaphony of *Refrains and Choruses* and the Darmstadt-like practices of *Précis* lies in the *Three Sonatas for Nine Instruments*, originally given the more characteristically Birtwistle-like title of 'Sonata Cantus Choralis', a work clearly modelled on Webern's Op. 24. Scheduled for performance in June 1960 at the Aldeburgh Festival, it was withdrawn after the first rehearsal and was until recently assumed lost. However, thanks to the work of David Beard,[83] the score has now come to light at the Paul Sacher Stiftung, Basel, where Birtwistle has deposited many sketches and manuscripts. Beard has revealed a work steeped in twelve-note practices: indeed, it proves to be Birtwistle's only thoroughgoing serial composition and thus an extremely important historical document in helping to locate the composer's early developments firmly in the context of the European avant-garde. Why he withdrew the work is uncertain; there is no doubt that it was a brave act for one so early in his professional composing career. It certainly confirms Goehr's observation above about Birtwistle's suspicion of 'academic technique'. No doubt he found the strict application of the method too restrictive; it did not allow his creative freedom full flight. Michael Hall has suggested that the work's symmetries 'turned out to be too obvious',[84] but the composer did not need to hear the work for this to be apparent. (Indeed, symmetry, being in essence a spatial concept, is often far more obvious to the score-reader than it is to the listener – hence, for example, Berg's general avoidance of retrograde forms other than the most overt palindromes.) More likely, it sounded too modish, too much like the Webern pastiche which was everywhere in Europe at that time, and not enough of an individual voice. The only reason Birtwistle gives for its withdrawal is that 'it wasn't any good'.[85] By contrast, *Précis*, for all its Darmstadtishness, remains recognizably Birtwistle.

Ex. 1.5. *Secret Theatre* (opening).

Ex. 1.5 (cont'd)

= 108
1
fl
cl
tpt
hn
trbn
vib
pno
very fast
ob to solo position
con sord. (metal)
without motor, hard sticks

Ex. 1.5 (cont'd)

Ex. 1.5 (cont'd)

Though he never again attempted a wholehearted twelve-note composition, the serial legacy continues to resonate through Birtwistle's music. This is most obvious in his treatment of horizontal melody and its relationship to the vertical. The rotation/cycling of notes within a limited collection of pitch classes (a mode) is characteristic both of Stravinsky and of serial practice (the 'mode' is distinct from a 'row' in that the rotations/transformations are rarely strictly systematic: the 'mode' tends to be unordered, the 'row' ordered). Take the opening of *Secret Theatre*. What is interesting here is that, though Birtwistle is careful to make a distinct opposition between horizontal cantus (flute) and vertical continuum (strings), cyclic/rotational procedures are common to both. The flute cantus is built from two symmetrically placed chromatic tetrachords (D–E♭–E–F; A♭–A–B♭–B) around which it moves freely (see Ex. 1.5). The rotations of the continuum are much more regular and are performed on a more limited set of notes in each voice ('ostinato'). Note that the cello and bass 'modes', like that of the flute, are characterized by chromatic segments.[86] Note also the scotch-snap rhythms in the continuum after fig. 1. So, cantus and continuum share materials and processes while asserting their differences. Birtwistle himself recognized this in his (unprecedentedly public) notes made prior to composition, in which he asked 'at what point does an ostinato cease to function as such, due to the number of notes present in it? or the amount of time for it to register as a repeat? . . . ostinato into melody perhaps'.[87] In this case, the different roles enacted by the melodic 'ostinato' and that of the continuum are highlighted physically: the cantus player stands on a raised dais behind the main ensemble. At other points in the piece, the roles of cantus and continuum are exchanged. But what this brings to our attention once again is how close Stravinskian and serial procedures of pitch rotation really are. Perhaps Birtwistle (with Stravinsky, Berio and others) might argue that serial repetitions are just an elaborate kind of ostinato. That one of Birtwistle's freely rotating melodies can itself become a more overt kind of ostinato is made clear by, for example, the omnipresent melodic line of *Melencolia I*, which turns, at the end of the work, into a simple ostinato (fixed pitch order – D–E–C♯–G(A)–G♯ – but free rhythms) (Ex. 1.6). The other important feature to note about the opening bars (up to fig. 1) of *Secret Theatre* is that they organize all twelve notes of the total chromatic, but do not present them as a single twelve-note row. Furthermore, Birtwistle (like Stravinsky) gives prominence to certain focal pitches – here the important D–F dyad in both cantus and continuum – which are an important point of reference throughout the piece and, indeed, re-emerge writ large in *Secret Theatre*'s orchestral companion piece, *Earth Dances*.

SATIE

This discussion of ostinatos leads us to the work of another early modernist who is important for Birtwistle. He had encountered Erik Satie's music at an early age. Much later he made an arrangement of Satie's ballet *Mercure*, to which no doubt he was drawn in part because of what Constant Lambert described as the music's 'static abstraction' (Birtwistle uses Satie's subtitle, 'Poses plastiques'),[88] and also in part because of Picasso's close involvement with the original project. The early sets of piano pieces, the *Gymnopédies* and the *Gnossiennes*, in a much simpler but not entirely dissimilar manner to Boulez's 'tropes', illustrate the idea of viewing the same object from multiple perspectives. Each of the set is distinct yet in essence the same. They also have a timeless quality – not just as a result of the slow tempi, or the absence of metre (barlines) in the *Gnossiennes*, but also because they appear completely undirected, going round in circles or spirals, as if we can glimpse only part of some much larger totality. The music is brought to an artificial halt; it does not end. Instances of such procedures are too numerous to mention in Birtwistle; perhaps the most obvious examples are to be found in the constant but varied returns to the same basic material in *Silbury Air* and *Endless Parade*. As already mentioned, the relationship between the movements of *Harrison's Clocks* is also of this kind, if less obvious, while the sense of a timeless music being brought to an arbitrary

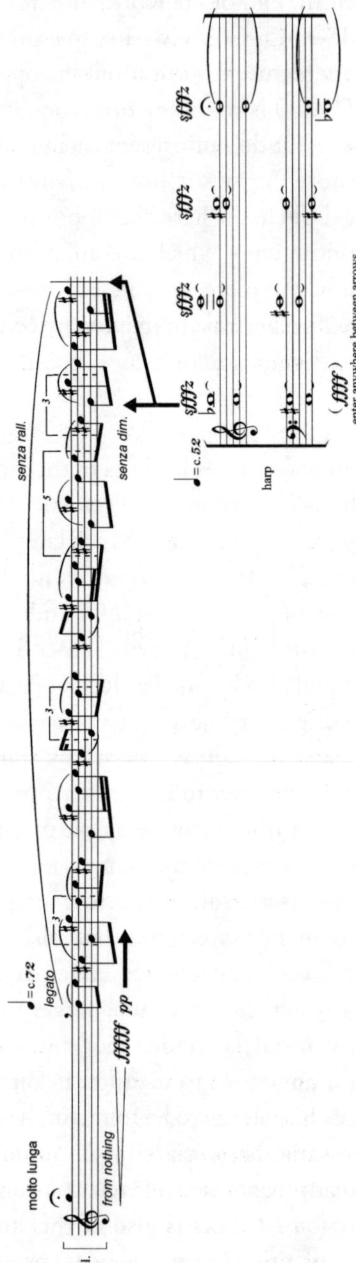

Ex. 1.6. *Melencolia I* (ending).

end is reinforced by the imitation of the clock mechanism unwinding. As Pruslin writes in his note on the work, 'Each piece begins *in media res*, and ends only because its clock-spring has wound down. The "heart" of the clock may have stopped, but the music could go on forever.'[89] The same could well be written of much Satie.

MESSIAEN

The name of Messiaen has already cropped up on a number of occasions as a significant influence: recall, for example, Birtwistle's student experience of *Turangalîla*. Goehr has written of the importance of Messiaen for all the Manchester group of composers in the 1950s:

> The most important event of my student life, however, was the impact of Messiaen. Messiaen, whom we became aware of at that time, represented . . . a kind of music which incorporated all the different ideas that concerned us: artificial modes, non-retrogradable rhythms, metrical experiments and number-generated structures.[90]

The general parallels with Birtwistle are obvious enough: bold, block structures defined by repetition; an interest in musical ritual and ceremony; structures where rhythm is the primary organizing parameter; a sophisticated modality; an interest in ancient, medieval and non-western forms and practices. It could, of course, be said that Messiaen himself derived such features in large part from Debussy and Stravinsky; one of the reasons why Messiaen so fascinated the young avant-garde across Europe might well have been his ability to suggest some sort of accommodation between the Franco-Russian line and Schoenberg's Austro-German line. In the context of the impact of the serial legacy on Birtwistle, Messiaen's use of modes of limited transposition bears useful comparison with Birtwistle's modes. A comparatively simple use of a mode which in some ways parallels Birtwistle's modal practice can be seen, for example, in the solo clarinet melody of the third movement ('Abîme des oiseaux') of the *Quartet for the End of Time* which begins in mode 2 (octatonic) and within which the melody moves freely, employing characteristic additive rhythmic patterns. Messiaen's influential 'twelve-note modes' (of pitches and durations) deployed in *Mode de valeurs et d'intensités* are not actually treated serially, regardless of the fact that the piece was one of the catalysts for the integral serialism of the 1950s. Like Birtwistle after him, Messiaen, despite the high degree of control of pitch, duration and dynamics, seems happy to use his 'rows' as freely as the compositional moment demands; he is not constrained by the system, but uses it as a starting-point. The end result is a beautifully layered music which seems to have neither beginning nor end; it shimmers but does not move: Stockhausen's description was of a 'fantastic music of the stars'.[91] In Messiaen's hands, even twelve-note music thus became some sort of mysterious cosmic ceremony. Elsewhere in Messiaen, the number-generated structures to which Goehr referred (such as the systematic 'personnages rythmiques') must have fascinated Birtwistle, even if, as with his own use of random numbers, they have little bearing on the expressive 'essentials' of Messiaen's music.

VARÈSE

One final element to be looked at in this constellation of musical modernisms of which Birtwistle's art is a part is the music of Varèse. Varèse's aesthetic (matched by his rhetoric) parallels that of Birtwistle in various ways. Once again, Stravinsky is the common link, while Klee and Picasso offer meaningful contexts. Birtwistle's sound-world – pre-eminently in the hard-edged works of the 1950s and 1960s – is that of Varèse: wind, brass and percussion; instrumental extremes (a shared penchant for clarinets – high, squealing E♭ clarinets and low, grumbling bass clarinets); a harmonic language of dissonant seconds, sevenths and ninths. Formally, too, Varèse's practice of building large forms or 'resultants' from individually coloured blocks or 'zones' is akin to the large-scale structure of many recent works of Birtwistle which do not depend on any ready-made formal given. The overall forms of works such as *Secret Theatre*, *Endless Parade*, *Earth Dances*, *Antiphonies* and *Exody* are hard to grasp, though the logic of the small- and medium-term repetitions (verse-refrain structures) is perfectly clear. Klee's idea of 'taking a line for a walk', so richly suggestive for Birtwistle, would also seem to be appropriate for Varèse. Take, for example, the opening of *Octandre* (1923). It is interesting that while Varèse was never a serial composer, he nonetheless organized the total chromatic in imaginative ways. Here it manifests itself as the progressive unfolding of all twelve notes, the first ten in the oboe, the eleventh (B♭) in the clarinet, and the twelfth (G) screeched *ffff* at the top of the oboe's range (bar 9). The rapid expansion of the music outwards at the completion of this line with the entry of the rest of the ensemble is an instance of the kind of movement and collision of sound masses of which Varèse spoke. Also important here is the symmetrical organization of the pitch space around this line. Thus, though the music gives the sense of being improvisatory and its linear progress is not always predictable, it is carefully contained by its symmetries and use of the total chromatic. The form of the movement as a whole proceeds in a moment-to-moment fashion by a series of 'collisions', a genuine 'resultant' stemming from taking the line for a walk. Birtwistle's *Refrains and Choruses* is his most Varèse-like work. Its symmetries, its only intermittently serial and flexible attitude to the total chromatic, its scoring (for wind quintet), its 'free' form, suggest obvious parallels with *Octandre*. It stands in stark contrast to the formalism of many of his works of the 1960s: 'I wrote it completely off the top of my head. I can't justify a single note.'[92] Compare Birtwistle's opening with Varèse's. It, too, is a free procedure where, starting from the horn's initial reiterated C, one idea leads to the next and is as much concerned with filling out the musical space as with any explicit generative process. First of all, the clarinet produces a descending line by progressive intervallic expansion (semitone–wholetone–minor 3rd–major 3rd), doubled by the flute. After a pause (bar 11), the next section (bars 12–20) reveals the proliferation of material by means of symmetry, a feature which is clearly on the surface of the music in the contrary motion of pairs of voices (see Ex. 1.7). But this is not Webern-like mirroring; it has the informality of Varèse: symmetry offers a procedural context but not a method to which the composer is rigidly bound. The music's rhetoric is clearly more important to him: hence, the important punctuating roles played by the horn (repeated focal notes), pauses and tempo fluctuations. The overall structure of *Refrains and Choruses*, like much of Varèse's music, cannot be evaluated in terms of a given form. It is through-composed where one section generates the next (in Birtwistle's own terms, the 'refrain, through repetition, becomes a predominant entity, and so [becomes] the chorus material of the following section'),[93] and where the regular (symmetry) is constantly being opposed with its irregular opposite. It is as if the piece defines its own rules, the mould being broken no sooner than the piece has been cast.

Elsewhere in Varèse, his love of percussion and his attempt to define instrumental roles within a purely percussive context (preeminently in *Ionisation*) find their match in *For O, for O, the Hobby-Horse is Forgot* – though the explicit role-play here of 'king', 'queen' and 'chorus' is more likely to have been derived from Birtwistle's understanding of, *inter alia*, the stylized ceremonies of Stravinsky (e.g. *Les Noces*). Comparison between Varèse's large-scale orchestral works, *Amériques* and *Arcana*, and *Earth Dances* is in many ways inevitable, in that the rhythmic energy, the structural layering and the instrumental imagination of the works of both composers exist in the strongly cast shadow of *The Rite of Spring*. Even in terms of their personalities, influences and respective historical positions, both composers have much in common: both are 'individualists' and belong to no particular school. While, in recent years, Birtwistle has engaged in more formal teaching activities (since 1994 he has been Henry Purcell Professor of Composition at King's College, London, and Director of Contemporary Music at the Royal Academy of Music),

Ex. 1.7. *Refrains and Choruses*, bars 1–20.

Ex. 1.7 (cont'd).

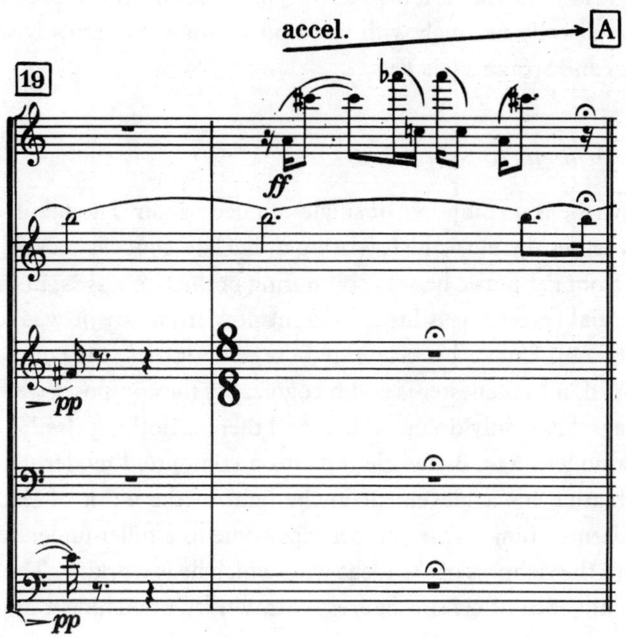

Ex. 1.7 (cont'd).

there is no 'Birtwistle School' as such, no generation of younger composers copying his style and compositional methodology – principally because there is no specific 'methodology' to be learnt.[94] A common interest in the visual arts, a propensity for geometrical structures and the influence of Cubism brings Varèse and Birtwistle together. One further point of contact is their reluctance to discuss compositional technique and a certain antagonism towards musical analysis. Jonathan Bernard has written of Varèse that he 'preferred to speak analogically, not analytically, of his music, often with reference to physical phenomena . . . Attempts to involve him in more narrowly defined, "analytical" discussions made him uneasy.'[95] The same words could easily have been written of Birtwistle. And they draw attention to the nature of Varèse's and Birtwistle's modernism: one which expresses a central – and, in part, instinctive – primitivism, and as such puts them directly in touch with the modernism of Picasso's *Demoiselles* and Stravinsky's *Rite*.

An Orpheus for our Time

Birtwistle is a composer of single-minded vision. Though in certain senses the music he is writing in the late 1990s is very different from the music he was composing in the late 1950s, in other essential respects it is little different now from how it was forty years ago. Unlike his celebrated contemporaries, the composer formed in Manchester is still recognizably the composer we hear today. 'I can only do one thing, and there is nothing else.'[96] In a postmodern age, Birtwistle remains a committed modernist. By evaluating his achievement in the light of the work of leading modernist thinkers we can perhaps come to a fuller understanding of the richness of the ideas with which he is working. Though the influence of certain figures – Stravinsky pre-eminent among them – may appear direct and ubiquitous, what is so fascinating about Birtwistle's music is the way it has renewed this inheritance, achieving an expression which seems both universal and particular, a music which gives the impression of being simultaneously ancient and utterly contemporary. Hence his preoccupation with myth and ritual, with formal theatre and stylized drama, with contexts that can give shape to deep feelings and ideas. And hence his obsession with simple musical structures and with the very basics of musical language, as if in every piece he were beginning again, as if every time he were inventing music itself all over again. Little wonder, then, that the story of Orpheus is so important to him. It is no exaggeration to say that every one of his works explores these musical fundamentals, these universal human truths.

2 *Episodion I* – Theatres

> For some composers, creating opera or music-theatre somehow requires a different, separate compositional process from the rest of their output. Harrison Birtwistle, however, like Hector Berlioz and the young Stravinsky, is a composer whose work in whatever form is 'theatrical' . . . [E]ven from the 1960s it is clear that Birtwistle's musical thought is inherently dramatic and that a sense of theatre pervades all his scores.[1]

We conventionally think of a theatrical drama – as indeed we do of opera – as something which is presented on a stage and which involves the relating of a story by means of dialogue and action. While such a narrow definition may well be true for many stage works, there is also the danger – especially in commercial contexts – that such theatre can turn into what Peter Brook famously described as 'Deadly Theatre':

> Deadliness always brings us back to repetition: the deadly director uses old formulae, old methods, old jokes, old effects, stock beginnings to scenes, stock ends; and this applies equally to his partners, the designers and composers, if they do not start each time afresh from the void, the desert and the true question – why clothes at all, why music, what for? A deadly director is a director who brings no challenge to the conditioned reflexes that every department must contain.[2]

The opposite, a living theatre, has those characteristics which Brook identifies in Elizabethan theatre where drama 'was exposure, it was confrontation, it was contradiction and it led to analysis, involvement, recognition and, eventually, to an awakening of understanding.'[3] For many reforming playwrights and dramatists of the early twentieth century, the naturalism and narrative inevitability of much nineteenth-century drama became a primary indicator of its 'deadliness'– what Nietzsche disparagingly described as 'the region of wax-work cabinets'[4] – and was codified perhaps most strongly in the naturalistic Method Acting of Stanislavsky. For Brecht, pre-eminent among such reformers, a drama became deadly when it tried to create the illusion of reality, where the audience 'suspended its disbelief' and identified directly with what was being represented on the stage. Brecht rejected the naturalism of classical and romantic theatre. By contrast, his epic theatre was anti-dramatic; that is, the audience was continually made aware that it was watching actors in the theatre, not real life: it was kept at a critical distance from the action by various devices of framing and estrangement (the *Verfremdungseffekt*). As Peachum states at the end of *The Threepenny Opera*, '. . . this is opera not life'. Meyerhold, too, challenged the Stanislavskian Method head on. Like Brecht after him, Meyerhold's theatre was concerned with the inner motivations of human behaviour rather than with plot and character. As both Stephen Walsh and Glenn Watkins have explored, Meyerhold's interest in, among other things, ancient popular theatres, masks, dance, mime and stylized gesture, resulted in a ritualized, anti-realistic theatre which was certainly an important influence on Stravinsky – especially evident in such works as *Renard* and *Les Noces*.[5] Similar interests in immediate, non-naturalistic, non-narrative ideas and techniques are echoed and pre-echoed in the work of many other early twentieth-century playwrights: the concern for masks and puppets in, for example, Jarry's shocking *Ubu roi*, Edward Gordon Craig's concept of the actor as *Übermarionette*, and in Cocteau's work; the related fascination (shared particularly by Meyerhold) with the characters of the *commedia dell'arte*, which further manifested itself in Stravinsky's *Petrushka* and *Pulcinella* and Schoenberg's *Pierrot lunaire*; a more general orientation towards what Brook calls the Rough Theatre of folk and popular traditions, such as Wedekind's and

Brecht's involvement with cabaret; a search outwards for models from oriental theatre, especially Balinese and Japanese; an obsession with theatre *qua* theatre, most famously in Pirandello's *Six Characters in Search of an Author* which begins with the stage instruction 'When the audience enters, the curtain is already up and the stage is just as it would be during the day'; and so on.

Such ideas were picked up and developed by later figures, too. Artaud's First Manifesto of the 'Theatre of Cruelty', for example, proposed that stage and auditorium should be done away with in order to bring about direct contact between actors and audience.[6] It also advocated a theatre concerned with myth, ritual and magic, with something metaphysical, which rediscovered 'the idea of a kind of unique language somewhere in between gesture and thought'.[7] Balinese theatre was thus important to him: 'In the Balinese theatre one senses a state prior to language, able to select its own language; music, gestures, moves and words . . . There is something of a religious ritual ceremony about them [Balinese productions], in the sense that they eradicate any idea of pretence, a ridiculous imitation of real life, from the spectator's mind.'[8] Such statements make it clear why Brook (on whose own directorial work Artaud was an enormous influence) designated Artaud's theatre a Holy Theatre. Important developments after World War II continued to challenge the expectations of conventional narrative theatre. Beckett's *Waiting for Godot*, in which as Estragon puts it, 'Nothing happens, nobody comes, nobody goes, it's awful',[9] is perhaps the best-known example of what has become known as the Theatre of the Absurd, a category to which such playwrights as Adamov, Genet and Ionesco, among others, are usually understood to belong. Interestingly, by Martin Esslin's definition, the Theatre of the Absurd also approaches Brook's category of the Holy Theatre:

> In expressing the tragic sense of loss at the disappearance of ultimate certainties the Theatre of the Absurd, by a strange paradox, is also a symptom of what probably comes nearest to being a genuine religious quest in our age: an effort,

> however timid and tentative, to sing, to laugh, to weep – and to growl – if not in praise of God . . . at least in search of a dimension of the Ineffable; an effort to make man aware of the ultimate realities of his condition, to instil in him against the lost sense of cosmic wonder and primeval anguish, to shock him out of an existence that has become trite, mechanical, complacent, and deprived of the dignity that comes of awareness.[10]

A still more experimental kind of innovation that emerged in both America and Europe in the 1950s, and which shared many of the attributes of the Theatre of the Absurd, was the cross-disciplinary Happening, reputedly initiated by Cage and his colleagues Rauschenberg, Johns, Cunningham and Tudor at Black Mountain College, North Carolina, and followed by all sorts of extraordinary examples of performance art which rejected traditional plot and character, even language itself. Cage's subsequent impact has been immense, drawing the attention of all musicians to the theatre involved in *any* musical performance – theatre on and off the stage or concert platform, a theatre in which both performers and audiences are directly involved.

This is the background against which Birtwistle began to produce a range of different kinds of theatre pieces from the 1960s onwards. Ideas about theatre and drama extend outwards from his stage works to embrace his entire compositional aesthetic (see Snowman's observations which head the present chapter), and the defining characteristics of that aesthetic put him in direct contact with many kinds of radical twentieth-century theatre and drama, through such aspects as his interest in anti-narrative, stylization, formalizing and framing devices, repetition, folklore, masks and puppetry; that is, through an engagement with both Holy and Rough Theatres. Birtwistle's theatrical sensibilities were perhaps most fully realized during his time as Music Director at the National Theatre, a period he regards as one of the most fulfilling of his compositional career. It was there that he was confronted directly with Brook's question: why music? If any piece of theatre is going to have music, then there must be a reason for it: it must spring from the theatre itself. This was also Brecht's view: 'When an actor sings he undergoes a change of function. Nothing is more revolting than when the actor pretends not to notice that he has left the level of plain speech and started to sing.'[11] In requiring his actors to become musicians by speaking rhythmically and singing in the Peter Hall production of Aeschylus's *Oresteia* trilogy (see the discussion in Chapter 3), Birtwistle was dealing directly with their motivation, reinforcing through music, for example, the structural changes in dramatic function from prologue to chorus to episode, and so on.

It is first and foremost the formality of ancient Greek tragedy which appeals to Birtwistle: the drama is not attempting to be naturalistic, it is not pretending to tell a story as if it were unfolding in the present tense. Its formal structure, its frames and articulatory points, are clear for all to see, enhanced in the *Oresteia* production by a stylized music with a strongly punctuating role (the very opposite of the mood-reinforcing character of so much contemporary film music whose presence usually goes entirely unnoticed). And this is also the reason why Birtwistle is so interested in opera and oratorio – not because of their narrative qualities but because of their formality: 'There are certain things you don't have to justify in an opera, and one of these is its formality . . .'[12] In such genres, recitative, aria, chorale, dance, and so on, all have a clearly defined musico-dramatic function and make no claim to be playing a realistic role. It should be no surprise, then, that in his most stylized theatre pieces – pre-eminently *Punch and Judy* and *The Mask of Orpheus* – such historically loaded formal types occur overtly. This, on one level, is what Pruslin means when he describes the work as a 'source opera'. On another level, this is blatantly nonsense: it cannot succeed in creating 'the illusion of having been written before' all other operas because our understanding of the work's structure depends on our recognizing these historical forms and their historical functions. Judy's Passion Aria, to give just one example, like Jocasta's aria in *Oedipus Rex*, is not an aria as such but an aria in quotation marks, an aria 'made strange'. When the stage characters step forward at the end of *The Rake's Progress* to sing the moral – just, indeed, as they do at the end of *Don Giovanni* – we have to recognize this moment for what it is: a theatrical device, a frame which draws attention to the fact that we are in a theatre watching actors. 'Our littel play is at an end', speaks Choregos at the end of *Punch and Judy*. Not a weak ending, but a very necessary device to signal the conclusion of proceedings which, given the cyclic nature of the work, might well begin all over again.

Birtwistle was not the only composer of the 1960s to be taking a renewed interest in 'rough' music theatre. The post-war disapproval of opera – that bourgeois genre *par excellence* – among the European avant-garde, further fed by the experiments of the Happenings and performance art, resulted in new kinds of music theatre dependent neither on inappropriate narrative forms nor on conventional institutions such as opera houses. In addition, it might well be argued that the high modernist concerns with structure – both in integral serialism and in electronic music which did not even require a visible performer – had failed to speak to any audience other than the most committed devotees found at such places as Darmstadt. A new eagerness to communicate with audiences, combined with a desire to engage with the politics of the left, fed the quest after novel expressive forms. The challenge to conventional opera in the late 1950s and 1960s in such large-scale anti-narrative works of total theatre as Zimmermann's *Die Soldaten* (an important precursor of *The Mask of Orpheus*) and Nono's *Intolleranza*, as well as Berio's *Passaggio*, *Laborintus II* and *Opera*, was matched by impressive smaller-scale music theatre experiments of the 1960s such as Maxwell Davies's *Revelation and Fall*, *Eight Songs for a Mad King* and *Vesalii Icones*, Henze's *El Cimarrón* and *Der langwierige Weg in die Wohnung der Natascha Ungeheuer*, Ligeti's nonsense *Aventures* and *Nouvelles aventures*, and so on. Their twin roots are to be found in *The Soldier's Tale* and *Pierrot lunaire*. And it is clearly to this tradition that Birtwistle's *Punch and Judy* belongs, the conjoining of the roughness of Stravinsky's eclectic, ritualized folk entertainment and the formalized, expressionistic violence of Schoenberg's latent theatre. Birtwistle's Manchester colleagues and other satellite musicians (principally Pruslin) were obsessed with *Pierrot* – in 1967 they were even to bless their own ensemble with its name. But while Maxwell Davies in particular was to explore the opportunities offered by the *Pierrot* model of individual characters *in extremis*, Birtwistle was to find greater musical possibilities in Stravinsky's more 'objective' models, with their emphasis on the collective rather than the individual, on non-narrative role-play. Even *Monodrama*, Birtwistle's work written for the first Pierrot Players concert performed alongside *Pierrot lunaire* and Maxwell Davies's *Antechrist*, while scored for Schoenberg's ensemble plus percussion, was a theatre of a very different (collective) order. However, one fascinating consequence of these developments was Birtwistle's so-called instrumental theatre, precedents and parallels for which can be found in the work of Berio (*Circles*, *Sequenze*), Boulez (*Domaines*) and Messiaen (most notably *Chronochromie* which, like *Tragoedia*, is structured according to the divisions of Greek tragedy). *Tragoedia* is a work of latent theatre which was to find its realization overtly in *Punch and Judy*. *Verses for Ensembles*, however, is the logical consequence of *Tragoedia*, where the physical movements of the players about the concert platform enact some kind of abstract drama – or, rather, their movements spell out spatially the dramatic oppositions of the musical structure. Subsequently *For O, for O, the Hobby-Horse is Forgot*, *Secret Theatre*, *Ritual Fragment* and (to a more limited extent) *Slow Frieze* have, among other works, developed this 'genre' in new and sophisticated ways. Even a work such as *Five Distances for Five Instruments* dramatizes spatially the differences between different wind instruments and their musical material.

These interests might help, in part, to account for Birtwistle's fascination with Greek tragedy. Aristotle's analysis of Attic drama in his *Poetics* offers further clues. In tragedy, for Aristotle, 'the most important [element] is the plot, the ordering of the incidents; for tragedy is a representation, not of men, but of action and life, of happiness and unhappiness – and happiness and unhappiness are bound up with action.'[13] This definition certainly fits well with Birtwistle's theatre pieces. It is not the story that is of primary importance, hence his reliance on mythical subject-matter; rather, it is the way in which it is told, the ordering of the incidents, that is most important – that is, its ritual formality. Aristotle reinforces this point by arguing that tragedies 'are not performed . . . in order to represent character, although character is involved for the sake of action. Thus the incidents and the plot are the end aimed at in tragedy . . . Furthermore, there could not be a tragedy without action, but there could be without character'.[14] Such a statement helps explain the dramatic effectiveness of *The Mask of Orpheus*, in which we learn little of the character of Orpheus *per se*: Orpheus is, at the highest level, just a function of the plot – a decidedly structuralist interpretation, but one which allows Birtwistle and Zinovieff to represent Orpheus in multiple form – but who nonetheless expresses passionate emotions of love and loss. After all, as Aristotle states in the very first part of the *Poetics*, tragedy is a form of imitation or representation. It helps, too, to account for the success of *Punch and Judy* – admittedly, like *Godot*, a tragicomedy (see Chapter 4) – despite the lack of a conventional narrative. (Certainly the apparent resolution at the end, when Punch finally gets his girl, is not the main point of the work, and the librettist is at pains to point out that it was not necessarily his intention to suggest 'a causal connection between Punch's aggression and his idealistic quest for Pretty Polly, so that he embarked on a series of murders in order to win her. The opera then became an amoral fable ending with the triumph of evil.')[15] *Punch* wears the structure of its plot on its sleeve and in many respects one might argue that the work is essentially about the way in which its interlocking cycles of repetition are organized. The puppet characters are necessary for the work to operate as myth and are involved, as Aristotle put it, for the sake of action, but I, for one, am not disturbed or frightened by the violence of *Punch and Judy* (it seems comical) and I am not moved to tears by the passionate expressions of love and rejection (they seem ironic). 'The plot, then, is the first essential of tragedy, its life-blood, so to speak, and character takes the second place.'[16]

Aristotle's analysis helps to account for the failure of *Monodrama*, an allegory without a plot. But it also helps provide a context for the dramatic effectiveness of Birtwistle's works of instrumental theatre. *Tragoedia* is a clear instance of a tragedy *with* action but *without* character – though the action is in part defined by the abstract roles played by the instrumentalists. The overall structure of *Tragoedia* is given in Fig. 2.1, indicating clearly how it takes on the formal aspects of Greek tragedy as defined by Aristotle:

> The prologue is the whole part of a tragedy that precedes the parode, or first entry of the Chorus. An episode is the whole of that part of the tragedy that comes between complete choral songs. The exode is the whole of that part of the tragedy which is followed by a song of the Chorus, and a stasimon is a choral song without anapaests or trochees.[17]

Neither *Punch and Judy* nor *Verses for Ensembles* was conceived explicitly according to Aristotle's tragic schema (though Pruslin enjoys Gabriel Josipovici's description of *Punch* as 'ancient Greek drama in the guise of popular puppetry').[18] Nonetheless, Fig. 2.1 also reveals how closely these works parallel the structure of *Tragoedia*. Each has a clearly defined prologue, the main body of each is built from a series of episodes, and the structure of each literally turns about a still centre, the stasimon.

This structural reversal brought about by the stasimon is one of two important constituents of the plot identified by Aristotle; indeed he goes so far as to describe them as 'the two most important means by which tragedy plays on our feelings, that is, "reversals" [*peripeteia*] and "recognitions" [*anagnorisis*]'.[19] The latter he goes on to define as:

> . . . a change from ignorance to knowledge, and it leads either to love or to hatred between persons destined for

FIG. 2.1. Comparison of overall design of *Tragoedia*, *Verses for Ensembles* and *Punch and Judy*.

a) *Tragoedia*

Prologue				
	Parados			
		Episodion: Strophe I	Antistrophe I	
				Stasimon
		Episodion: Strophe II	Antistrophe II	
	Exodos			

b) *Verses for Ensembles*

Prologue			
	Parados		
		Episodion: I	
			Stasimon
		Episodion: II	
	Exodos		

c) *Punch and Judy*

Prologue					
		Melodrama I	Passion Chorale I	Quest I	
		Melodrama II	Passion Chorale II	Quest II	
		Melodrama III			
					Nightmare
			Passion Chorale III	Quest III	
		Melodrama IV			
	Punch Triumphans				
Epilogue					

> good or ill fortune. The most effective form of discovery [or recognition] is that which is accompanied by reversals, like the one in *Oedipus*.[20]

In other words, *anagnorisis* 'is the moment at which the characters understand their predicament fully for the first time, the moment that resolves a sequence of unexplained and often implausible occurrences; it makes the world (and the text) intelligible'. This summary of Aristotle is made by one of the most important writers on *anagnorisis*, Terence Cave, whose own generally preferred translation of the term is 'recognition', though its slipperiness is made clear by Cave's catalogue of other translations, among which number discovery, revelation, self-recognition, wakening, illumination, recovery of knowledge and so on. It is, Cave begins his book by stating, 'unquestionably the least respectable term in Aristotelian poetics'. This is because it is often perceived as a contrivance, 'a shoddy way of resolving a plot the author can no longer control'. He goes on to define recognition in terms of 'scandal' (after the French *scandale*), and not just because so many recognition plots are actually about scandalous goings-on. From a critical perspective, *anagnorisis* is a 'stumbling block, an obstacle to belief; it disturbs . . . it seduces the reader into a trap or snare (*skandalon*) – hunting . . . is a metaphor endemic in the topic'. From this, the shock rendered by recognition, he moves towards a reverse interpretation; that is, the fact that recognition can also bring about 'a shift into the implausible: the secret unfolded lies beyond the realm of common experience; the truth discovered is "marvellous" (*thaumaston*, to use Aristotle's term), the truth of fabulous myth or legend'.[21] He even allows for the possibility, as in *Waiting for Godot*, for what he describes as 'imperfect recognition' where 'an expected recognition wholly fails to materialize'.[22]

What has this to do with Birtwistle? For a start, not only are the majority of his theatre works based on the formal precepts of Greek tragedy in one way or another, but it is also characteristic for their plots to turn on moments of *anagnorisis*, as detailed below.

• 'Truly the light is sweet, and a pleasant thing it is for the eyes to behold the sun', speaks and sings the defiant chorus of women towards the end of *The Mark of the Goat*. Though Lucus has been killed by Capran's troops, the women's discovery of the power of his symbol, the sun, brings about the disablement of the soldiers: 'We are helpless, useless, crippled with fear before the defiance of women!' The women turn, the narrative turns, through the illumination of the sun.

• By contrast, it is in the darkest 'Nightmare' section of *Punch and Judy* (the point of structural *peripeteia*) that Punch the protagonist is forced to confront his previous crimes. The entire section is built of disguises (Polly as witch, Judy as fortune-teller, dream as reality) and at the height of the tarot game Punch literally recognizes Judy – she reveals herself; she is unmasked.

• It could certainly be argued that the essentials of the plot of *Bow Down* are made almost entirely from recognitions (unmaskings) of one kind or another, where a member of the chorus is revealed as a principal character, and vice versa. The key dramatic moments are similarly brought about by *anagnorisis*, first when the Miller's Daughter goes to the water with her bucket and discovers the body of the Fair Sister, and later, just before the work's conclusion, when the King recognizes the voice of his daughter who has been transformed into a harp.[23]

• The Orpheus myth, whose multiple retellings form the substance of *The Mask of Orpheus*, is built around a moment of literal turning, of recognition, of tragic reversal. Having journeyed to Hades and had Eurydice restored to him, Orpheus was, as Virgil tells the tale, overcome by madness:

> . . . he halted
> And on the very brink of light, alas,
> Forgetful, yielding in his will, looked back
> At his own Eurydice. At that same instant
> All his endeavour foundered . . .[24]

Or, as Boethius tells the tale, and as set by Birtwistle in his madrigal *On the Sheer Threshold of the Night*, 'Orpheus saw Eurydice. Looked, and destroyed her.' In Act 2 of *The Mask of Orpheus*, Orpheus's moment of *anagnorisis* takes the form of his awakening, and his realization that his journey into the underworld had been entirely imaginary.

• *Yan Tan Tethera* turns on Hannah's recognition that the dark-haired twin boys with Caleb Raven are *not* her own sons, but that she must nonetheless accept them: 'I'll take them in care to save them from you.'

• In the light of Cave's observations quoted above, it is interesting that Gawain's self-recognition in Act 2 of the opera occurs after the ritualized Hunt, itself an allegory for the seduction and entrapment of Gawain. At the Green Knight's third swing of the axe, Gawain recognizes his own shortcomings: 'Not greed and love? I'm guilty of both. I wanted fame. I loved myself too much. I'm guilty of cowardice, too.' Morgan's magic shape-shifts the Green Knight, who is revealed as Bertilak. This moment of *anagnorisis* prompts *peripeteia*: 'Become yourself', Morgan sings to Gawain, 'your purpose has just begun. Now you must go back, taking with you everything you've gained: greed, self-love and cowardice.' The plot turns; Gawain journeys back to the court of Arthur.

• The moment of *anagnorisis* in *The Second Mrs Kong* comes in the opera's last scene. Kong has undergone many trials and temptations in order to reach Pearl. When they finally meet – the moment they have longed for, one of physical recognition – they try (to terrifying, electrifying music) to touch, but cannot. They plead with the Mirror to say their loneliness is over and their happiness can begin, but of course the Mirror cannot. She not only accurately reflects the reality of their situation – that Kong is only an idea and Pearl only an image – but her appearance at this point is also an *act* of reflection, of *anagnorisis*. Kong and Pearl cannot have each other. The characters recognize that it is the yearning for what cannot be that moves the world from night to morning. The presence here of Orpheus and Eurydice reinforces this.

It is also interesting to note here Birtwistle's use of 'two' soprano voices combined in rhythmic unison to represent the Mirror – the singer sings with her own pre-recorded reflection – a technique he had already employed in *On the Sheer Threshold of the Night* where tenor and counter-tenor are combined for the role of Orpheus. An obvious precedent is to be found in the use of two singers combined to represent the voice of God in Stravinsky's *The Flood* (1961–2), itself – arguably – cribbed from the same procedure in Britten's *Canticle II: Abraham and Isaac* (1952). Though the dramatic situations employing this technique are different, the combining of voices nonetheless seems to be symbolic of the possession of greater knowledge on the part of that character (God, Orpheus, Mirror) than those around him or her. Aristotle defined *anagnorisis* as a change from ignorance to knowledge, and for Cave the term 'carries within its etymology and its definition . . . the theme of knowledge'. Cave quotes the critic F. L. Lucas who defines it as 'the realization of the truth, the opening of the eyes, the sudden lightning-flash in the darkness.'[25] For Britten and Stravinsky, an omniscient God is self-evidently a personification of *anagnorisis*. Birtwistle's Mirror, too, brings about 'the opening of the eyes'. In Orpheus's case, his knowledge comes from the combination of the masculine and the feminine, a division dramatized in the work by the antiphonal arrangement of the singers on the platform: the multiple Orpheus is in the centre with the women and Eurydice (soprano) ranged to his left and the men and Hades (bass) to his right.

• Into the twelve-character *dramatis personae* of *The Last Supper* Birtwistle and Robin Blaser have introduced a thirteenth called Ghost, the only woman amidst twelve men who has the Choregos-like function of *anagnorisis*, of commentary, of illumination, of revelation of meanings to the audience: 'I am the ghost of you', she sings.

Anagnorisis, according to Cave, is 'a means of knowing which is different from rational cognition. It operates surreptitiously, randomly, elliptically and often perversely, seizing on precisely those details that from a rational point of view seem trivial.'[26] This reading rings true for the plots of Birtwistle's operas which can turn on the most apparently insignificant details – a green sash in *Gawain*, a mere turn of the head in *Orpheus*. But it also offers the possibility of reading the structure of purely instrumental works in terms of *anagnorisis*. Birtwistle is interested in the musical world of the 'beyond-word', in the expression of deep and important ideas that lie beyond rational cognition but can be accessed through myth and ritual. Furthermore, Cave's assertion that the 'interest of recognition scenes in drama and narrative fiction is perhaps that, more than any other literary motif or element, they have *the character of an old tale*'[27] offers additional evidence for the significance of the *anagnorisis* trope for all Birtwistle's music – where each new work, to appropriate Pruslin's words once again, becomes a source work which, though written after all others, gives the illusion of having been written before them. This 'ancient', monumental quality is apparent in so many works, from *Nomos* to *Silbury Air*, from . . . *agm* . . . to *Earth Dances*. And it is in part achieved – to return to Snowman's opening observations – as a result of the inherently dramatic nature of Birtwistle's musical thought.

Michael Hall talks in similar terms. For him, Birtwistle's music is 'not merely dramatic in the sense that Beethoven's music is dramatic; it is as if the platform were a stage and the players *dramatis personae*.'[28] Hall's subsequent identification of protagonists and other kinds of role-play becomes a little obsessive, his reading of the 'drama' perhaps too literal, but it is interesting that in a handful of pieces he uncovers a decisively Aristotelian conjunction of *anagnorisis* and *peripeteia*. In his analysis of *Verses* for clarinet and piano, for example (see Chapter 5), he discusses a moment of mutual recognition of formerly opposed materials for the two instruments about which the structure of the whole turns. The climax of *Refrains and Choruses* is defined, in Hall's terms, by role reversal and the absorption of the horn into the rest of the ensemble. But working with Cave's more open-ended interpretation of the functions of *anagnorisis*, it can be shown to be useful to extend the concept to a wider range of Birtwistle's instrumental works.

Take, for example, the percussion piece *For O, for O, the Hobby-Horse is Forgot*. Birtwistle was working at the National Theatre on music for *Hamlet* at the time of the work's composition, but why did he select this seemingly trivial moment of pantomime (from Act 3, scene 2) to form the basis for an extended instrumental composition? Birtwistle was not deceived by its apparent simplicity; the trivial may actually be fundamental. Following the enactment of a dumb show by King, Queen and Poisoner, Ophelia asks Hamlet what it might mean. 'Marry, this is miching mallecho; it means mischief', responds Hamlet. 'Belike this show imports the argument of the play', observes Ophelia. And so it proves to be. By the end of *Hamlet*, with the Queen poisoned and the King stabbed, we – as does Hamlet himself before he is wounded by the poisoned rapier – retrospectively recognize the prophetic meaning of the dumb show. The device of the play-within-the-play is, for Cave, associated with recognition, 'creating shifting relationships between life and text'.[29] The dumb show is thus itself an act of *anagnorisis*. Birtwistle, it would seem, has recognized its profound significance. His preoccupation, like Stravinsky's, with seemingly primitive kinds of theatre is a result of his recognition of their profound mythopoeic power.

This fascination with the 'dumb show', with the secondary, symbiotic drama, occurs elsewhere in Birtwistle. Perhaps the most obvious examples are the Passing Clouds and Allegorical Flowers of *The Mask of Orpheus*, literally dumb shows (mimes). They are allegorical interludes within the larger allegory and take the shape of tales told by Orpheus to the trees after losing Eurydice for the second time. There are six interludes in all, three stories of violent deaths (the Clouds of Abandon: the stories of Dionysus, Lycurgas and Pentheus) and three lyrical stories of love, but also containing deaths (the Flowers of Reason: the anemone, the hyacinth and the lotus). They reflect both the violence of the death of Orpheus and the lyricism of his love for Eurydice, yet they remain independent of the principal drama. They have the function of *anagnorisis* in that they illuminate the main narrative. It is also worth noting that each mime is danced purely to the sound of the harp (albeit electronically transformed), not only representing the self-accompaniment of Orpheus's laments on the lyre, but also symbolizing the act of *anagnorisis*, just as did the figure of the Harp-Sister in *Bow Down*, and just as the related sound of the cimbalom is always associated with the reflections of the chorus-like Mirror in *Mrs Kong*. The filmic interpolations in *The Second Mrs Kong* function like plays-within-the-play: they are windows on to a different narrative (one that we all know, but a story that is only alluded to and never actually told in full in the opera) which illuminates the principal plot while remaining differentiated from it. The comic pantomime, the mummery of *Down by the Greenwood Side*, theatre as theatre, acts as a commentary on Mrs Green's tragic tale. The coming-together of the two narratives at the end is the moment of mutual *anagnorisis* (discussed more fully in Chapter 4 as an aspect of pastoral tragicomedy).

But there are instances of the discovery of something only symbiotically connected to the main narrative in instrumental works too. One of the most striking is the 'discovery' of *The Fields of Sorrow* at the heart of *The Triumph of Time*. It is a clear moment of recognition, literally for those listeners who know the earlier work, but rhetorically too, with its striking focus on E and its chiming bell-like sounds (note the symbolic presence of the harp once again). Structurally, though, the key act of *anagnorisis* occurs around fig. 26 where the amplified soprano saxophone's recurrent three-note motif finally blossoms into a melody, an event which is recognized by the woodwind who take up that very melody and present it as a kind of chorale.

This leads us to the role of the chorus, which is so important to Birtwistle as, *inter alia*, a representation of the collective. But the chorus – as observers and commentators – can also be understood to have an *anagnoristic* role. In Act 3, scene 2 of *Hamlet*, following the dumb show, the players begin their play proper with the entry of a Prologue who, like Choregos in *Punch and Judy* (itself with something of the character of a dumb show about it), entreats the audience, 'For us and for our tragedy, Here stooping to your clemency, We beg your hearing patiently.' Hamlet once again interprets the action, prompting Ophelia to describe him as 'a good chorus'. For Cave, the Greek chorus is an example of 'a reader in the text . . . Narrators present themselves as observers, unravelling the half-hidden deeds and motivations of the character proper.'[30] This role-play is crucial for Birtwistle, whether derived from Greek drama, from Stravinsky (*The Soldier's Tale*, *Oedipus Rex*, etc.), or wherever else. But as in Stravinsky, as in Messiaen, the purely instrumental chorus (refrain) is also significant. Here it is the rhetoric of the chorale that is important. The exemplar is the chorale at the end of Stravinsky's *Symphonies of Wind Instruments*, towards which the work as a whole appears to move and which Cone argues brings about 'synthesis', which he defines as 'some sort of unification . . . [whereby] diverse elements are brought into closer and closer relation with one another, all ideally being accounted for in the final resolution.'[31] The significance of this chorale is not so much that it unifies or resolves – indeed, it resists closure even as it enforces it – but (merely) that it signals a temporary halt, leaving the work ambiguously open-ended. Pieter van den Toorn describes it as 'a terminating convenience, an expedient, a "device"'.[32] It is thus a structural device of recognition and is clearly a goal of some kind, helping to make sense of the kaleidoscopic fragments that lead up to it. This generally seems to be Birtwistle's understanding of the function of the chorale, too: it clarifies, it illuminates, it accompanies moments of stillness, of revelation, of self-recognition.

A clear example is the gentle chorale for wind and brass that occurs near the end of Act 1, scene 3 of *The Mask of Orpheus* to accompany Orpheus's First Shout of Gratitude (Shout of Triumph) where he finally realizes the meaning of what the Oracle has been telling him. His words, 'I remember the arches . . .', are spoken over this music: he understands from the Oracle's three clues that he must journey to the underworld and back. The chorale signals this moment of recognition. But there are also chorales in purely instrumental works. The chorale-like writing which closes *Carmen Arcadiae Mechanicae Perpetuum* functions in a manner not dissimilar to Stravinsky's *Symphonies*. In *Panic* the wind chorale, which parallels that found in *Orpheus,* is the moment where the chorus achieves greatest coherence. The brief *Chorale from a Toy-Shop* (significantly written *in memoriam* Stravinsky, just as Stravinsky's *Symphonies* chorale was written *in memoriam* Debussy) is another of the objects 'discovered' in *The Triumph of Time*. While the invented Passion Chorales of *Punch and Judy* signal a structural engagement with what Pruslin calls the 'invisible theatre' of Bach's *St Matthew Passion*, an actual Bach chorale is used (and abused) in *Medusa*. And in one particular case, the chorale is magnified (seizing on the 'trivial' detail) into a twenty-minute orchestral composition: *Chorales for Orchestra*. Like *The Triumph of Time*, Birtwistle draws analogies between this music and a Bruegel painting, in this case *The Martyrdom of St Catherine*, a work in which Catherine herself is an insignificant detail, as the portrayal of an individual death is subordinated to the dominant presence of the landscape. (All decidedly Birtwistle-like characteristics – compare again with the themes of *Orpheus* where, by the end, personal tragedy has been subsumed by the landscape.) What is interesting in *Chorales* is how not only an entire work is built principally from a single moment of *anagnorisis* (the 'frozen' moment) but, if one accepts Hall's interpretation, its structure again accords with the formalization of Greek drama: 'The search for the chorale creates the tension, the recognition of it [at] the climax, at which stage the structure turns back to its point of maximum repose.'[33]

There might appear to be a contradiction at the heart of this account of Birtwistle's theatre. On the one hand, an examination of the historical contexts for Birtwistle's experiments with different kinds of theatre emphasizes both the contemporaneity and originality of his achievements. This is a process in which the composer himself has attempted to participate, aligning himself with the high modernist enterprise of the post-war years in which the likes of Boulez were arguing for an abandonment of the past, for the destruction of all opera houses and so on. In relation to *The Mask of Orpheus* Birtwistle claimed that he 'wanted to invent a formalism which does not rely on tradition . . . I didn't want to hark back any more; I wanted to create a formal world that was utterly new.' On the other hand, his ongoing interest not only in classical subject-matter but in the very forms and techniques of Attic tragedy, of Baroque opera, even of Wagnerian music drama, shows a composer acutely aware of and responding creatively to past traditions. In practice, Birtwistle's theatres seem to strike a fascinating balance between these two tendencies. The bold violence of his music theatre works of the 1960s is given meaning by being contained within ancient archetypes. The rite is renewed for contemporary sensibilities. Herein lies its originality and its expressive power. Though his subsequent works have never been quite so uncompromising in their confrontations, similar concerns adapted to new contexts echo through even his most recent pieces.

To conclude, two brief case studies follow in order to try to get a sense of how theatre and music operate together and comment on each other in Birtwistle's work, and how old debates between modernism and tradition achieve an exciting equilibrium in his theatre pieces. His works of instrumental theatre are among his most innovative contributions to recent music, and it is the structural integration of music and theatre (away from the convenient prop of a text) that is so satisfying about many of these works.

The overall structure of *Verses for Ensembles* in terms of a (latent) Greek tragedy is only one aspect of its drama. Another is its concern for the dramatic confrontation of boldly defined blocks of musical material – at its most acute in the two Episodion. But in this work, the drama is also actually realized, it is 'enacted': by their spatial distribution and simple movements about the platform, the players present to the audience a stylized drama whose plot is not explicit but where the physical relationships between individuals and groups is always changing. It is, like *Tragoedia*, an abstract drama, a ceremonial, but where the visual theatre now mirrors the processes at work inside the music.

Firstly, as in so many of Birtwistle's works, a carefully specified arrangement of the players on the concert platform represents, in spatial terms, the divisions between groups of instruments within the music.[34] The woodwind, seated at the front of the stage, use one block of seating on the left when they are playing as a high-pitched ensemble, and another block on the right when they play as a low ensemble. Hence, when the bassoonist takes up the contra bassoon, for instance, s/he has to move from the left to the right of the stage. A change in the instrument's role is thus articulated musically by the change in the instrument's range and timbre and physically by the change in the player's position within the performing space. Seated behind the woodwind is the brass quintet, and behind this are two further levels, one for the untuned percussion and one for the tuned. The two different types of percussion are played by the same players so that movement between the two levels becomes necessary; however, each distinct group always plays as an ensemble (tuned and untuned are never mixed) so again their movements articulate timbral changes. The brass play as a full ensemble less frequently. The horn has an important solo role whilst the two trumpets demonstrate a tendency to break away and continue an independent musical 'conversation'. This too is represented theatrically as each soloist moves to a new position at one of four solo platforms around the stage, two at the back and two at the front. The trombones never take on the roles of soloists, so remain permanently seated in their ensemble positions. It is a reminder, perhaps, of another kind of drama, one where the stage becomes a church. Here, the rows of players make up the choir, while 'lessons' are read from lecterns, and musicians call to one another from the galleries. This is a Holy Theatre where ritual movement, repetition and stylized role-play become the principal focus of attention.

The horn and the trumpet have important roles in marking the beginnings and endings of blocks of material. With the exception of the central horn/woodwind verses, it is only they who move to occupy the solo platforms and it is often from these positions, detached from the rest of the players, that they announce new sections or bring others to a close. Like the Greek chorus, they can both stand outside the main action to comment on it and announce the arrival of new characters, and participate in the drama from within the ensemble. At these major moments of articulation, the physically remote soloists present musical material which is quite distinct; indeed, Michael Nyman has observed that 'the formation of a new and entirely convincing cadential "language" is one of the most original features of the score'.[35]

It is generally the horn that signals the start of each main section: it plays its familiar role of protagonist. Conversely, the role of the trumpets is one of closure; like the horn, they repeat certain striking musical ideas at moments of structural importance. They have two quite distinct musical ideas associated with different structural blocks (and, hence, different parts of the platform), although they are related in terms of their antiphonal writing. The first idea is built around a perfect fourth and brings both the Prologue and the entire work to a conclusion (Ex. 2.1a). On both these occasions, like masters-of-ceremonies, the trumpeters step forward to the solo desks at the front of the stage and announce the beginning and end of the 'drama' (compare with Choregos's fanfare, 'Let's trumpets sound', at the start of *Punch and Judy*). The second group of ideas appears only in the two Episodion where the trumpets gradually assert their independence, eventually escaping entirely the metrical hegemony of the main ensemble (fig. 28 – see Ex. 2.1b). The musical isolation of the trumpets is echoed in theatrical terms by their occupying the two rear solo platforms whose stereophonic positioning also gives a spatial representation to the antiphonal nature of the writing. At fig. 29 they rejoin the main tempo, their musical reintegration being signalled by a return to their positions within the ensemble. The trumpets' behaviour here illustrates the more general relationship in this work between solo writing, limited indeterminacy and spatial

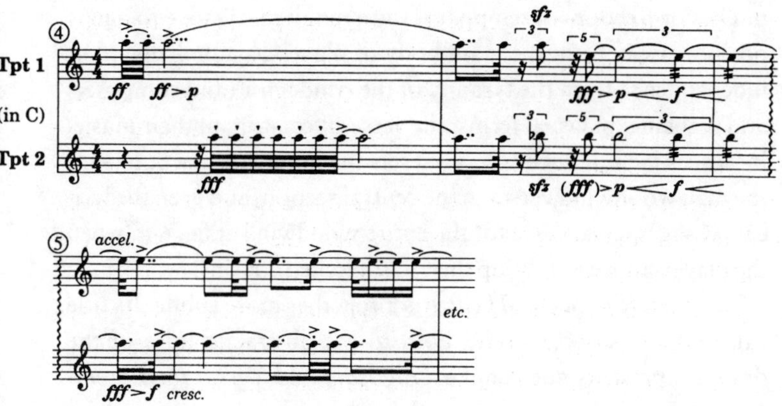

Ex. 2.1a. *Verses for Ensembles*, figs 4–5.

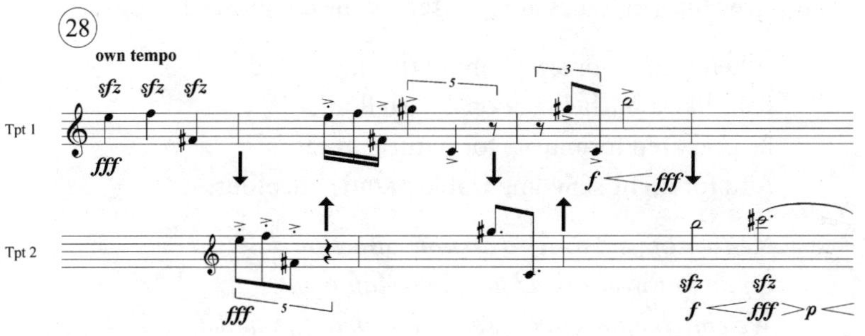

Ex. 2.1b. *Verses for Ensembles*, fig. 28.

separation. On each occasion that players are given choices of pitches or freedom of tempo, they are required to move to a new position away from the main body of players, symbolizing their independence from the tyranny of the conductor (and composer) and realizing, in visual terms, the verse-like nature of their music. Instances include such solo verses as the horn cadenza at fig. 13, the high woodwind verses in the central section, and even the lyrical passages (chorales?) for the entire woodwind at fig. 6 ff. when the players move to take up their low-pitched cousins.

The theatre of *Secret Theatre* is altogether more subtle. Its title can be understood to refer both to the abstract nature of the drama it presents and, unlike *Tragoedia* and *Verses for Ensembles*, to the less overt 'rules' by which that drama is enacted (there is, for example, no underlying classical schema). Its source is a poem of the same name by Robert Graves, quoted in abridged form in the front of the score, and which suggests a change in the tone of the drama away from the bold conflicts of the works of the 1960s (the lines in italics are omitted by the composer):

When from your sleepy mind the day's burden
Falls like a bushel sack on a barn floor,
Be prepared for music, for natural mirages
And for night's incomparable parade of colour.

Neither of us daring to assume direction
Of an unforeseen and fiery entertainment,
We clutch hands in the seventh row of the stalls
And watch together, quivering, astonished, silent.

It is hours past midnight now; a flute signals
Far off; we mount the stage as though at random,
Boldly ring down the curtain, then dance out our love:
Lost to the outraged, humming auditorium. [36]

As Arnold Whittall has proposed, it 'evokes the private celebrations of human love rather than the public rituals of epic drama'[37] and thus parallels the shift in dramatic emphasis also to be found between *The Mask of Orpheus* and *Gawain*. Here, the members of the ensemble still play roles (Birtwistle even describes them as the *dramatis personae*) and they are divided between two groups – the main ensemble, designated the continuum (seated), and the soloists or cantus (standing behind the continuum). Certain players move at certain times from the continuum to the cantus. Though the work enacts 'an unforeseen and fiery entertainment', the overt confrontation of soloist and ensemble, of verse and chorus, is generally eschewed here in favour of an apparently more continuous music whose ideas are heard to flow between the two groups.

For the most part, it is the cantus that is associated with continuous melodic ideas. A certain location is thus identified with a certain kind of musical material and a player 'mounts the stage' only when s/he has a narrative to deliver, a song to sing. Even when the cantus consists of more than one player (which, apart from the very opening, is almost always the case), it always speaks with a single voice: in unison or octaves, heterophonically, or in a complex kind of organum. However, as has already been suggested, this piece, unlike its progenitors from the 1960s, is not merely concerned with setting up a bold opposition between groups which is then maintained throughout the work. Rather, the musical drama enacted by the players' movements explores the changing relationships *between* the two ensembles – Whittall has written of an exchange of characteristics between groups 'that question[s] the logic of the basic Cantus/Continuum distinction at the same time as it is being reinforced'.[38] Indeed, one might go so far as to say that the form of *Secret Theatre* is built from processes of recognition, from a series of acts of *anagnorisis*. An opposition is established at the start which is then continually challenged as the two groups come to recognize their mutual *similarities*, paralleling the undermining of the distinction between stage and auditorium articulated in Graves's poem.

Take, for instance, the passage initiated by the flute's temporary physical return to the continuum at the very moment the trumpet and horn begin to play with the cantus (just after fig. 6). When the flute starts to play from within the ensemble (fig. 7), its rather hesitant falling dyads ('quivering, astonished') stand apart from the rest of the ensemble's music, as they do not seem to belong. By fig. 9, it is participating in organum-like writing with strings and vibraphone whose formation is highly reminiscent of the flute's melody from the beginning of the work; this is accompanied by contra bassoon, double bass and piano rotating pitches in a manner similar to the continuum at the opening. Meanwhile, the cantus (oboe, clarinet, trumpet, horn) contributes another stratum to the texture – a unison melody with the important D–F dyad which had been a prominent component of the opening *continuum* music. This exchange of ideas and roles, this moment of recognition, is brought directly into the foreground when, at the change of tempo (bar 9 of fig. 9), the continuum suddenly suspends its motion with a sustained chord while the cantus 'blurts out' a kind of compressed echo of the continuum's material, only for the idea to return hurriedly to the continuum. The flute initiated this change in relationship and it is the flute which now signals an explicit link between cantus and continuum (as implied by the poem: 'signals far off'). At fig. 12, still from within the continuum, the flute plays four times a short, varied 'refrain' figure while the other instruments pause (Ex. 2.2). On the fourth occasion, the work's opening opposition is resumed (mechanistic continuum, sustained cantus), the flute's held F merges with the cantus (fig. 14), and finally the flute moves back to its solo position to play the refrain for the fifth and last time. This prompts a return to the musical opposition of the opening (melodic cantus, ostinato continuum) but varied in recognition of the preceding events, of the changed context.

Ex. 2.2. *Secret Theatre*, fig. 12.

Though the musical context at this point in *Secret Theatre* is much more fluid than in *Verses for Ensembles*, the movements of the players serve a similar function in articulating physically the changing musical relationships between distinct groups of players. That said, the expressive character of the two works could not be more different. Where *Verses* seems 'merely' to enact a non-specific ceremony – for the most part engaging in a kind of ritualized game-playing – *Secret Theatre* is a love dance, adopting and renegotiating certain familiar musical topics of romance.

What emerges from these accounts of *Verses for Ensembles* and *Secret Theatre* is that theatre is not a preoccupation of Birtwistle's merely for its own sake. Through role-play, through the formality generated by the adoption of certain archetypal dramatic schemata, through an awareness of the theatricality of any musical performance, comes a strong sense of ritual. And through ritual he arrives at an expression of deep human emotions which lie beyond words and whose motivation is often unconscious. This is the very stuff of myths, and it is with the fundamental significance of myth and ritual for Birtwistle that the next chapter is concerned.

3 *Episodion II* – Myth and Ritual

Myth is a central preoccupation of Birtwistle. A quick glance down the list of his works for the stage will reveal that they all, in different ways, engage with mythical subject matter, whether Greek (*The Mask of Orpheus*), British (*Punch and Judy*, *Yan Tan Tethera*, *Gawain*, etc.), Biblical (*The Last Supper*) or imaginary (*The Second Mrs Kong*). Similarly, most of his choral works have a mythical dimension, from the invented, stylized narrative of his dramatic cantata for schoolchildren, *The Mark of the Goat* (to a text by Alan Crang), to the mysterious and ambiguous fragments of Sappho set in ... *agm* ... Even in his purely instrumental music Birtwistle often invokes characters, places and ideas with mythical resonances, as in *Linoi*, *Medusa*, *Silbury Air*, *The Cry of Anubis* and *Panic*. In typical fashion, then, Birtwistle has continued to explore and re-explore the ongoing function, significance and power of myth today.

The Penguin Dictionary of Psychology gives its definition of myth as a 'narrative or tradition, without historical or scientific basis, embodying a popular idea regarding natural phenomena, or historical events, or deeds of gods, heroes, etc.'.[1] While the blandness of these words suggests little of the richness Birtwistle finds in myth, they nonetheless indicate the concern of myths with essentially collective representation and with the presentation of a 'popular' narrative, a story that everyone knows and that can stand multiple retellings. The fact that myth is 'without historical or scientific fact' (though this is by no means always the case) means that both listener and story-teller become more concerned with the way in which the story is being (re)told than – necessarily – with the subject matter of the story itself. One of the essential aspects of a myth is that, though it may represent a particular individual (who may or may not have existed in history), it universalizes that individual's experiences. Claude Lévi-Strauss's structural analysis of the Oedipus myth,[2] for example, makes this abundantly clear. His interpretation of this myth depends not on any individual telling or version of the story, or on any particular individual participant within the story, but on the structural relationships between the elements of the story ('system'). One of Lévi-Strauss's comments has a particularly interesting bearing on Birtwistle: 'we define the myth as consisting of all its versions; or to put it otherwise, a myth remains the same as long as it is felt as such'.[3] In the light of Birtwistle's and Zinovieff's bringing together of many different versions of the Orpheus legend in *The Mask of Orpheus*, it is clear how they, too, view myth not as a simple narrative, as a story to be told which may or may not affect the listener, but as a tradition, a living tradition which continues to be relevant. A myth is timeless: it 'remains the same as long as it is felt as such'. Hence, perhaps, the preoccupation of *The Mask of Orpheus* with the idea of time itself, the representation of a multiple time, a multiple present which contains both past and future. Indeed, the work begins with remembrance of things past – 'I remember . . .', sings Orpheus in his First Poem of Reminiscence – and is continually reviewing past events from new perspectives, while the final act is an extraordinarily rich and complex interweaving and repetition of events and ideas from the past in a new, eternal, timeless present.

The collective dimension of myths has been fully explored by Carl Gustav Jung who considered them 'fundamental expressions of human nature'.[4] Myths, for Jung, are a direct expression of the collective unconscious, a deeper part of the psyche than the personal unconscious which provides the 'unknown material from which our consciousness emerges.'[5] The collective unconscious can be recovered through certain archetypal images and emotions, and these archetypes can appear in dreams as well as myth whose nature – 'the creative urge it represents, the feelings it expresses and evokes, and even in large part its subject-matter' – is defined by the collective unconscious.[6] Jung brings religion, poetry, folklore and fairy-tales within the ambit of myth (the central figures of all the major religions, he argues, are archetypal in nature) and stresses that the capacity for myth-making is a *creative* dimension. He thus anticipates Lévi-Strauss's view that myth is about much more than either idle play or crude philosophical speculation, and while Lévi-Strauss rejects Jung's idea of the archetype carrying a specific meaning (for Lévi-Strauss the archetype is just another arbitrary sign), they agree on the fact that myths in similar forms exist among peoples of all times and places. For Jung, it is again the universality of myths which is of importance.

Jung discusses at length the archetypes of the collective unconscious. One such, which exists primarily in the personal unconscious but also manifests itself as a collective phenomenon, is the 'shadow'. The shadow, writes Frieda Fordham, 'since it is unconscious, cannot be touched by ordinary education; it has remained much the same since infancy, when our actions were purely impulsive. It has probably remained much the same since man first walked the earth, for the shadow is the natural, i.e. the instinctive man . . . "The shadow", says Jung, "is a moral problem which challenges the whole ego personality"; it is moreover a social problem of immense importance.'[7]

The archetypal shadow frequently treads the boards of Birtwistle's stage. It can be witnessed, for example, in the untrammelled, amoral, violent and sexual urges of Mr Punch. It can be witnessed in the dialectic of the shadow (unconscious) and the light (conscious) in the violent, jealous drowning by the Dark Sister of her Fair Sister in *Bow Down*. (Indeed, in the context of the above observations, it is interesting to note that Tony Harrison, the librettist, drew on more than one version of the 'Ballad of the Two Sisters'; the fact that these girls are unnamed is just one of the means by which the universal, mythical dimension of the narrative is achieved.) Perhaps the most extensive representation of the shadow in mythical form is to be found in *The Second Mrs Kong*. For the work's librettist, Russell Hoban, no less than for Birtwistle, myths – particularly that of Orpheus and Eurydice – have been an enduring obsession. Certain mythical archetypes and images recur like leitmotifs across his writings – not just Orpheus, but Medusa, Hermes, the Sphinx, the Kraken, the young woman's head from Vermeer's painting *Head of a Girl with a Pearl Earring*, and many more. In fact, it is usually *just* heads that interest him, disembodied: 'The head of Orpheus is its own body and the Kraken is its great deep brother whose dark mind is wild with the terror of itself.'[8] This is once again the world of the shadow, the unknown region from which our conscious fears and feelings emerge; the fact they are only heads reinforces both their mythical (stylized) and their emotional (purely psychological) dimensions. The head of Orpheus makes an appearance in *The Mask of Orpheus*. In one version of the myth, Orpheus is decapitated and dismembered by the wild Maenads and his head and lyre float down the river Hebrus; the head reaches the Aegean Sea and eventually is carried to the island of Lesbos where the skull, which has magical powers and makes magical sounds, becomes a new oracle. In Act 3, Orpheus as Oracle is represented on stage by a puppet singing in an invented, magical (and – to the audience – unintelligible) Orphic language. In his libretto, Zinovieff writes that the skull of Orpheus has huge flaming eyes; for Hoban, 'the look in the eyes of the Vermeer girl is the look in the eyes of the unseen Kraken in the blackness of the ultimate deep, the great head looking for ever into the blackness'.[9] Or, as Vermeer sings in Act 1 of *The Second Mrs Kong*, 'In her face I see time's ancient shadow reaching forward, reaching back.' One head is the same as another; one myth is the same as another. Faust becomes Orpheus. The power of a myth lies not in its subject matter but in what it points to beyond itself, what it points to in us: the archetype generates specific and personal associations. The less 'real' the characters (even only heads or eyes), the more powerful their role in myths. As Hoban puts it, 'The real reality, the flickering of seen and unseen actualities, the moment under the moment, can't be put into words; the most that a writer can do . . . is to write in such a way that the reader finds himself in a place where the unwordable happens off the page.'[10] And where the words can say no more, the music takes over. This is certainly what happens at the end of both *The Mask of Orpheus* and *The Second Mrs Kong*.

Hoban's singing Head of Orpheus reappears in *The Second Mrs Kong*, cast as a counter-tenor. So do Vermeer's girl (now under the name of Pearl) and the Sphinx (Madame Lena), along with an almost music-hall-like cast list of other mythical characters including Anubis (the jackal-headed creature from Egyptian mythology), Inanna (the Sumerian goddess of love and fertility) and Eurydice. Many of these characters are to be found in Hoban's *The Medusa Frequency* (1987) which explores, in the form of a novel, many of the ideas which were to re-emerge in the libretto for *Mrs Kong*. The one mythical creature not yet mentioned is King Kong himself. The key point about Kong for both Hoban and Birtwistle is that he never actually existed. He was only a celluloid creature, a product of stop-frame photography, a 50 cm puppet – though there was a life-size head and hand. Yet what Hoban calls the *idea* of Kong is very real. There can hardly be anyone who, even if he or she has never seen the 1933 RKO film, does not know about the giant ape, his destructive power, the fear he instilled in the people of New York, his fatal love for a beautiful girl (Fay Wray) and his inevitable death by falling from the top of the Empire State Building. One of the reasons why the idea of Kong is so powerful is that it seems to represent our collective shadow, those deep fears, those inaccessible forces of violence and lust which shape our conscious minds. Kong represents the primitive (plucked by 'civilized' man from the jungle), instinctive, impulsive, preconscious, infantile in all of us – 'from his eyes look the wild and wordless, lost and lonely child of all the world'. He is a manifestation of a specific archetype of the collective unconscious.

This is the world in which *The Second Mrs Kong* begins. In complete darkness, starting out of nothingness, the lowest instruments of the orchestra – bassoons and contra bassoon, cellos and basses, tuba, muted horns, later the exotic sounds of the cimbalom – paint a picture of a dark, mysterious, unknowable realm. The music is gloomy, brooding, angst-laden. There is little that is immediately recognizable for the listener to grasp hold of: no melodies as such, just intervallic fragments, predominantly bare fourths, fifths and tritones. This place Hoban names the World of Shadows and is populated by the dead. Anubis appears, rowing his boat, ferrying souls to this deathly world. He encourages the dead to tell him of their passions and dreams (the very stuff of the unconscious): 'Have I not fed upon the carrion of your longing and your crazy dreams of love that cannot be?' The dead repeat endlessly (and here comically) their memories and desires in a kind of self-conscious parody of the usual Birtwistle journeys through the same material. 'Again!', calls Anubis, sadistically. He knows that their desires can never change and can never be fulfilled: the longing for what can never be is the central theme of the opera – Vermeer's longing for Pearl, Kong and Pearl's mutual longing, Inanna's longing for Kong, Orpheus's longing for Eurydice. The characters may be different but the 'narrative' of the myths is universal. Jung tells us that in the unconscious nothing changes. In Jungian terms, these characters are immature because they have not individuated, that is, they have not reconciled their conscious and unconscious selves. In representing the idea of Kong as an archetype, we are invited to confront our own shadow. It is interesting to note that Kong himself emerges from the shadows such that in Act 2 he is forced to confront *his* own shadow in the form of Death of Kong.

It might be said that the dialectic of conscious and unconscious could be understood, following Hoban's observation above, as the dialectic of words and beyond-words (music). Birtwistle clearly understands this. Indeed, as shall be explored more fully in relation to pastoral in Chapter 4, such oppositions are crucial to Birtwistle's aesthetic: line and circle, verse and refrain, cantus and continuum, even personal lament and collective dance. Throughout this opera, purely on a practical level, the distinction between voices (text) and orchestra (music) is carefully maintained. Birtwistle knows when to allow the words to be heard, and when to let the music dominate – though sometimes to a degree that the word-setting becomes almost perfunctory, and often unnecessarily (and unwittingly) draws attention to itself (for example, the setting of Anubis's line 'My contract stipulates a one way trip. I come in heavy but I go back light'). Nevertheless, there is much that is very witty in the text, and every joke can be understood, such as the hilarious encounter in Act 2 between Kong and Lena. The composer's view is that comical music is impossible – music simply does not operate in those terms – and so you just need to let the music take a back seat while the words speak directly. This is recitative at its simplest. Elsewhere, one finds examples of the orchestra supporting the surface text almost like a film score (a not altogether inappropriate comparison in this context). A good example is to be found in the penultimate scene of Act 1 where Pearl uses the Internet to communicate with Kong. Much of the text of this scene is typed, letter by letter, on to a big stage computer screen. The actual typing speed is precisely notated in the score, and it is the gradual emergence of the (again highly witty) text which principally captures the audience's attention. The orchestra is dominated by the sound of the accordion playing rapid demisemiquaver figurations which articulate the frantic 'mood' of communication, albeit suggesting an age more of mechanical telegraph printers than of contemporary silent computers. The rest of the orchestra plays mainly ostinatos and pedals so as not to draw attention to itself. Nonetheless, the accompaniment also has an important role in supporting the growing emotional excitement of the scene: as Kong and Pearl begin to recognize their love for one another, the music builds in intensity to reach a breathless climax as they share the declaration 'I love you'. Even if the technological context is of the late-twentieth century, musically this scene must be one of the most conventionally operatic that Birtwistle has ever written. It is a love story in the best nineteenth-century tradition.

In general terms, the distinction between voices and orchestra is maintained throughout the work: the voices ride on the surface as carriers of the text while the orchestra follows its own course underneath – an almost Wagnerian structure where the singers represent the conscious mind, the orchestra their unconscious (unsung) motivations. At the opening, the orchestral music attempts to represent the dark, formless, ungraspable realm of the unconscious. At the entry of Anubis, it continues to grow from the materials it established at the start, while Anubis's line has its own distinct structure, moving outwards from its initial G♭ in a familiar – albeit informal – wedge pattern (see Ex. 3.1). Anubis's soliloquy culminates in somewhat prosaic self-identification: 'I'm Anubis'. Yet, at key points here, voice and orchestra work together, because both are making conscious aspects of the unconscious. Just as Anubis emerges out of the darkness, out of the shadows, so his musical line emerges out of the orchestra, and disappears back into it.

Ex. 3.1. *The Second Mrs Kong*, Act 1 (Anubis's first entry).

Throughout much of Birtwistle's music (even the purely instrumental pieces) an important distinction is made between what one might generally term recitative and aria. Once again, this can be understood, at base, as an opposition between the linear and the circular, the cantus and the continuum – and, in the specific case of this opera, between words and music. Conventionally, in recitative the plot unfolds, the drama develops, characters interact, the words and their meanings dominate, while the music is subsidiary; in aria the narrative 'stops' while a specific idea or emotion is explored through the music, usually by one character alone (a situation beyond words) – what Birtwistle has tellingly described as 'the poetic flowering of the moment'. This distinction can be seen at its most overt in Baroque opera: the formality, the extreme stylization of, for instance, Handel's *opere serie* (the very opposite of 'naturalistic' nineteenth-century opera) clearly interests Birtwistle and can certainly be seen to have influenced the structure and aesthetic of both *Punch and Judy* and *The Mask of Orpheus*. In *The Second Mrs Kong* the librettist has carefully provided the composer with moments whose rhetoric is clearly distinguishable between that of recitative (conversational, prosaic) and aria (reflective, poetic). This is matched musically. (It is worth pointing out here that there was an unusually close collaboration on this opera between composer, librettist and director/designer – Tom Cairns – and the success of the first Glyndebourne production in 1994 was a result of this genuinely three-way discussion. It should be clear by now why Birtwistle was attracted to Hoban: they are not only similarly obsessive, but are creatively obsessive about similar ideas and in similar ways. Hoban knew nothing of Birtwistle's music before the composer made contact by letter; Birtwistle's first encounter with Hoban's writing came after he had finished work on his previous opera, *Gawain*. At the suggestion of the baritone, Omar Ebrahim, who created the role of the Fool in *Gawain* at Covent Garden, Birtwistle read Hoban's novel *Riddley Walker*. He immediately recognized in it a kindred voice. Furthermore, Hoban's preoccupation with King Kong coincided with Birtwistle's growing interest at the time in film.) Here is a brief illustration from Act 1, following the first interpolated film sequence, where Kong himself has projected on to a screen an excerpt from the 1933 film, including the original sound track, during which all stage action and live music is suspended.

Inanna Kong! Kong!
Kong What?
Inanna Are you all right?

Kong I don't know.
Inanna What's bothering you?
Kong Everything.
Inanna What do you mean everything?
Kong I'm not the giant head, the giant hand, the little puppet moving on the screen . . . there never was a giant ape!
Inanna I know.
Kong Sometimes I dream the misty mountains of an island that I've never seen,
Sometimes a jungle painted all in glass
Sometimes I dream I'm up so very very high and falling.
And sometimes only colours in darkness.

The dialogue between Kong and Inanna emerges out of the film sequence: the film is faded out as a sustained orchestral chord fades in. The text setting here is as one would find in conventional recitative: syllabic and following – on the whole – the contour and rhythm of the words. When, for example, Inanna repeats Kong's 'everything', it has exactly the same intervallic and rhythmic profile, just transposed up a tone. The accompaniment is built mainly of fragments and is unobtrusive, allowing the text to be heard. When Kong moves into 'aria' mode, the music becomes more expansive and lyrical. Whereas Kong's recitative line involved much repetition of single notes, here he now sings wider leaps and self-absorbed 'contemplative' melismas. However, Birtwistle still takes careful account of the words by, for instance, providing a musical rhyme (a rising minor 7th) for the repetition of the word 'sometimes' at the beginning of the first and second lines, and by indulging in some basic kinds of word-painting with high tessitura on the words 'very, very high' and falling figures on the word 'falling' (twice repeated, each statement lower than the preceding one) – see Ex. 3.2. The orchestra provides supporting cantabile lines of similar character to Kong's, as if his dreamy melismas have proliferated outwards; the mystery of his dream of something he's never seen and yet which is part of him is reinforced by the orchestra – once again, the 'voice' of the unconscious. It is

Ex. 3.2. *The Second Mrs Kong*, Act 1, figs 99–102.

particularly worth noting how each statement of 'falling' is connected by the orchestra's own brief semiquaver falling idea, a kind of reworking of similar figures from the film's soundtrack, suggesting that Kong's 'memory' of falling is actually derived from his own viewing of the film (the fact of which he seems to be unaware). Inanna follows Kong with a self-absorbed arioso of her own ('Whatever love I had was never what I wanted').

The most distinctive aria of the opera occurs towards the end of Act 2 and is for Inanna alone, focusing on her personal emotion, expressing its *Affekt* in the Baroque manner. Such an aria, on similar subject matter, is not without precedent in Birtwistle: as here, the confluence of song ('aria'), dance and the flute, symbolizing love and courtship, can be found, for example, in Punch's danced

'Serenades' for Pretty Polly in *Punch and Judy*, and in Lady de Hautdesert's 'dance aria' in Act 2 of *Gawain*. Inanna sings mournfully, twice over, 'All my life and all my death I've wanted something and it never happened', yearning for what can never be – the central theme of *Mrs Kong*. The dramatic and musical moment is frozen, and in the larger scheme provides a moment of stillness before the long, final scene. Cello and bass each have an almost clockwork-like ostinato typical of Birtwistle, which continue until the aria is over. The accordion, which has more of a continuo role here – binding together the other elements of the aria – has its own, more complex repeating line, sequences of chords rich in the interval of a second and employing dancing scotch-snap rhythms. Together, cello, bass and accordion form the continuum. The cantus line is a continuous flute melody which soars freely over the top, providing a lyrical counterpoint to Inanna's own melody. Punctuating this, and connecting the end of each of Inanna's phrases with the beginning of the next, is a short alto saxophone phrase, marked 'a bit bluesy'. As one might expect of a jazz instrument, each of its phrases is a varied version of the first. The music as a whole here poignantly articulates Inanna's personal unconscious which her conscious words can only weakly hint at. The cantus points forward (conscious yearnings) but can never reach fulfilment because of the circularity of the continuum (opposing unconscious forces); the two are held in eternal equilibrium. If this musical situation is familiar, it is because we encountered it at the start of *Secret Theatre* (see Chapter 1): an essentially forward-moving flute cantus ('a flute signals far off . . . then dance out our love') accompanied by interlocking low string ostinatos and a piano continuum playing scotch snaps. The idea of aria is clearly not confined merely to Birtwistle's stage works. And, as if to confirm this, a very similar situation to that in Act 2 of *The Second Mrs Kong* occurs in the most recent large work, *Exody* (beginning around bar 487). Here, too, the texture thins right down to strings/vibraphone and solo flute offering a brief moment of reflection – in what is a very busy work – before the final, unrelentingly turbulent denouement. The flute begins in the role of the cantus playing a characteristic rhythmicized melody (triplets predominate), while the string/vibraphone continuum sustains a resonant G pedal (the open string of the violin). The marimba punctuates with reiterated Gs in a rallentando figure. In keeping with the identity of the rest of *Exody* which is texturally one of the densest pieces Birtwistle has written, this simple situation is quickly elaborated: the pedal expands outwards, chromatically, in wedge fashion while the flute melody proliferates into counterpointing woodwind lines. But the rhetoric of this moment remains immediately recognizable.

If this account of recitative and aria gives the impression of highly conventional opera, then in some senses this *is* the case. Though stylized in many (quasi-eighteenth-century) ways, *The Second Mrs Kong* also continues *Gawain*'s tendency towards a more direct (nineteenth-century) narrative structure. Birtwistle's two most recent stage works are his most conventionally *operatic* (indeed, these are the only two dramatic works to date to which he gives the designation 'opera'). While Act 1 of *Mrs Kong* might be understood to take the episodic dimensions of a classical Greek tragedy, Act 2 has all the characteristics of a quest opera. Kong sets off on a journey, he passes successfully through various trials that are set in his way (resisting the four temptations, answering the Sphinx's riddle, overcoming his own nemesis in the shape of Death of Kong), and finally gets his girl – though, ironically, having found Pearl, the two are condemned to be eternally together yet eternally apart. It is a postmodern *Magic Flute*: the journey without a final destination, the conflict without resolution. Thus, though it focuses on individual character development in a way unprecedented in works before the 1990s – in Kong, Birtwistle presents us with a believable operatic character who, like Gawain, grows and develops as the narrative unfolds – the opera's concern with myth nonetheless remains a familiar and central concern. The moments of recitative and aria in *Mrs Kong* serve a similar function of formalization as they do in *Punch and Judy* and *The Mask of Orpheus*; here, though, they are more thoroughly integrated, less boldly opposed.

In addition to extended moments of recitative (where the conscious comes to the fore), there are also what may be described as extended moments of aria (which, by contrast, focus on the unconscious), the most powerful of which forms the final scene of the work. This scene is dominated by one of Birtwistle's 'favourite' notes, E, the note which has consistently formed the starting-point or focus for so many of his works throughout his composing career. Birtwistle has never given an adequate reason for his obsession with this particular pitch class . . . but, then again, why should he? On a number of occasions when asked, 'Why E?', he has wryly retorted, 'Why not? It's as good a note as any other'. In the knowledge that the final scene of *Mrs Kong* took much longer to complete than had been anticipated (the final double bar of the full score is followed by the inscription 'Lunegarde. 19. Aug. 94', a mere two months before the opera's première took place at Glyndebourne on 24 October 1994), Birtwistle offered the explanation that when he suffers from a compositional block, he will 'stick down an E' and see where it takes him.[11] Another instance of taking a line for a walk. There may also be very practical reasons for the choice of this note: it is the lowest open string of the four-string double bass and the highest of the violin; it is the lowest written note on Birtwistle's own instrument, the clarinet. It also, arguably, brings with it associations of the Phrygian mode (the octave of 'white notes' on the piano starting on E) – that mode's characteristic E–F upper semitone and E–D lower tone occurs frequently in Birtwistle, for example, as the punctuating D–E–F device of the melancholic, E-dominated *Four Songs of Autumn*, or as the focal D–F dyad asymmetrically placed about E throughout *Secret Theatre*. It should be obvious to anyone who hears it that the E at the end of *The Second Mrs Kong* is more than just a compositional convenience. The scene begins immediately after Inanna's aria and is marked by reiterated sextuplet semiquaver Es in the violins, later opening outwards in symmetrical fashion, the open string E nonetheless remaining ever-present. As the scene unfolds and the hopelessness of Kong and Pearl's situation strikes home (the Mirror sings: 'This is the moment when reality begins. You cannot have each other'), so the presence of the E also becomes more and more aurally apparent. To begin with, it is generally only Pearl's vocal line that reveals the E. Nearly every one of her phrases either begins on or is built around E (in the same register as the violins). Kong enters, and he too is gradually drawn into the world of E ('Pearl, this is the moment we have waited for' is sung to reiterated Es). Their joint appeal to the Mirror ('Please say that our loneliness is over and our happiness begins') reveals a shared concern for E, each line moving in essence around a symmetrically focal E (see Ex. 3.3). A richly layered texture of lines is built around the voices and these too eventually coalesce around a common E. The defining moment comes with the arrival of an E pedal in the closing minutes of the opera. From here onwards, the E is omnipresent: as a pedal; as a centre of symmetry for the vocal lines; as the point either from which linear figures proliferate outwards or to which they return (Klee's 'line accompanied by complementary forms'

Ex. 3.3. *The Second Mrs Kong*, Act 2, final scene.

– the parallels with the E-based section of *Refrains and Choruses*, discussed in Chapter 1, are striking, and draw attention to how little the essentials of Birtwistle's technique have altered in forty years). This circling around E, as Kong and Pearl are left only with their memories – 'I remember', 'You remember?' – continues to the end of the work and can do nothing else but fade into nothingness, into the darkness of the endlessly repeated memories with which the opera had begun, into the inexpressible obscurity of the unconscious.

The Second Mrs Kong ends in the realm of the shadow. Any individuality that Kong and Pearl may have achieved up to this point is lost again. They are merely the product of their (and our) half-remembered memories. Comparison with Act 3 of *The Mask of Orpheus* is fruitful. The Act is structured, musically and conceptually, by the Aura of the Tides (an electronic tape). The ebb and flow of the tides is represented by a change in octave of the focal note, E; as the Act proceeds, so the E seems to predominate more and more. By the end of the Act, events have become so attenuated that the E of the tides is about all one can fix on. Fragments are layered on top of this – moments from earlier in the work, the voice of Apollo calling 'Rufi' ('Love'), and so on – but we are left in something like a dream world, an eternal present, the product only of memory. In their remembered love duet, Eurydice (singer and puppet) and Orpheus call for one another (see Ex. 3.4); strikingly, Orpheus and Eurydice reappear at the

Ex. 3.4. *The Mask of Orpheus*, Act 3.

end of *Mrs Kong* too, calling one another's names in a not dissimilar fashion: the myth of two lovers condemned to be together forever yet forever apart – it matters not whether they are called Orpheus and Eurydice or Kong and Pearl. *The Mask of Orpheus*, like *The Second Mrs Kong*, fades into the nothingness from which it sprang as Orpheus's skull is silenced by Apollo. Clearly, for Birtwistle, the note E symbolizes this realm beyond the everyday, where the mystical, the mythical, the unconscious all coincide. And when Es recur in instrumental works such as *Silbury Air* or *Panic* – significantly both 'arias' of an instrumental kind – we should be alert to the possibility that similar associations are being explored and expressed.

Another way of looking at the opposition of conscious and unconscious which is so frequently explored in Birtwistle is via the opposition between the mythical gods of Apollo and Dionysus, as presented in Nietzsche's *The Birth of Tragedy*, first published in 1872. Dionysus was the ancient Greek god of revelry, of wine, music and dancing, whilst Apollo was the god of beauty, sculpture, order and logic. For Nietzsche, Apollo and Dionysus are conceived as representing the worlds of, respectively, dreams and intoxication. Apollo is 'the deity of light', and represents the 'higher truth, the perfection of these states in contrast to the incompletely intelligible everyday world' as well as of 'measured restraint, that freedom from the wilder emotions, that calm of the sculptor god.'[12] Nietzsche, after Schopenhauer, goes on to assert that Apollo himself is 'the glorious divine image of the *principium individuationis*'.[13] It is at the collapse of this *principium* that Nietzsche argues we steal a glimpse of the nature of the Dionysian, resulting in both terror and blissful ecstasy. In such orgiastic rituals as those of the Bacchic choruses and the Dance of St Vitus, we are thrown into self-forgetfulness; 'nature which has become alienated, hostile, or subjugated, celebrates once more her reconciliation with her lost son, man.'[14] Later in his tract, Nietzsche goes on to discuss myth in relation to the Dionysian: 'for the myth wants to be experienced vividly as a unique example of a universality and truth that gaze into the infinite. The truly Dionysian music presents itself as such a general mirror of the universal will'.[15] Nietzsche has, of course, Wagner in mind; in these terms, it is the Dionysian, even the Wagnerian aspects to the music at the close of both *The Mask of Orpheus* and *The Second Mrs Kong* that gives its mythopoeic power. In both cases we witness – dramatically – the collapse of the *principium individuationis* resulting in both a certain terror and (certainly on the part of the stage characters, if not ourselves) a self-forgetfulness (though in the case of *Orpheus* it is interesting that this 'collapse' is engineered by, and in the presence of, Apollo).

Just as Jung and Lévi-Strauss (along with Birtwistle) recognized the parallels across many different myths, so Nietzsche argued that the only stage hero of the pre-Euripidean tragedies was Dionysus – that is, Prometheus, Oedipus, and the rest were all mere 'masks' of the original hero. In other words, these were at once tragedies of particular individuals and also universalized, representations, 'not of men, but of action and life'.[16] The tragic heroes were Dionysian archetypes. One particular Dionysian archetype which Nietzsche discusses is that of the satyr:

> The satyr . . . is the offspring of a longing for the primitive and the natural . . . Nature, as yet unchanged by knowledge, with the bolts of culture still unbroken – that is what the Greek saw in his satyr who nevertheless was not a mere ape. On the contrary, the satyr was the archetype of man, the embodiment of his highest and most intense emotions, the ecstatic reveler enraptured by the proximity of his god, the sympathetic companion in whom the suffering of the god is repeated, one who proclaims wisdom from the very heart of nature, a symbol of the sexual omnipotence of nature which the Greeks used to contemplate with reverent wonder.'[17]

What better analysis could one find of Kong! The Kong of the film is clearly the primitive creature of nature who understands nothing of the constraints of culture. But in his love for Fay Wray, and, in the opera for Pearl, Kong shows himself – like the satyr – to be not just an ape but half-man, half-goat. His intensely felt emotions and his suffering speak to us directly because they are primal, pre-verbal, deep; for Birtwistle, it is only in the beyond-words, in music, that such feelings can be expressed at all.

As a 'simple' creature of nature, the satyr has much in common with the pastoral shepherd, an idea which will be explored more fully in Chapter 4 – though Nietzsche saw the man of the idyll as only a weak and mawkish shadow of the satyr. But the satyr makes regular appearances elsewhere in Birtwistle – as the singing sheep of *Yan Tan Tethera*; in the wild choral dances of the satyrs – the dithyramb – of *Tragoedia* (literally, 'goat dance') as well as in such other places as (negatively) the screeched, wordless 'Hysterical Aria' of the Oracle of the Dead in *The Mask of Orpheus*, in the climactic moments of *Earth Dances*, and pre-eminently in *Panic*; even, by implication, the satyr is present in the dark character of Capran, marked by the sign of the goat in *The Mark of the Goat*, and in the half-man, half-jackal who sings (wordlessly) out of the tuba in *The Cry of Anubis*. Nietzsche also makes the point that the satyr was usually part of a chorus, reinforcing the collective nature of Dionysian expression which is at the heart of myth. Furthermore, the satyr was always masked, symbolizing his lack of individuality and identifying him with the collective. It is significant that it is the Chorus of the Dead at the start of *The Second Mrs Kong* which populates the World of Shadows, and which sings preconscious nonsense words, groping towards an articulate meaning which is only later revealed. Here is another parallel with *Orpheus* in which The Oracle of the Dead sings horrible, wordless noises. The idea of chorus – whether a group of people, individuals speaking on behalf of or out of a group, a choric figure (Choregos), or all kinds of instrumental choruses – is vital to Birtwistle. The chorus adds nothing to the actual subject matter of the telling of the myth, but its role is crucial in universalizing, and indeed ritualizing, the narrative.

Panic is a work which the composer actually describes as a 'dithyramb', and is a kind of song for the nature god Pan. The score is prefaced by the following (misquoted) lines:

O what is he doing, the great god Pan
Down by the reeds by the river
Spreading ruin and scattering ban[18]

Like the excerpt from the Robert Graves poem which prefaces the score of *Secret Theatre*, these lines offer a key to interpreting *Panic* without ever reducing it to the status of mere programme music. Panic is a feeling of terror or anxiety. Pandemonium is the familiar Birtwistle realm of wild confusion and uproar. And Pan himself was another mythical half-man half-goat creature. *Panic* is, like *Tragoedia*, a goat dance, but here the controlling forces of Apollo (the abstract formalism of Greek tragedy) are far less strong and Dionysus runs riot. The alto saxophone soloist takes on the the role of chorus leader (Choregos), inciting mischief, creating chaos, 'spreading ruin and scattering ban'. The outbursts of the main body of the chorus (wind and brass) portray the fearful, collective response to Pan. Once again, Birtwistle has utilized a mythical character to help unleash the powerful forces of the unconscious.

It is possible to identify the musical and expressive origins of *Panic* in *The Second Mrs Kong*. There are some very bluesy/jazzy sounds for saxophones and percussion in Act 2. They accompany the character of Death of Kong, whose association with the World of Shadows is reinforced by the fact that he is sung by the same singer as Anubis (compare with the psychologically resonant doubling of roles in Berg's *Lulu*). Aggressive wind and percussion writing (including drum-kit instruments such as the hi-hat) support Death of Kong's violent actions and the showing of the film sequence where the celluloid King Kong falls to his death from the top of the Empire State Building. The saxophone writing here is unremittingly loud, and characterized by rapid rising or falling roulades leading to single sustained notes, trills or tremolandos. There is little that could be described as contemplative or melodic. This is music which is seemingly instinctive; it is raw and immediate. It is *not* improvised but might give the impression of being so. Birtwistle uses the jazz instruments not necessarily as a jazz composer would, but for their associations with an unpremeditated music. Images of brutal death and destruction are accompanied by a music of similar character. And such writing – in a more exaggerated form – predominates in *Panic*. We begin, inevitably, with reiterated Es from Pan, crudely called out, roughly decorated with grace notes. The accompanying wind chorus (note the lack of strings – the voice of civilized culture) play demi-semiquaver roulades echoing those of *Mrs Kong*. Melody (Pan's song) only gradually emerges, and even then it rarely takes full flight. At their most 'primitive', saxophone and drums rebel completely against the temporal order of conductor and ensemble (see Ex. 3.5) to play independent, repeating figures which amount to little more than primordial grunts and bangs. This Pan is undoubtedly of a much 'harder' nature than the one found in earlier modern contexts, such as in Debussy's *Syrinx* or *Prélude à l'après-midi d'un faune*.

The work's primary impulse is rhythmic. The relationship of the drum-kit to the saxophone and to the rest of the ensemble is

Ex. 3.5. *Panic.*

an interesting one, playing a kind of 'continuo' role like the accordion in *Mrs Kong*. Sometimes it plays with the soloist, sometimes with the group; sometimes it binds the two together, sometimes it does the opposite and disrupts. However, the energy, violence and rhythmic dynamism of the Dionysian dance does subside from time to time, allowing the chorus to cohere (there is a beautiful wind 'chorale') and the saxophone to sing with a softer, more lyrical voice. This, too, parallels the second style of writing for saxophones found in *Mrs Kong*, such as seen in Inanna's aria, or just before Kong's encounter with Death of Kong when he speaks to Pearl on the telephone. Birtwistle here exploits the blues associations of the instrument: by turns seductive, pleading, raunchy. It is also, appropriately, the sonic language of the dance band. Ex. 3.6 shows one version of the saxophone melody from Inanna's aria and a lyrical moment from *Panic* where the soloist and drum-kit are again playing independently of the conductor's beat. It should be immediately apparent that these melodies share the same rhetoric, the same contours, rhythms and harmonic sphere.

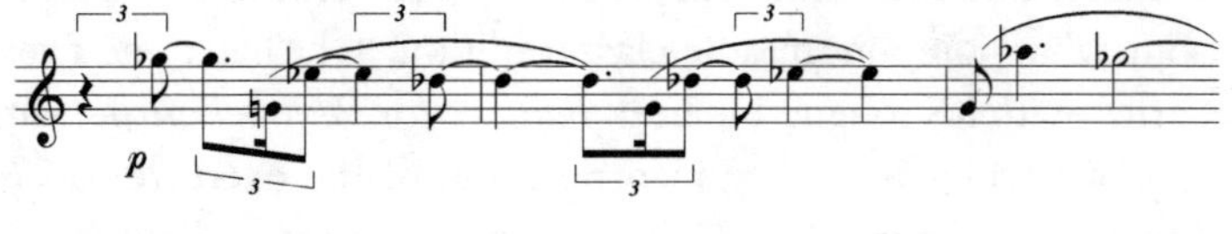

Ex. 3.6. Comparison of saxophone lines in *Panic* and *The Second Mrs Kong*, Act 2.

The extraordinary thing about *Panic* is that, despite its seeming chaos, it is carefully ordered. Literal pandemonium would, of course, be incomprehensible. There seems to be an uncanny inevitability, a momentum driving the music forward; as in so many of Birtwistle's works, the timing of events is skilfully controlled. Furthermore, a framework is provided for the unruly behaviour of Pan and his followers by certain points of harmonic focus: the E of the opening; elsewhere, D♭, D, E♭[19] Just as the soloists move in and out of the rhythmic control of the conductor, so the music as a whole flows towards and away from these pitch centres.

That *Panic* seemed to touch deep fears is evinced by the ferocious public response to the work, echoed in the tabloid newspapers, following its premiere at the Last Night of the Proms in the Royal Albert Hall, London, on 16 September 1995. The uproar was in part a response to the apparent effrontery of a knight of the realm in providing challenging modernist music in the context of the traditional Last Night fare of Parry's *Jerusalem* and Elgar's *Pomp and Circumstance* march. Worse still, listeners' sensibilities had been offended by introducing the brashness of proletarian saxophone and drum-kit into this citadel of bourgeois manners and restraint. Was Birtwistle just cocking a snook at a somewhat pompous middle-class tradition, as he had done a year earlier with his tongue-in-cheek *Fanfare for Glyndebourne*, with its not particularly witty incorporation of the overture to *The Marriage of Figaro*? Or did the outrage generated by *Panic* reveal a deeper horror at being confronted by the terrors of the shadow, of the repressed unconscious? For me, it is undoubtedly a music with a primordial expressivity. Its power, its excitement, even its danger, come from its predominantly Dionysian directness, from the pleasure it takes in the immediate (sonic, rhythmic), from its celebration of the rough bodily physicality of its soloists seemingly uninfluenced by the rational Apollo. It is this powerfully erotic aspect of the work which is the source both of its strength and its discomfort. It is this which places *Panic* in direct line of succession with other Dionysian dances of the twentieth century such as *The Rite of Spring* – whose *succès de scandale* was similarly due, at least in part, to its forthright representation of the violent and erotic dimensions of myth and ritual. Stravinsky and Birtwistle recognize the closeness of music and dance and the ability of both those forms to express aspects of that deep, primitive, pre-verbal realm of the unconscious. In *Panic*, they unite in a celebratory dithyramb.

Nietzsche's distinction between Apollo and Dionysus is part of an elegant argument aimed at showing how in tragedy – those of Aeschylus and Sophocles especially – the two poles are brought together. Great tragedy is born of the spirit of music (the Dionysian) but is contained and understood through art (the Apollonian). This can certainly help account for Birtwistle's preoccupation with Classical tragedy. In tragedy, the revelation of the most basic and literally horrible passions in the mythical narratives – jealousy, lust, blood lust, hatred, fear, revenge – are brought out into the open, yet are controlled by the formalized structure of the plays themselves. Put simply, they are ritualized. A play (and, indeed, a piece of music) is not real life; we can witness and learn to come to terms with feelings and emotions that in reality we would find too horrible to contemplate. For Aristotle, this was the necessary process of *catharsis*, the purging or purification of the emotions through the evocation of pity and fear. For Nietzsche, this is no less than a justification of the aesthetic, of the very necessity of art:

> She alone [art] knows how to turn these nauseous thoughts about the horror or absurdity of existence into notions with which we can live.[20]

Despite Theodor Adorno's arguments to the contrary,[21] this is where the tragic power of a work such as *The Rite of Spring* lies (and hence, perhaps, Birtwistle's lifelong fascination with that work). The violence of *The Rite*, its exploration of unconscious collective emotions through a mythical narrative, is nonetheless objectified – ritualized – by means of the obvious structural elements of block organization and repetition. For Adorno, this means that, as listeners and observers, we relinquish our subjectivity to the collective will, so becoming crucially distanced from the violence and thus making us side with the perpetrators of such violence. (It is important to remember that Adorno's interpretation was deeply coloured by what was happening in Germany in the 1930s and 1940s.) The alternative was the free exploration of the personal unconscious in a work such as Schoenberg's *Erwartung*. But if we follow Nietzsche's lead, we can see that the distancing that ritual brings, far from suspending our individual critical and moral faculties, actually enables us to make sense of and come to terms with our otherwise inaccessible fears and urges. In Jungian terms, we individuate; or, in Michael Tippett's Jung-inspired formulation in *A Child of our Time*, 'I would know my shadow and my light, so shall I at last be whole'.

In 1975, just at the time he was finishing Act 2 of *The Mask of Orpheus*, Birtwistle was appointed Music Director at the National Theatre, London. For a period of eight years (until 1982, when he became an Associate Director), he worked closely with directors and playwrights, and also alongside the younger composer Dominic Muldowney (born 1952), producing music for a very broad range of theatrical productions from *Hamlet* to *Amadeus*. This was a key appointment for him and seemed to result in a period of codification, simplification and reorientation in his music of the late 1970s and early 1980s: a focusing on musical essentials, on the basics of rhythm, melody and gesture. Muldowney has spoken of this in terms of what he learned as a colleague of Birtwistle's: '. . . what's rubbed off is not the sound of his music but a much more abstract and simple thing: how gestural it is, and how simple those gestures are'.[22] Undoubtedly, his most important undertaking at the National was the three-way collaboration on director Peter Hall's production of Tony Harrison's verse translation of Aeschylus's *Oresteia* trilogy. Clearly Harrison and Birtwistle share similar attitudes to the significance of myth: Harrison's more recent *Medea: A Sex-War Opera* (1985), for example, is prefaced by the words of Lévi-Strauss quoted above on a myth consisting of all its versions. They are alike, too, in the Northern directness, even abrasiveness, of their expression of ideas – witness, for instance, such lines as those spoken by the Watchman just before the first entry of the Chorus in *Agamemnon*: 'As for the rest . . . I'm not saying. Better not said. Say that an ox ground my gob into silence.' Hall's production was in tune with Birtwistle's attitudes to the formalized, stylized presentation of mythical narratives, the plays being given in the Greek manner, employing a masked, all-male cast. This had a direct influence on his own work, as far as employing many of the same production team (designer Jocelyn Herbert with masks by Jenny West) for the première of *The Mask of Orpheus*. Harrison's exciting verse translation made little attempt to keep close to the original Greek in terms of the text but rather aimed to match its formality of expression, especially in the choral odes which are rich in rhyme, repetition, assonance and alliteration. The end result was what Harrison describes as a 'rhythmic libretto', produced jointly with Birtwistle. The production was first given in London on 28 November 1981 (just as Birtwistle had resumed work on the composition of Act 3 of *Orpheus*) and repeated in the ancient amphitheatre at Epidauros in July 1982.

Birtwistle's score was for the familiar combination of voice (Jane Manning in the original production), three wind, harp and three percussionists. The sparse music is predominantly rhythmic, with the recitations of the chorus (as individuals or as a collective) being carefully specified and pulsed, spoken over simple drones. Just as Pruslin wrote of his and Birtwistle's aim in *Punch and Judy* as 'the collective generalisation of known operas into a "source opera"',[23] so the music for the *Oresteia* has the quality of being utterly modern and yet appears as ancient as the text itself. The combination of highly stylized poetic text and hieratic music along with the simple, bold design and masks of the production make for a powerful telling of the myth, as far removed from naturalistic representation as could be imagined. The blocks of text governed by a clear pulse, the regularly repeating drum beats with unpredictable accents, the ominous and omnipresent drones, the modal melodic fragments, these all reinforce the ritual, collective aspects of the choral passages, so making the events recounted appear timeless. Even the most horrible accounts of, for example, Clytemnestra's bloody murder of Agamemnon are contained by the stylized manner of presentation. Personal tragedy becomes mythic; through music the familiar narrative is invested with mythopoeic power. By these means we are able to 'gaze into the infinite'. Music here is shown to be not peripheral but central to the representation of the tragic myth because – as Harrison's verse translation makes abundantly clear – its very origins lie in music itself.

The above discussion makes apparent the mutual dependence of myth and ritual; indeed, many thinkers regard them as homologous. Lévi-Strauss summarizes: 'Regardless of whether the myth or the ritual is the original, they replicate each other; the myth exists on the conceptual level and the ritual on the level of action.'[24] (In fact, for his own purposes, Lévi-Strauss questions this homology on the basis of his examination of accounts of the mythologies of particular societies, preferring to see myth and ritual in a dialectical relationship.) For Birtwistle, ritual is the outcome of myth while myth can only successfully be articulated through ritual. In other words, myth provides the formalized, anti-naturalistic context within which the ceremonial repetitions, incantations and role-play of ritual can take place. Myth gives meaning to ritual.

But this is not to say that Birtwistle does not also produce musical rituals or ceremonies that have no specific mythical context. A number of his important works of instrumental theatre seem to play out non-specific ceremonies. *Tragoedia*, as we have seen, gives a clear indication of such thinking in its adoption of the form of Greek tragedy: 'It contains a specific drama, but this drama is purely musical . . . [T]he work is concerned with the ritual and formal aspects of Greek tragedy rather than with the content of any specific play.'[25] *Verses for Ensembles* seems to portray both an abstract drama and a non-specific act of religious worship. His only work explicitly termed a ritual is *Ritual Fragment*.

It is, in many ways, an audacious piece – a simple overall concept constructed from the most basic of musical materials. Yet in Birtwistle's hands these elements are moulded into a music where each instrumental 'character' is able to speak for itself, and where the whole possesses an extraordinary momentum, a powerful ritualistic inevitability.

Like *Secret Theatre* before it, *Ritual Fragment*'s fourteen players are seated in a semicircle and, during the course of the piece, ten of them move in turn to the front of the platform to occupy a solo position. The other four instruments (bass drum, piano, cello, double bass) remain immobile and form a kind of continuo group, helping to accompany and link the solos and to signal moments of structural importance. Like so many ancient rites, this contemporary ritual begins with a 'call to order' from the drum (the absence of a conductor reinforces the impression that we seem to be witnessing an intimate ceremony). The drum's brief fragment, together with the familiar trochaic (scotch-snap) pattern on the piano which always follows it, periodically punctuates the development of the 'drama'. The first solo instrument, the trumpet, quickly moves to the front of the stage and initiates a melodic procession which continues virtually uninterrupted to the end of the work. Where the soloists in *Secret Theatre* articulated a single melody heterophonically, *Ritual Fragment* presents a heterogeneous sequence of discrete melodic fragments. Each solo melody is distinguished by its own timbre and tempo, and by a short, characterizing motif which can also occur independently of the melody (reminiscent of the recurring saxophone and cor anglais motifs in *The Triumph of Time*). For example, the trumpet's motif, a four-note falling figure played six times at the end of its solo (and overlapping with the next), appears a further eight times during the course of the piece from within the ensemble. Whenever any one of these solo motifs recurs, it remains a fixed object – unchanging in pitch, contour and tempo – but always heard against the continuously changing background landscape.

It is this context which helps bind the melodic fragments together (without undermining their essential differences) and which prevents the work from descending into the incoherence of mere collage. When the instrumentalists are not playing the role of soloist ('protagonist'), they move back into the ensemble to become accompanists ('chorus'). Sometimes they take their material directly from the solo line, as is the case with the trumpet solo, as a kind of commentary on it; at other times they paint a new landscape of pedals and ostinatos, as for instance in the accompaniment to the viola solo. Occasionally they take a more active role in order to make a transition from one solo to the next. At the end of the work, there is a ritualistic 'roll call' of the principal motivic fragments in the presence of a long pedal D (a pitch which has served as a recurrent point of reference throughout). The flute, the final soloist, reiterates its motif no fewer than nine times to which, in turn, each of the other solo instruments responds. Yet this is no climactic synthesis; though the fragments have elements in common, they nevertheless remain independent of one another. Their proximity here merely signals that the ritual has come to a temporary halt. As the final violin D disappears into the distance, we are left with the expectation that the ritual will continue on another day, in another place.

Thus, the ritual aspect of *Ritual Fragment* is expressed through the formalized manner in which the instrumentalists interact, enhanced by their stylized movements about the concert platform. It is a 'fragment' in two senses: firstly, it is as if we, the audience, are only part-witness to an event which has already begun and which could continue *ad infinitum* (a necessary characteristic of all rituals) – we hear just a fragment of the music's endless melody; secondly, each solo participant possesses his or her own musical fragment and thus has an independent role to play in the ritual, despite always being reined in by the collective.

Ritual Fragment is a specific example of what in general can be seen to characterize Birtwistle's rituals: a 'primitive' music (dealing with 'basic', 'unformed', 'preconscious' or fragmented materials) with a primacy on rhythm; a highly formalized, stylized structure which depends on repetition at many levels; an 'open' or 'unending' structure which is brought to a temporary halt but which could repeat infinitely; music where the individual usually springs from and can only be understood in relation to the collective – hence, the preponderance of verse-refrain forms. This again suggests a neo-medieval aspect to Birtwistle's aesthetic: he is concerned both with *musica practica* (that is, a music that is never abstract but always part of some sort of ritual) and *music speculativa* (that is, a metaphysical music, a music which suggests possibilities beyond the everyday). It also directs our attention, once more, to the profound connections between Birtwistle and Stravinsky. Not only are ritual and myth central to the subject matter of many of Stravinsky's key 'stage' works from *The Rite of Spring* through *Les Noces* and *Oedipus Rex* to *The Flood* (based, in part, on medieval mystery plays), but virtually all his works have a ritualistic aspect through their structural formality (blocks, frames, verse-refrain forms), repetition (structural, rhythmic and melodic), instrumental role-play and, often, a formal open-endedness. Those works of Stravinsky's which Birtwistle most admires – *The Rite of Spring*, *Symphonies of Wind Instruments*, *Symphony of Psalms*, *Agon* – are those works in which such ritualized formality is especially prominent. The framing and role-play in the first of the *Three Pieces for String Quartet* where each string instrument has its own individually characterized, repeated 'fragment', where each element seems almost to be spatially as well as musically distinct, where a potentially infinite number of repetitions are framed by the viola's 'call to order', and where also an overall formality is suggested by a careful proportional scheme,[26] are very close to what Birtwistle achieves in *Ritual Fragment*. Similarly, the formalized block/spatial organization of 'fragments' in the *Symphonies of Wind Instruments* results in a structure – 'an austere ritual which is unfolded in terms of short litanies between different groups of homogeneous instruments'[27] – which has clearly influenced Birtwistle's instrumental rituals in fascinating ways. (Richard Taruskin's recent interpretation of the *Symphonies* in terms corresponding to the Orthodox Office of the Dead serves further to reinforce the powerful ritual dimension of this work.)[28]

One work of Stravinsky's which Birtwistle has not often discussed but which offers a model for so many of his own works is *Oedipus Rex*. We are here presented with a familiar mythical narrative from ancient Greece (after Sophocles) yet the substance of the work is not concerned with story-telling. The basics of the plot are swiftly disposed of by the Speaker (a kind of Choregos figure) in the vernacular, who according to the librettist, Jean Cocteau, 'expresses himself like a conferencier, presenting the story with a detached voice'. The main body of the work is in Latin:

> . . . the events and characters of the great tragedy came to life wonderfully in this language, and, thanks to it, assumed a statuesque plasticity and a stately bearing entirely in keeping with the majesty of the ancient legend.
>
> What a joy it is to compose music to a language of convention, almost of ritual, the very nature of which imposes a lofty dignity![29]

This is monumental, ritualistic, anti-naturalistic theatre. Stravinsky's 'statuesque' chorus of tenors and basses comment on the action, a stylization reinforced (according to instructions in Cocteau's prefatory note) by rough, two-dimensional décor, the use of masks, and a stylized acting style where only arms and heads move. Narrative continuity is eschewed. And just as the structure of the plot is overtly signalled by the Speaker, so through various devices of repetition, the music signals its own functions as structural punctuation and frame. The myth of Oedipus is told through ritual.

Birtwistle's two most stylized stage works can usefully be understood in the light of Stravinsky's model. Both *Punch and Judy* and *The Mask of Orpheus* rely on folk/mythical stories which he assumes are so well known, or at least so simple, that they release him from the need to concern himself with the exposition of narrative. The important point is that the subject matter already appears to belong collectively to the audience (this is true of all his stage works).[30] They will thus be drawn into the theatre's *musical* dimension, into its ritual. As in *Oedipus*, in both Birtwistle's works the 'chorus' has a vital function, though in neither case is it present in the way it is in Stravinsky. In *Punch and Judy*, different characters at different times come together to take on the role of the chorus, while Choregos both comments on and participates in the drama. Just as Cocteau's narration framed his 'play', so *Punch* opens with Choregos in front of the curtain inviting the audience 'to enjoy our littel play'. Choregos also appears in *Monodrama* to a text by Pruslin written immediately after *Punch and Judy*, but subsequently withdrawn. Here a Stravinskian speaker (actually named Choregos) takes on various dramatic functions though only his amplified voice is heard: he is never seen on stage. The work's failure is instructive and Hall's diagnosis is an accurate one.[31] *Monodrama* exists on too abstract a level: it is a virtually plotless allegory, so there is nothing in an audience's experience for them to engage with. It has neither the appeal of an individual narrative nor the resonance of a collective tradition – the very things which attract us to (and, indeed, implicate us in) the tales of Oedipus, Orpheus and Punch.

Mention should perhaps also be made here of another work based in part on Greek mythology. *Medusa* was first composed to a BBC commission for the Pierrot Players in 1969 but withdrawn because the composer felt it was too obviously symmetrical. The following year he revised and extended it, though he now disowns this version too. *Medusa*'s title refers both to the girl of mythology whose beautiful hair was changed into serpents and whose gaze would turn anyone who looked on her to stone, and also to the name of a type of jellyfish and its unusual means of reproduction. Birtwistle intended the piece to be concerned with both these aspects: the formalism of the classical myth and the organicism of the natural creature – that is, a kind of 'mechanical pastoral', to appropriate the term later coined for *Yan Tan Tethera*. *Medusa* quotes – or rather parodies – a Bach chorale and chorale prelude (an aspect of its formalism) while the jellyfish refers to the more amorphous aspects of the work's structure. Listening to it, one is immediately struck by a sound-world quite unlike anything else he has written, involving everything from Maxwell Davies-style parodies of the found material (possibly a response to the vogue for such quotation in much experimental music of the 1960s) to a manic Xenakis-like amplified viola cadenza in the context of somewhat alien electronics (the work of Zinovieff). Birtwistle's own verdict on the work is uncompromising: '*Medusa*'s a piece with something stuck here, something stuck there without rhyme or reason. There's nothing in it which has the right to be placed next to a Bach chorale, least of all to be transformed into one. It's a lie, and I didn't see through my own lie; that's why I don't like it.'[32] *Medusa* is, in many respects, a rough piece, certainly one of Birtwistle's most experimental.[33] He was not quite able to bring it off on this occasion. The relevance of the myth remains hidden for the most part and does not imbue the work with universal perspectives – on the contrary, our attention is focused on the very individuality of the ideas presented. Nonetheless, *Medusa* is significant because it points forward to important compositions of the 1970s, such as the more assured incorporation and transformation of 'found' objects in *The Triumph of Time* and the integral use of electronics in *The Mask of Orpheus*, and to the balancing of the circular ('formal', continuum) and the linear ('natural', cantus) in key works of the 1980s and 1990s. It also shows Birtwistle thinking about form in a new way: rather than relying on ready-made structures from earlier music or on dramatic forms, he is beginning to think here about how form can be developed out of the work's own material. One source of ideas at this time, to which he has often referred, is D'Arcy Thompson's book on form in nature, *On Growth and Form*.[34]

The archaic Latin and closed forms of *Oedipus Rex* are matched by the formality of language and structure in both *Punch and Judy* and *The Mask of Orpheus*. Pruslin's text is highly structured with over a hundred separate 'numbers', full of clever rhyming games, puns, assonance and alliteration; Zinovieff's text is similarly intricately organized and makes little attempt to allow the meaning of the words to be understood immediately – indeed, the invented Orphic language entirely precludes this, so that the actual 'events' of Act 3 (for example, Orpheus's Terrible Deaths by suicide, by a thunderbolt, and at the hands of the Dionysian women) are not part of the sung text at all. The shattering of both linear plot and naturalism in *Oedipus Rex* is matched by the music which Stravinsky described as a *Merzbild*, moving freely from one musical 'topic' to another (Handelian oratorio, Verdian opera, and so on). This is also certainly true of *Punch and Judy*, the 'source' opera, the 'opera about opera'. When Pruslin writes that 'as far as the scenario and libretto are concerned, I consider the St Matthew Passion as an ideal in that the very layout and structure of the work constitute a kind of "invisible theatre" which does not depend on theatrical realisation to make its point',[35] the Baroque, tableau-like aspect of *Oedipus*, designated an 'opera-oratorio', is brought immediately to mind. *Punch and Judy* has two Passion Arias and three Passion Chorales (unlike the unsuccessful use of Bach in *Medusa*, these take over the *Affekt* and function of Baroque chorales without the need for direct quotation) while Birtwistle's own *Merzbild* further includes Baroque dances, a nineteenth-century-style recitative (preceding Judy's Baroque *da capo* Passion Aria II) and mock nursery rhymes (Punch's 'Right tol de riddle dol'). Such eclecticism is not so obvious a feature of *The Mask of Orpheus* (aside from the inevitable stylistic caesura between Acts 2 and 3) but the formality of the dramatic distinction between, say, recitative and aria, is musically clearly articulated and fully contributes to the work's undeniable monumentality.

The first Love Duet in Act 1 of *The Mask of Orpheus* (subtitled Duet of Hope) is dominated by Orpheus and Eurydice (both sung simultaneously, on and off stage, by the singer and the puppet) quietly but ecstatically calling one another's names. These lines are punctuated by one pair or the other rhythmically speaking of their love, Orpheus once again using the words 'I remember', while Eurydice expresses a progressive change in attitude to Orpheus's love for her. (Birtwistle had already tried out this manner of presenting simultaneously more than one idea through the use of contrasting modes of vocal delivery in *Nenia: The Death of Orpheus* – also to a text by Zinovieff. In this work the single soprano vocalist is required to switch rapidly between speech, humming and singing so that she can, for example, both invoke the name of Orpheus and comment on it. Though an ancient funeral dirge, the mood of the music is not at all far removed from that of the Love Duet of *Orpheus*, not least as a result of the sustained writing for homogeneous groupings of three wind instruments found in both – three bass clarinets in the case of *Nenia*.) The Love Duet is focused throughout on the pitch G, and more generally on the interval G–B♭. In chanting their lovers' names, the singers' sustained melodic lines begin on G and gradually move outwards (in a non-symmetrical manner) by decorating it; but they can never escape the pull of G and always return to it. The woodwind lines freely echo the calls of Orpheus and Eurydice, proliferating outwards from G and B♭ to create a rich, multilayered texture but which is in essence expressive of the one idea. The marimba and vibraphones have ostinatos also built from the same material, beginning with reiterated Gs. The whole is underlaid by the presence in the background of the tape of the Summer Aura, which includes distant references to the buzzing of the bees of Aristaeus the bee-keeper, son of Apollo, and Virgil's 'Arcadian master' (principal protagonist of Book 4 of the *Georgics*, one of Zinovieff's and Birtwistle's key sources) whose later pursuit of Eurydice leads to her being fatally bitten by the snake.

As the Duet proceeds, further related yet independent elements are layered on top of those already present, such as the punctuating falling figure played by harp and Noh-harp, or the distinctly active piccolo line (joined by oboe and claves) which is associated only with the spoken texts of Orpheus Singer and Eurydice Singer and (like those texts) is in a different metre from the prevailing one which belongs with the lyrical calls of Orpheus Puppet and Eurydice Puppet (a sample is given in Ex. 3.7). In keeping with the anti-linear narrative of the work as a whole, the Duet is periodically interrupted, only to resume after the interruption from where

Ex. 3.7. *The Mask of Orpheus*, Act 1, 'First Love Duet'.

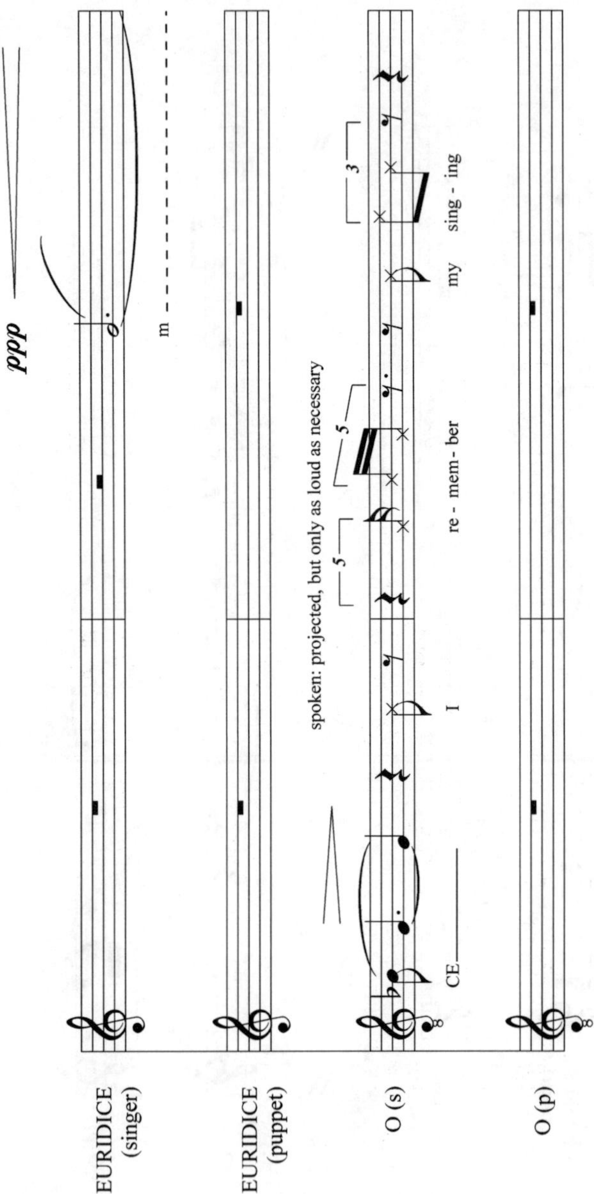
EURIDICE (singer)
EURIDICE (puppet)
O (s)
O (p)
ppp
m
spoken: projected, but only as loud as necessary
CE
I
re - mem - ber
my sing - ing

Ex. 3.7 (cont'd)

E (s)
E (p)
O (s)
O (p)
OR—— (m) - - - PHE—— (m) - - - US——
echo pp
OR - PHE - US
pp
p
(p)
EU—— RI - DI - CE—— EU——
pp
EU - RI—— DI - CE——

Ex. 3.7 (cont'd)

it left off (compare this with the 'interlock' of blocks of music in Stravinsky, pre-eminently in the *Symphonies of Wind Instruments*). The initial suspension of the Duet is brought about by the first Passing Cloud of Abandon which tells the story of Dionysus:

> The body of Dionysus was torn to shreds by the Titans. The pieces were boiled in a cauldron and turned into a pomegranate tree. Nevertheless Rhea, his grandmother, was able to reconstitute him.

The three Passing Clouds of Abandon and the three Allegorical Flowers of Reason are sequences of electronic music in which a mime troupe enacts other mythical stories which had been told by Orpheus to the trees after losing Eurydice for the second time. Each lasts about three minutes, and each causes the main action to be suspended. As myths within a myth, allegories within the larger allegory, they have a symbiotic relationship to the principal drama: they reflect both the violence of the murder of Orpheus and the lyricism of his love for Eurydice, yet they remain independent. The extraordinary electronic music, realized at IRCAM from Birtwistle's rhythmic and metrical schemes by the New Zealand composer Barry Anderson (1935–87), is formed from just four sampled harp notes and chords which were analysed, resynthesized and transformed by the computer at the Pompidou Centre. Magical, mysterious and almost timeless sounds are the result – Birtwistle describes them as 'a mad, mechanical percussion instrument'. Just as, for instance, he was later to extend the sonic and expressive scope of the solo piano in *Antiphonies* by the use of tuned percussion, so here the computer extends the harp (Orpheus's lyre) outwards throughout the audible spectrum and the entire auditorium. It is interesting that when the Duet resumes, three harps take on a punctuating role as if to suggest that Orpheus's story of the death of Dionysus can be heard to echo through his own love story (moreover, one of these harps is tuned flat to make its sounds less 'natural' and more like the electronically transformed harps of the Passing Cloud).

The next interruption[36] to the Duet is brought about by the first Ceremony, the wedding of Orpheus and Eurydice, itself punctuated by further extensions of the first Love Duet. This is an important choral moment for three priests, or Troupe of Ceremony, who sing collectively to invoke Hymen and speak individually to pose ritual questions. The music here stands in stark contrast to that of the Love Duet, being primarily rhythmic in impetus. The music is dominated by an incessant quaver pulsation in untuned percussion and cowbells (beginning at crotchet = *c.*138) along with the imprecise sound of three blown conch shells ritually calling the priests to order and suggesting some sort of ancient and primitive ceremony. Once again, the music proliferates outwards from these basic materials: the conches are extended by a quartet of low trombones and a trio of high clarinets playing close, sustained chords, while other percussion (tuned and untuned), three bassoons and three harps take up the quaver pulsation. The unremitting quaver pulse drives the music through to the end of the first scene. This music clearly stands at the head of a renewed interest in pulse that Birtwistle was to explore in the later 1970s following the completion of Act 2 of Orpheus. The percussive ceremony of *For O, for O, the Hobby-Horse is Forgot*, which ends with five minutes of (soft) regular quaver beats, or the 'primitive' rhythms and drones of the *Oresteia* score, invoke ritual situations of the same kind as *The Mask of Orpheus*'s first Ceremony. In all these cases, we are in the realm of the chorus, in the preconscious world of the mythopoeic collective. The first Ceremony thus stands in direct opposition to the Love Duet, whose subject matter (courtship, the yearning for a love which is fated not to be) and musical presentation (melodic cantus, ostinato-based continuum, periodic flute [piccolo] obligato) share those familiar characteristics of Birtwistle's 'arias' where the dramatic moment is frozen. It is also significant that the first Immortal Dance (Wedding Dance) which closes the first Ceremony evinces another instance of that Birtwistle topic brought about by the confluence of the intense song ('Come closer to will wildness . . .'), dancing rhythms and the flute (piccolo).

It is perhaps also worth remarking here that everywhere there are 'threes'. The intricate interlocking cycles of three events across the three acts, the threefold representation of the principal characters, and so on, is echoed in Birtwistle's predilection for grouping instruments in threes. Similar structural groupings of events in threes (Passion Chorales, Quests for Pretty Polly, and so on) are also to be found in *Punch and Judy*. Three is a significant ritual number: threefold repetition suggests a circularity and temporal infinity and is therefore an important ritual symbol. Compare this with the threefold choral shouts of 'Gloria!' which close Act 1 and open Act 2 of *Oedipus Rex*.

One of the central concerns of *The Mask of Orpheus* is with time itself, and its attempt to create new kinds of musical and dramatic (mythical) time. The revisiting of events from different perspectives is a fundamental aspect of the non-linear way in which the work 'tells' the myth, and the principal focus of this is in what Zinovieff calls Time Shifts. There are striking parallels here with the texts of both Cocteau's *Oedipus* and Pruslin's *Punch*: for example, Walsh writes of *Oedipus* that 'the narrator brings into play successive shifts in time sequence which re-introduce irony as a function of the music. By the end of each of his short speeches he has carried the story forward to its next crisis, but the music which follows must revert every time to the situation as at the start of the speech.'[37] This is what happens in the first Time Shift where we return, in distorted fashion, to the events leading to the death of Eurydice. Zinovieff describes this as 'caricature', and it certainly results in a degree of ironic distancing.

1st Look of Loneliness (Act 1, scene 2)	*1st Human Lie* (Act 1, scene 3)
. . .	
Kissed by the snake,	Kiss the snake,
Cracked shadow.	Cracked memory.
Speak to the water.	Speak to the dire land!

Kicked in the dust,	Cry in the dust,
Dead shadow.	Dead tears.
Listen to the dried grass.	Listen to the silent grass!
Killed by the river,	Kill by the river,
Dark shadow.	Dark blood.
Remember the white snake.	Remember the yellow sand!
Clipped . . . Eurydice . . .	Clipped Eurydice!
Orpheus, Orpheus, Orpheus.	Orpheus, Orpheus, Orpheus,
Change it.	Change it.
. . .	. . .

Aristeus's words are a parody of the first occasion on which they were uttered; the music does not follow this parody exactly, but it is still audibly a variant of the original with new layers added. The simplest example of this can be seen by comparing the calls of 'Orpheus', which in the Look of Loneliness are on the notes C and B but which are extended to B–C–G♯ in the Human Lie. Compare these musical and textual procedures of 'distortion' with those in *Punch and Judy* (Moral/Morale), discussed in Chapter 1, which are strikingly similar. The sense of the same story being retold many times is fundamental to any experience of myth; for Birtwistle, this becomes a structural feature of both drama and music, and is taken into the structure of his purely instrumental works too.

The passion of the individual represented in the formal context of a ritual; spontaneous and ecstatic behaviour balanced by the rational and the ordered; nature and culture; music and word; Dionysus and Apollo, even. Not just the choice of different kinds of mythical subject matter for all of his stage works, but his representation of these stories in a stylized, ritualized manner invests Birtwistle's 'narratives' with a universal significance while never necessarily denying the vitality of the portrayal of individual characters. And these concerns for ritual echo outwards into the instrumental works too. Myth is important to Birtwistle because it attempts to articulate the often overwhelming feelings, urges and emotions we all experience but which are beyond (indeed, which precede) words. For Birtwistle, it is music, not words, that best expresses these feelings. Music exists in the realm of the beyond-word; and thus through music we have unique access to the mythical.

4 *Episodion III* – Pastoral

The idea of the pastoral is at the heart of many of Birtwistle's music-theatre projects. He has only explicitly employed the term twice for theatre pieces: in the subtitles of *Down by the Greenwood Side* (a 'dramatic pastoral') and of *Yan Tan Tethera* (a 'mechanical pastoral'). However, it is clearly central to the concept of his Orpheus project (originally suggested by a reading of Virgil's *Georgics*),[1] culminating in *The Mask of Orpheus*, as well as to such works as *Entr'actes and Sappho Fragments, Narration: a Description of the Passing of the Year, The Fields of Sorrow, Carmen Arcadiae Mechanicae Perpetuum, Gawain*, even the purely instrumental *Silbury Air* and *Panic*. The series of flute miniatures, the *Duets for Storab*, also contain a 'Stark pastoral' and a 'White pastoral'. On closer examination, it would appear that Birtwistle's understanding of the idea of the pastoral has had a profound impact on many aspects of his musical as well as his dramatic thinking. Indeed, to approach his music from the perspective of the pastoral opens up fascinating possibilities for interpreting narrative and opposition in *all* his works.

Birtwistle's fondness for the pastoral may in part betray his 'Englishness' – to observe that the English have long had a penchant for the pastoral is not to say anything of startling novelty. Drawing on the pastoral texts of antiquity, especially the writings of Theocritus and Virgil, the interest in pastoral as a poetic and dramatic genre flourished in the sixteenth and seventeenth centuries in the hands of Spenser, Sidney, Marvell and Shakespeare. The dramatic pastorals of Tasso and Guarini in Renaissance Italy (from which emerged the pastoral *intermedi* such as the allegorical tableau *The Triumph of Time*, and which led to the early pastoral/Orphic operas) were widely imitated in England. Such English musical pastoralism passed from the naïve, idealized love of the Elizabethan madrigalists to Blow's *Venus and Adonis*, Purcell's *Dido and Aeneas* and Handel's *Acis and Galatea*. Yet outside the Orpheus pieces, and the sheep of *Yan Tan Tethera*, such texts and issues would appear to have little immediately to do with Birtwistle. Arcadia, with its nymphs and shepherds, Rosalind and Colin, its idealization of love and its unspoiled natural landscapes, 'an ideal realm of perfect bliss and beauty, a dream of ineffable happiness',[2] is hardly the territory of *Punch and Judy* or *Down by the Greenwood Side*. But this is to define pastoral too narrowly: an innocent, idealized, rural simplicity in absolute opposition to a corrupt, urban complexity. A closer look at the pastoral quickly reveals that it is usually tempered, at the very least, by an air of 'sweetly sad'[3] melancholy. In Poussin's famous paintings of *c.*1630 and 1635, the eponymous 'Et in Arcadia ego' is inscribed on the side of a tomb, which has led to the Latin being rendered by many as '*Death* is even in Arcadia'. This is certainly more like the world of *Down by the Greenwood Side*, at the start of which Mrs Green sings:

> There was a lady near the town,
> Low so low and so lonely,
> She walked all night and all around,
> Down by the greenwoods of Ivry.
> She had two pretty little babes,
> She thought one day she'd take their lives,
> Down by the greenwoods of Ivry.
> She got a rope so long and neat,
> Low so low and so lonely,
> She tied them up both hands and feet,
> She got a knife both keen and sharp
> And pierced it through each tender heart,
> Down by the greenwoods of Ivry.[4]

The art historian Erwin Panofsky writes of the *c.*1635 Louvre version of Poussin's painting that 'the behaviour of the figures . . . expresses . . . quiet, reminiscent meditation', 'a contemplative absorption in the idea of mortality . . . undisguised elegiac sentiment'.[5] Death is even in Arcadia. Panofsky's reading of Virgil is telling in this context: 'In Virgil's ideal Arcady human suffering and super-humanly perfect surroundings create a dissonance. This dissonance, once felt, had to be resolved in . . . [a] mixture of sadness and tranquillity.'[6] Guarini, for one, had recognized this mixture: he defended his pastoral drama, *Il pastor fido* (1585), as 'tragicomedy'. Birtwistle's and Pruslin's *Punch and Judy* is similarly subtitled 'a tragical comedy or comical tragedy'.

William Empson picks up this theme in his still fresh and provocative essays of 1935, *Some Versions of Pastoral.* In tragicomedy, he argues, the comic part usually 'provides as sort of parody or parallel in low life to the serious part' – a manifestation of the 'tragic king – comic people' convention.[7] A situation is repeated for 'high' and 'low' characters: 'this puts the main interest in the situation not the characters . . . The situation is made something valuable in itself, perhaps for reasons hardly realized; it can work on you like a myth.'[8] This account is paralleled by what happens in the two interleaved narratives of *Down by the Greenwood Side*, where the comedy (of Father Christmas, St George, Bold Slasher, Dr Blood and Jack Finney) provides a 'low life' parallel to the tragedy narrated by Mrs Green.

Tragicomedy, then, is not concerned with the naturalistic representation of events or characters (allied to this, Empson also discussed its 'looseness of structure'),[9] perhaps helping to account for the pastoral's appeal to certain twentieth-century composers. Geoffrey Chew supports such a view:

> In some works composers did not merely cultivate 'simple' idioms but also rejected nineteenth-century notions of realism . . . at the same time succeeding in returning to a more profound, moral version of pastoral . . .[10]

whether in the so-called 'soft' pastoral of Debussy, Ravel and Vaughan Williams, or the 'hard' pastoral of *The Rite of Spring.* This interest in situation rather than character coincides with Birtwistle's ongoing fascination with landscape and perhaps, in passing, reminds us of his love of the paintings of Cézanne, whose landscapes (situation) are arguably more effective than his portraits (character). As Birtwistle said in his interviews about music and painting,

> That's why I've made the analogy of landscape, you see, in that it's a place that's *there*. There are certain elements in certain places, and I choose to compose my way through them. It's as if I compose all the elements first, and move through them, and can return to them – which introduces the element of repetition.[11]

Repetition is also at the heart of Empson's definition of the pastoral tragicomedy. Furthermore, this view brings Birtwistle's interest in pastoral into line with his understanding of classical tragedy, which is concerned less with narrative continuity and development than with exploring certain *recurring*, volatile *situations*. In terms of the theatre, this results in something stylized, something more concerned with ritual and repetition than with story-telling *per se*. As Empson puts it, this 'makes the characters unreal, but not the feelings expressed or even the situation described'.[12]

In all Birtwistle's stage works, this unreality is exaggerated in that he and his librettists choose to represent blatantly 'unreal' characters: the puppets Punch and Judy, the mythical Orpheus (also represented, in part, by a giant puppet) and Father Christmas, the celluloid King Kong, and so on. The preface to *Down by the Greenwood Side* emphasizes the fact that the acting style and costumes should be stylized and non-realistic and recommends the wearing of masks. It is a 'strongly gestured pantomime' representing simple people who can yet utter profundities. Empson raises this issue too:

> The simple man becomes a clumsy fool who yet has better 'sense' than his betters and can say things more fundamentally true; he is 'in contact with nature' . . . he is in contact with the mysterious forces of our own nature, so that the clown has the wit of the Unconscious . . .[13]

The pastoral process at the heart of Birtwistle's aesthetic is one of 'putting the complex into the simple'.[14]

In his operas of the 1990s – *Gawain* and *The Second Mrs Kong* – there seems to be a greater concern with character. Gawain grows, matures and changes as a result of his experiences, and his musical characterization is strong; Kong is a 'believable' operatic character who similarly develops as the narrative unfolds. The stage characters of the 1960s and 1970s are more like archetypes, less like individuals, less capable of development ('primordial images', according to Jung, 'a priori, inborn forms of "intuition" . . . of perception and apprehension', 'typical images which recur in the psyche').[15] Though, for example, Punch breaks free of his cycles of violent murder and erotic quest and finally wins Pretty Polly, he is no different at the end. It is the formal situation that has changed, not the objects within it. The pastoral, as Chew reminds us, is a 'mode' (of experience, of discourse) rather than a genre or style.

Another important aspect of the pastoral is that of music and song. Virgil's Fifth Eclogue (which had made such a strong impact on Poussin) contains the laments of Mopsus and Menalcas over the tomb of the shepherd Daphnis:

> . . . there's a song I wrote out the other day on the green bark of a beech and set to music, marking the turns of voice and pipe.
>
> . . . a song – sweeter, to my ear, than the music of the South Wind gathering way, or beaches beaten by the surf, or the streams that hurry down through rocky glens.[16]

Certainly this melancholic song echoes through many of Birtwistle's instrumental works, notably in such laments as *Linoi*, *Grimethorpe Aria, Melencolia I* and *The Cry of Anubis*. *Down by the Greenwood Side* begins with Mrs Green singing the lamenting, strophic song quoted above, her entrance prefaced by a repeating alto flute obbligato, and her singing accompanied by the dancing dotted rhythms of bass clarinet, bassoon and cello.

(Birtwistle took the work's instrumentation from the words of the nineteenth-century 'Cornish Floral Dance': 'We danced to the band with the curious tone of cornet, clarinet and big trombone; fiddle, cello, big bass drum, bassoon, flute, euphonium'.) At the end of the work, Mrs Green finally joins with the mummers in a jaunty song and dance, a kind of masque, 'the symbolic dance of ordered function (or the dance of abandonment) in which the whole of society is engaged'[17] (compare this ritual of spring, the awakening of the dead, with the end of *Punch and Judy*: 'Spring has come, shattering the prism, dispelling the eclipse, unfreezing the stars'). Once again, the confluence of song, dance and the flute symbolizes for Birtwistle the passions and rituals of love and courtship.[18] Though the origins for the composer of this symbolism remain relatively obscure, one might hazard that they have occurred frequently enough in pastoral literature and in painting to make their recurrence seem 'natural'. To give just one example here, the Robert Graves poem which prefaces the score of *Secret Theatre* signals an explicit connection between the pastoral flute and the love dance: '. . . a flute signals far off; we mount the stage . . . then dance out our love'. At the beginning of the work, the flute sings its rustic song (cantus) to a dancing accompaniment (continuum), while the music's furious climax (fig. 78) is achieved when cantus and continuum finally join together in a dance of love. In this context, the use of the flute at the opening of *Down by the Greenwood Side*, though not here suggesting a love dance, is nonetheless significant: it signals a song in the pastoral mode, as in Colin's melancholy 'December' complaint to the god Pan in Spenser's *The Shepheardes Calender* of 1579:

> I thee beseche (so be tough deigne to heare,
> Rude ditties tund to shepeards Oaten reede,
> Or if ever sonet song so cleare,
> As it with pleasaunce mought thy fancie feede)
>   Hearken awhile from thy greene cabinet,
>   The rurall song of carefull Colinet.

This opening song of *Down by the Greenwood Side* also bears comparison with Punch's opening song of *Punch and Judy* – and not only because of their shared subject matter of infant murder. Both are strophic songs (Punch's more obviously so), yet neither involves simple repetitions. Each strophe is varied in such a way as to generate a sense of increased tension across the song and is achieved through the progressive layering of materials and an increase in musical density by means of rhythmic diminution; that is, a Stravinskian kind of varied repetition rather than a Schoenbergian sort of developing variation. The artifice matches that of Virgil's song contests in the *Eclogues*, where the emphasis is more on the skill of the poet, on the nature of the form's repetitions and variations, than on its meaning.

But Mrs Green's ballad of the Cruel Mother and Punch's murderous Melodramas are only one thread in their respective works. *Down by the Greenwood Side* is also based on the traditional mummers' play in which Father Christmas (the Choregos-like 'master of ceremonies, not personally involved in the various happenings')[19] oversees the repeated ritual killing and awakening from the dead of St George. In *Punch and Judy*, each murder cycle is complemented by Punch's Quests after Pretty Polly, overseen literally by Choregos. In each case, the two narratives move in different directions; they are independent yet complementary.

Commenting on a much more recent work, Birtwistle has remarked:

> [T]ake the string quartets and the songs in *Pulse Shadows* – what I'm saying is that they're both functioning as the ritornello to the other, simultaneously . . . I'm very excited by this idea of two simultaneous cycles, each with its own identity.'[20]

Pulse Shadows is fascinating because of the genuine independence of the two cycles (written at different times and in different ways) and it raises difficult aesthetic and analytical issues about why they belong together at all. But this was not a new idea for Birtwistle: he had attempted a similar thing in *Entr'actes and Sappho*

Fragments. The work began in 1962 as a cycle of five simple movements (the 'entr'actes') plus coda for flute, viola and harp. Both in their scoring and in their delicate lines, they recall the 'soft' pastoral of Debussy's late second sonata. In 1964, Birtwistle added a connecting movement for an expanded ensemble and wordless soprano, followed by five settings of Sappho translations (called 'cantus') alternating with reworked versions of the original entr'actes and ending with a new coda. All the songs articulate pastoral themes and each is tinged with melancholy. The fifth is the most explicitly pastoral:

> Like the wild Hyacinth flower which on the hill is found.
> Which the passing feet of shepherds for ever tear and wound
> until the purple blossom is trodden under foot.

The new entr'actes are Boulez-like reworkings of the originals, sometimes (as in the case of Entr'acte II) following their model closely, sometimes (as in Entr'acte V) proliferating out from the original to generate a movement many times longer. The songs and the new entr'actes remain mutually independent, and yet they share a similar *Affekt*. Each throws light on the other; each provides a 'refrain' for the other.

The symbiotic relationship between the two narratives of *Down by the Greenwood Side* re-emerges in *The Mask of Orpheus* where the principal action is periodically interrupted by the six interludes of Passing Clouds and Allegorical Flowers. It is interesting that Virgil adopts a similar technique in Book 4 of his *Georgics*. The stories of Aristaeus and Orpheus are in the form of a short kind of epic called an 'epyllion', a story within another story, 'directly or obliquely, relevant to it, if only by way of contrast'.[21] Here the Aristaeus story is told in the Homeric style, objectively, while Orpheus's inset story is told subjectively, full of pathos. Virgil thus interweaves two contrasting stories that are both concerned with life and death, 'of life newly granted and ever again to be rewon; and life lost, sought with passionate love, almost snatched from death, and then for ever sinking back into the underworld'.[22] In other words, the *same* situation repeated for *different* characters. In *Down by the Greenwood Side*, the mother's murder of her boys is reinterpreted in the context of the killing of St George. Or, in Empson's words, the 'two parts make a mutual comparison that illuminates both parties'.[23] This, again, is tragicomedy. Both musically and theatrically, Mrs Green and the mummers are kept separate until the end (Mrs Green circles round but never enters the acting area defined by Father Christmas). Broadly speaking, Mrs Green operates according to the principle of 'aria' (reflexive, strophic, lyrical, sung) while the mummers operate according to the principle of 'recitative' (dynamic, through-composed, spoken), though this is perhaps to overstate their differences; on another level, both 'stories' or cycles are locked in to differing patterns of recurrence, a situation not so dissimilar from Birtwistle's account of *Pulse Shadows*, where 'they're both functioning as the ritornello to the other, simultaneously'.

This is confirmed at two key moments – the curing or bringing back to life of St George. A melody marked 'dolce' appears on both occasions, the first time on clarinet, the second on flute (the only two instruments from the ensemble which could possibly equate to the 'shepherd's oaten reed'), constituting a kind of motif of resurrection or renewal (Ex. 4.1). Its outwardly expanding shape represents this, reinforced in an appropriately comic manner on the second occasion by a figure which rises from contrabassoon through bass clarinet to piccolo. (Birtwistle is never averse to such obvious pantomime or film-score gestures: witness the coconut-shell horses' hooves at the arrival of the Green Knight in Act 1 of *Gawain*, and the 'falling' music as the film is shown of Kong toppling from the Empire State Building in Act 2 of *The Second Mrs Kong*.) In *Down by the Greenwood Side*, this melody is an important marker: the comic part takes over the mode, the rhetoric of the serious. It also suggests a way of interpreting Mrs Green's story – that is, the narratives of both the mummers and Mrs Green are to be understood as allegories of seasonal death and renewal:

> What is displayed on the tragi-comic stage is a sort of marriage of the myths of heroic and pastoral, a thing felt as fundamental to both and necessary to the health of society.[24]

Birtwistle himself thinks not just of his stage works in these terms: witness those works from the 1960s which project dramatic concerns into the concert hall. *Tragoedia* is shaped according to the principal categories of Greek tragedy in order 'to bridge the gap between "absolute music" and theatre music', while the literal translation of its title – 'goat dance' – again suggests a pastoral association. *Verses for Ensembles* takes on the external features of Greek tragedy and the physical movement of the players about the concert platform suggests the enactment of some kind of ritual. But more than this, it is productive to interpret a work such as *Verses for Ensembles* in terms of the pastoral, especially since it was being written simultaneously with *Down by the Greenwood Side*.

Take the central section (the 'stasimon') made up of two interlocking cycles: a series of five woodwind solos over a horn ground, interlaced with and framed by brass ritornelli (Ex. 4.2). These ritornelli are always the same yet always different: the total object is represented on the page but never fully realized because on every occasion it is played in a different way. 'It's like looking at an object,' Birtwistle has said; 'every view is unique but the object exists irrespective of the way it's viewed'.[25] The verses present a similar process but involving different materials and players: each statement of the horn ground is slightly varied, such that one cannot distinguish original and variant – multiple views of the same object which is never actually present in its entirety (discussed in more detail in Chapter 5). Thus, there are two interlocking cycles working in *similar* ways with *different* materials, the one lyrical (verse), the other more obviously fragmentary and repetitive (ritornello). Or, put another way, a pastoral situation of 'nature' (simple, lyrical woodwind – i.e. the urban and/or courtly). Though opposed and independent, one idea nonetheless throws fascinating light on the other: 'they're both functioning as

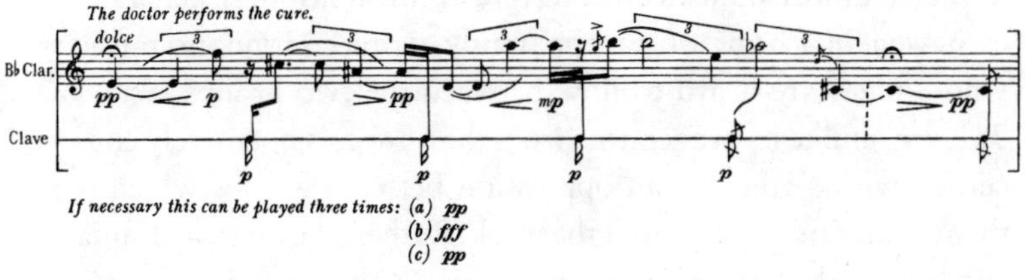

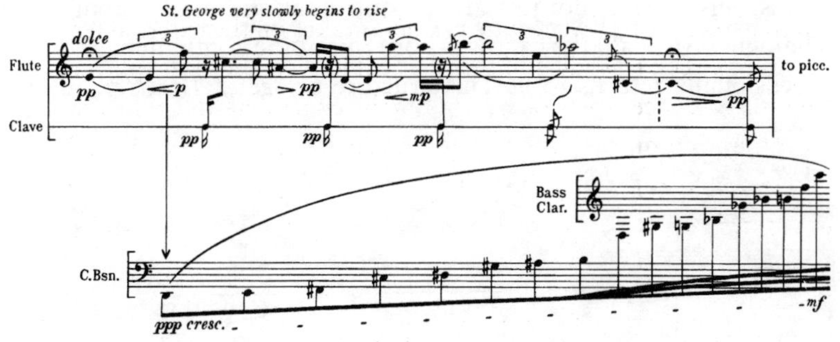

Ex. 4.1. *Down by the Greenwood Side*, 'The curing of St George'.

the ritornello to the other, simultaneously'. A situation, as Emerson told us, is repeated for 'high' and 'low' characters, which 'puts the main interest in the situation not the characters . . . The situation is made something valuable in itself . . . it can work on you like a myth.'

'*Verses* is the most extreme piece I've written.'[26] The bold juxtapositions, the uncompromising nature of the musical materials of *Verses for Ensembles* and many other of his works of the 1960s, allowed Birtwistle to explore certain extreme situations. It laid the ground for everything that has come since. What there is in *Verses for Ensembles* is, in embryonic form, an idea that was to materialize fully in *Secret Theatre* as cantus and continuum. Cantus is lyrical, linear, horizontal, the pastoral song; continuum is more fragmented, rhythmic, circular, vertical. But if this suggests another bold opposition of foreground and background, of melody and accompaniment, of verse and chorus, its working out is much more sophisticated. Overt confrontation is generally eschewed in favour of an apparently more continuous music whose ideas are heard to flow between the two groups. *Secret Theatre*, unlike its progenitors from the 1960s, is not merely concerned with setting up an opposition between groups which is then maintained throughout the work. Rather, the musical drama enacted by the players' movements about the concert platform explores the changing relationships between the two ensembles. Thus, this work is not just about confrontation but also about dialogue. After all, the cantus is born out of the continuum, and occasionally returns to it. The structure of *Secret Theatre* had

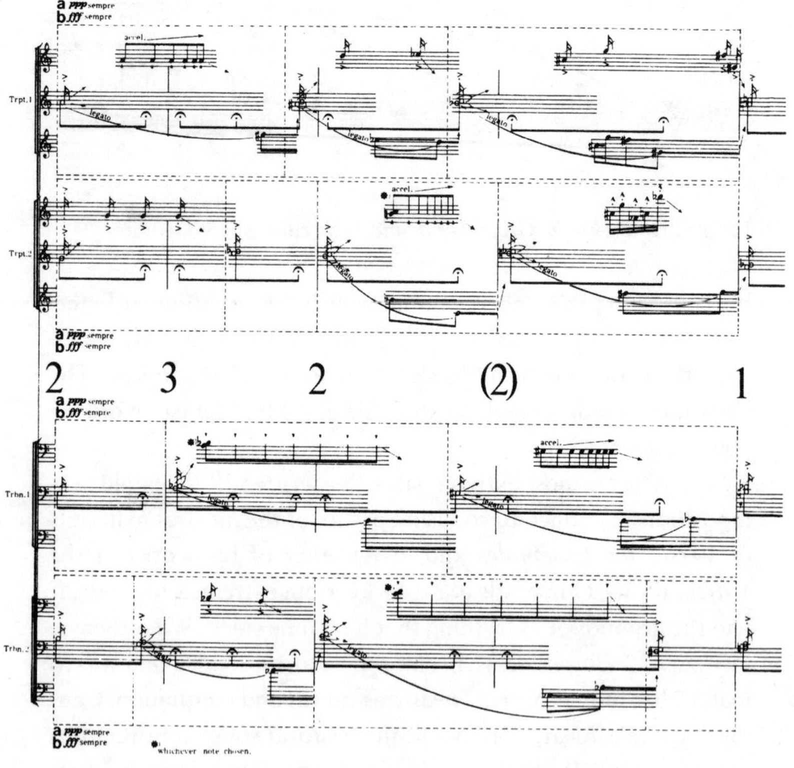

Ex. 4.2. *Verses for Ensembles*, 'Ritornello'.

already been suggested in *Down by the Greenwood Side*: the pastoral song interweaved with its 'other' with which it nevertheless shares much; the 'other' adopting, from time to time, the pastoral rhetoric of the song; the two coming together in a final danced masque. This pastoral song (and endless melody) resonates throughout Birtwistle: in the music for Orpheus, in the Arcadian song of *Carmen Arcadiae Mechanicae Perpetuum*, in the air of *Silbury Air*, in the landscapes of *Earth Dances*. Indeed, the craggy, pastoral landscape of *Earth Dances* can be understood as an extension of *Secret Theatre* with six rather than two layers, independent yet interdependent, like the shifting strata of the earth's crust. Dance once again points in the direction of the pastoral – here the 'hard' pastoral of *The Rite of Spring*, with which *Earth Dances* (and many other of Birtwistle's works) has so frequently been compared.

In this context, it is useful to look briefly at Geoffrey Chew's fascinating interpretation of Stravinsky's *The Rake's Progress* using pastoral theory:

> Stravinsky's neoclassical language in this opera sets up an elaborate network of differentiated relationships of congruence and lack of congruence, continuity and discontinuity, and of different structures and styles . . . [The] effect of Stravinsky's juxtapositions is rhetorical: oppositions are set up between principles of structure, and gain symbolic significance within the narrative . . . Yet the subtlety and complexity of the process is greater than has been noticed: there is no unchanging contrast throughout between 'old' and 'new', tonal and atonal, diatonic and chromatic, but these oppositions group and regroup as the music proceeds, acquiring new symbolic force in the process, and resisting schematic systems of interpretation.[27]

He could equally well be writing of *Secret Theatre* or *Earth Dances* ('oppositions group and regroup as the music proceeds, acquiring new symbolic force'). There are striking parallels between *The Rake's Progress* and *Punch and Judy*. Locating

Birtwistle's music within a general discussion of the oppositions of Stravinsky's neoclassicism opens up the fascinating possibility of writing the history of a certain strand of musical modernism – identified initially with Stravinsky and characterized by its ritualized anti-narrative, its discontinuities, its focus more on objective form than subjective content – in terms of the pastoral mode, a history to which Messiaen, Tippett, Birtwistle and Xenakis, to name just the most obvious candidates, all belong.

The pastoral, then – 'dramatic', 'mechanical' or otherwise – encourages us to look again at the oppositions in all of Birtwistle's music. Using the extremes of the music of the 1960s as paradigm, it proves possible to evaluate Birtwistle's music less in terms of obvious exclusive absolutes and more in terms of degrees of accommodation between similarity and difference, continuity and discontinuity. Music speaking or singing in the pastoral mode invites examination in terms of situation rather than character; the idea of the pastoral would thus appear to be appropriate more to a music concerned with exploring ritual than to that interested in developing a narrative argument. One kind of music can coexist with another, can share the same situation, can even come within the sphere of influence of the other, without its identity, its difference, being subsumed by the other. In the case of *Verses for Ensembles*, for example, Greek tragedy provides its dramatic frame, the pastoral its mode of discourse. This perhaps suggests a way round the difficult aesthetic and analytical issues raise above, of how and why different objects and ideas belong together at all. If we think primarily in terms of opposition – though clearly in tune with the modernist concerns of many of these works – this may deafen us to the more subtle connections and continuities between opposed terms, between opposed musics. To privilege – as does pastoral theory – situation over character is to enable a more appropriate balancing of continuity and discontinuity in this music without giving primacy to either. As Geoffrey Chew suggests, a resistance to schematic systems of interpretation is necessary in the study of Birtwistle's music; in the light of development in his music of the 1980s and 1990s, the bold oppositions, the verses and refrains, of his music of the 1960s need to be understood in terms which make plain the flexibility, not the granite-like rigidity of their structures.

5 *Stasimon* – Verses and Refrains

> *There are things that keep repeating, but if you listen to them or look at them closely, they're not repeating. It's like the leaves of a tree. You know what an oak leaf looks like, but if you take one, then look at the next one, they're all different.*[1]

The stasimon of *Tragoedia* for wind quintet, string quartet and harp is its still centre. It is the central panel of the work's symmetrical scheme and thus the point about which the work turns (the equivalent of the reversal or *peripeteia* of Greek tragedy). This is symbolized both in the prominence given to the harp (which stands centrally in the work's instrumental symmetry between the two 'choirs' of wind and strings) and in the essentially static character of this section. No overt verse-refrain structure is employed here: it is the episodes which stand either side of it that are made up of strophes, anapaests and antistrophes, where the second episodion is a freely reworked commentary on the first. This is in keeping with Aristotle's description of the stasimon as 'a choral song without anapaests or trochees.'[2] Nonetheless, this music shares in the character of so many of Birtwistle's verses – a soft, sparse, almost lyrical cantus. All of the music of *Tragoedia* reappears in one guise or another in *Punch and Judy*; the music of this stasimon returns – transformed but still readily recognizable – in Judy's Passion Aria II ('Be silent, strings of my heart') as a part of Melodrama III, that is just before the 'Nightmare' section, the opera's own stasimon and the moment of structural *peripeteia* and Punch's *anagnorisis*. Judy's Aria shares aspects of *Tragoedia*'s stasimon's scoring (harp, flute), motivic and rhythmic figurations, and general *Affekt*. Retrospectively, this certainly confirms the possibility of a reading of *Tragoedia*'s stasimon as verse/aria. If further confirmation is required, then a comparison with the virtually contemporary

Verses – discussed below – is instructive, whose writing for piano and clarinet strongly echoes that of this stasimon, and whose title is a definite clue to the musical identity of *Tragoedia*'s stasimon.

The notion of structural turning is embodied in the very gestural character of this section's principal material: a wave-like phrase, usually moving from high to low and back again, with a tendency also to turn back on its own pitches (though never employing obvious retrogrades), and which is present throughout in the harp. Despite their regular quaver durations, the harp's phrases never repeat exactly, giving the impression of an informal series of verses which continually show new facets of the same basic idea. The harp's material is always changing and yet never appears to be moving anywhere different. Hence the static character of the stasimon. The other instruments reinforce this either by echoing and reinterpreting the harp's figurations at different speeds (flute in quavers at the beginning, violin 1 in triplet quavers, later semiquavers) or else by adding new static layers either as pedal points or as regular rhythmic ostinatos (including the use of claves). Only in the second half of the movement does the music's song-like character begin to assert itself as violin 1 and flute (in triplet minims and triplet crotchets respectively) attempt to build around the harp more sustained cantus lines out of their formerly more fragmented ideas.

This is circular music, continually turning. There are moments (after fig. 23, for example) when at least five durational schemes are layered and operate simultaneously. The result, however, is not the kind of mechanical music to be found in some of Birtwistle's experiments with pulse during the the 1970s (see Chapter 6) but something more ritualistic, a secret, ancient ceremony in keeping with the abstract dramatic concerns of the work as a whole. The music is brought to a halt by two strokes on the claves and unpitched cello pizzicatos, as if this music wanted to continue to turn *ad infinitum*.

Everything I've written is a multiple object.[3]

The brass ritornello of the central 'stasimon' of *Verses for Ensem-*

bles is a paradigm for Birtwistle's attitude to varied repetition, an object complete on the page but one which is never viewed in the same way twice. This ritornello, like its Baroque counterpart, both frames and punctuates a series of episodes, in this case, five woodwind verses over a horn ground, the latter itself derived from an important independent horn phrase heard at the start of the work. The horn, as protagonist, has a central role in this work: indeed, this particular figure – or versions of it – always occurs at moments of structural opening, signalling the start of each main section: at the beginning ('prologue'); at figs. 13 and 14 (pre-echoes of 'episodion I'); at fig. 18 (the start of 'episodion I' proper); throughout the 'stasimon' as ground, figs. 34–53; and at fig. 57 (the start of 'episodion II'). The importance of the horn's role is signalled physically by the movement of the player about the platform.[4] Significantly, Birtwistle's original title for this work was to have been 'Signals'.

The horn ground's pitches are self-evidently derived from the version as it first appeared played from within the ensemble, a figure built principally of fourths and fifths in characteristic hunting-horn fashion. But its character in this central 'stasimon' is very different, as befits the verse-nature of the section: that is, a fanfare-like figure (*fff*, hard accents, even quavers), which clearly signals a beginning, has been transformed into something much more expansive and 'discursive'. Like the ritornello, however, each time the ground recurs, it is never quite the same; in engaging in dialogue with the solo woodwind instruments, it seems almost to respond to and take on some of the characteristics of each instrument. Ex. 5.1 gives examples of two forms of the ground: those which accompany the bassoon (no. 1) and the E♭ clarinet (no. 4). Note the 'wrong' notes, like the unpredictable variants that occur in the retelling of a story or in the oral transmission of a song melody. Which is 'original' and which is 'variant' is impossible to determine here; like the Orpheus story, the point is rather that multiple views of the same object are presented but it is an object which is never actually present in its entirety.

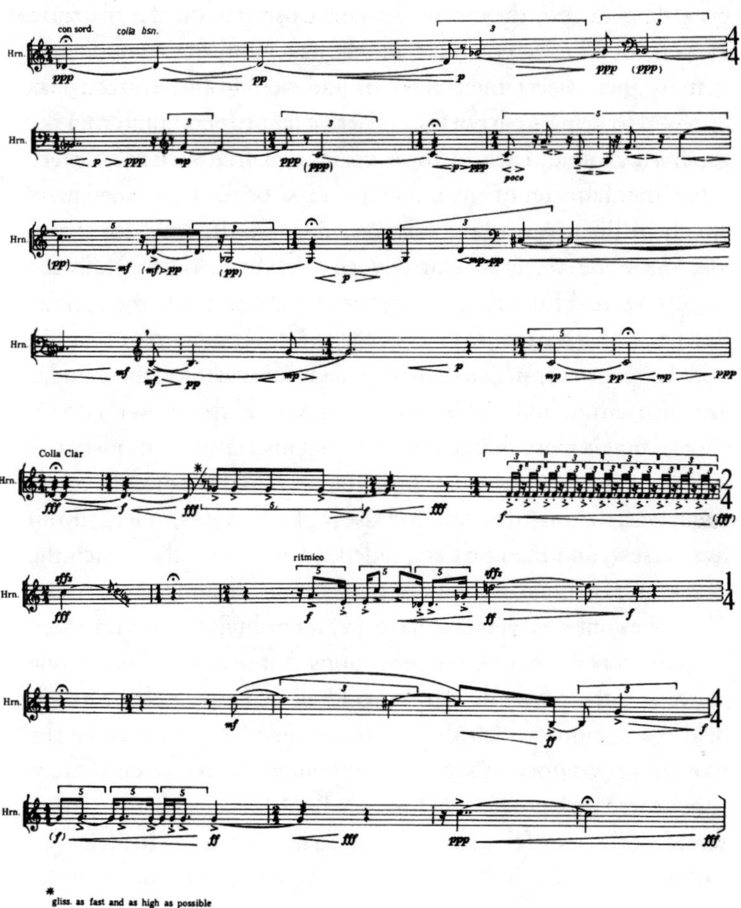

Ex. 5.1. *Verses for Ensembles*, horn ground (bassoon and clarinet verses).

This is true, too, of the woodwind verses. Each player is given a number of alternative routes through the music so that again a three-dimensional view of the musical object becomes possible. Such musical freedoms are part and parcel of the soloistic nature of verse writing in general, and in this work in particular are further identified with physical freedoms. Whenever players can choose their notes or are able to disengage themselves from the prevailing tempo, they move to new positions on the platform away from the main ensemble and the hegemony of the conductor; that is, they assert their roles as individuals (verse/cantus) as opposed to being a part of the collective (chorus/continuum). Like the horn ground, each of these verses is a free variant of every other, the character of any individual verse being determined principally by the nature of the solo instrument itself. Thus, for example, the oboe verse is relatively sustained, melodic, while the piccolo verse is full of rapid repeating- and grace-note figurations (see Ex. 5.2). To be more precise, each verse is built around certain nodal pitches over which there is an element of choice; these nodes are then connected by writing (over which the player has no choice) that is most characteristic of that instrument. For instance, in Ex. 5.2 it can be seen that both the oboe and the piccolo verses begin with a choice from pitch classes F, D and C (as, indeed, do all five verses), and then proceed independently until they reach the next common node, a choice of pitch classes A♭ and G, and so on. Thus, the common elements have greater in-built freedoms to help disguise in performance the repetitions that exist on paper, while conversely there is no need to provide choice in those elements not held in common – which also, ironically, involve writing that is the most improvisatory in style. (To my mind, there are clear resonances here with procedures found in Boulez, such as in the 'parentheses' of the Third Sonata as discussed in Chapter 1.) In fact, even within these individual verses, there is yet another kind of verse-refrain structure, where the nodes form the refrains and the free writing in between forms the verses. Verses embedded within verses embedded within verses, one might say.

Despite the apparently static nature of the 'stasimon' – the predictable alternation of verse and refrain, the symmetrical still centre of the work as a whole – it is nonetheless possible to perceive a progression through these verses in that both the horn ground and the solo verses become progressively more elaborate rhythmically, a movement supported by the ever-increasing density of activity in the percussion instruments. In relation to the symmetry of structure of *Tragoedia*, Birtwistle wrote that:

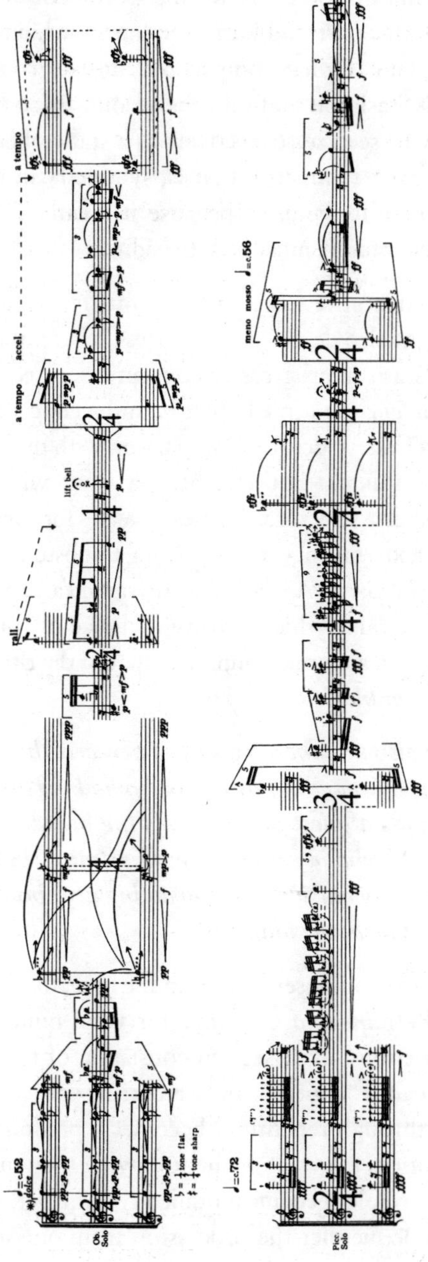

Ex. 5.2. *Verses for Ensembles*, oboe and piccolo verses.

> Although the Episodion is symmetrically complete in the small, it is also part of a larger symmetry which is not yet complete. This is what compels the music forward across the central Stasimon and into the second Episodion. Symmetry may be seen retrospectively as a static phenomenon; but incomplete symmetry, that is, symmetry in process of being formed, is dynamic because it creates a structural need that eventually must be satisfied.[5]

The same considerations appear to operate in *Verses for Ensembles*. One might also describe this process, after Günter Grass, as an aspect of 'stasis in progress', a concept discussed more fully in relation to *Melencolia I* in Chapter 7, and a concept at the heart of the verse-refrain structure. Comparison with the virtually contemporaneous *Cantata* is useful here, a work which adopts an unambiguous verse structure. A series of verses for soprano (singing fragmentary texts taken variously from tombstone inscriptions, Sappho and *The Greek Anthology*) are framed and punctuated by instrumental refrains which involve a choice of routes for each instrumentalist in a manner similar to that of the ritornellos from *Verses for Ensembles.*

> *... I think also that there's a sort of perverse thing in me, in that when you have a refrain, or something that repeats obviously, it's a question of what's the bread, and what's the filling. Maybe my pieces are all refrains, but I like to think that in my music there's an ambiguity about what the bread is and what the filling is.*[6]

According to the composer's programme note, the compositional scheme for *Refrains and Choruses* for wind quintet is 'simple, having five sections, each section consisting of two elements: a constant one called "chorus", and a recurring one called "refrain". The refrain, through repetition, becomes a predominant entity, and so the chorus material of the following section. In the final section, the two roles become modified . . .'[7] In fact, the scheme is far from simple: neither the procession from one section to the next, nor the roles of refrain and chorus are as clearly defined as either the composer's comments or the work's title would seem to imply. Indeed, more recently Birtwistle has *dismissed* the existence of any carefully worked-out compositional scheme, the work's through-composed nature being a result of the fact that he 'wrote it completely off the top of my head. I can't justify a single note. I don't know why I was doing it or why it is like it is.'[8] He is obviously playing a game with us here. Birtwistle's works of the 1960s were often accompanied by quite detailed notes in keeping, perhaps, with a high modernist climate which expected composers to be able to justify their compositional choices and to articulate clearly their works' structures. ('Structure', Boulez famously proclaimed, was the key word of the post-war era.) Despite the profound impact that Boulez, Stockhausen and other leading figures of the avant-garde had on Birtwistle in the 1950s, he nonetheless kept at arm's length what he saw as the over-intellectualization of high modernism – typified for him by the ideas of Babbitt. Over the years we have seen Birtwistle invent for himself a distinctive public persona which makes full play of his northern roots and tries gruffly to understate the fact that he is engaged in an intellectual activity, that he could be seen as part of some sort of cultural élite. The image that follows him everywhere – in books, articles, programmes, and promoters' and publishers' publicity – is of the Romantic creative artist concerned with the noumenal rather than the phenomenal, concerned not with the superficial niceties of grooming but with his art. We are thus always confronted by a man with tousled hair, an unkempt beard, never smiling but with an unnerving, intense glare straight at the camera, as if to say, 'This is who I am. This is my music. Take it or leave it.' The change in the way he chooses to talk about *Refrains and Choruses* is entirely in keeping with the way he has chosen to project his own identity.

In whatever ways Birtwistle might wish to manoeuvre our listening towards some kind of direct, unmediated sonorous object, he cannot deny that his music has been self-consciously composed, not merely discovered serendipitously. Though there are clearly aspects of *Refrains and Choruses* which do seem to be relatively 'unpremeditated' – that is, where the composer seems to proceed from one moment to the next purely on the basis of the exigencies of the local context (see the discussion of the opening of the work in Chapter 1) – this should not distract us from the fact that there is an underlying structure. To listen to the foreground processes of *Refrains and Choruses* against the background of a model drawn from verse-refrain structures *can* tell us interesting things about the different functions of different kinds of music within the whole. The final section (from bar 132) is, in essence, a horizontal 'chorus' of material derived from a twelve-note row punctuated by a vertical five-note 'refrain' chord (A–B♭–C♯–D–E). Chorus and refrain have much in common: both have a fixed resource of pitch classes (as was mentioned in Chapter 1, both are concerned with cycling through a fixed sequence of pitch classes); both demonstrate a process of contraction through the section, the chorus moving towards a single clarinet voice, the refrain chord collapsing from its widest to its narrowest spacing. Yet the functional distinction between chorus and refrain is maintained throughout. Birtwistle's attitude to his verse model, like his attitude to his twelve-note 'row', is not prescriptive: it generates situations within and against which he can operate.

> *My attitude to time, if time is the right word, is concerned with repetition – about how repetition changes our perception of how things happen.*[9]

Residues of verse-refrain structures occur in more recent instrumental music (though less overt since the 1970s, they are still there). Take, for example, *Antiphonies* for piano and orchestra of 1992. The music is written as a continuous whole without any obvious large-scale repetitions and to this extent it is in keeping with most of his major works since the mid-1980s, all of which are through-composed: *Secret Theatre*, *Earth Dances*, *Exody*. Its principal climax comes about a third of the way into the piece. (Though the composer has been keen to challenge the classical norm of the climax arriving two-thirds of the way through a piece, this for me at least is one of the factors which contributes towards a sense of a less-than-satisfactory overall shape. I have to confess that I find it difficult to hear my way through *Antiphonies*, and I find it difficult to remember where I am in the piece at any given moment. I have similar difficulties with *Exody*, too.) *Antiphonies* and *Exody* share similar beginnings and endings. Birtwistle has spoken of *Antiphonies* beginning and ending as if a door were being opened and closed, as something almost arbitrary, a work encountered, as it were, *in media res* – a feature of so many of his processionals (as will be explored more fully in Chapter 7). But the initial sonorities of *Antiphonies* are like the opening of a door in another respect, too, in that Birtwistle has suggested that the entire work is a composing out of the (intervallic) possibilities inherent in these chords. They return at the end to signal the closing of the door. This is not a structural closure, only a 'temporary suspension of activity', an interpretation borne out by the fact that *Exody* begins precisely where *Antiphonies* left off – that is, with the extremes of low double bass Cs and high violin C harmonics – though then proceeding in entirely different directions before returning to where it began. (Other works have also proceeded in new directions from the same material, most notably *Still Movement,* exploring new avenues suggested in *Yan Tan Tethera.*) In *Exody*, too, the opening and closing events provide a frame for everything that happens in between, and here Birtwistle has again used the analogy of doors opening and closing. 'Exody',[10] in Birtwistle's usage, is derived from the Greek *exodia* (going out), meaning a departure or journey, and the piece is intended to be a celebration of leaving in general. This certainly suggests connections with *Gawain* where the opening and closing of doors is a central image, events that coincide with moments of structural musical importance, and further by the fact that both acts of *Gawain* could be considered to be concerned in essence with issues of departure and journeying. *Antiphonies*, Birtwistle's first major work following the completion of *Gawain*, locates itself in the same kind of sound world as the opera and might well be considered a response to some of its musical concerns, just as

The Cry of Anubis was a response to *The Second Mrs Kong*.

Though the overall shape of *Antiphonies* is through-composed, this does not preclude smaller-scale portions of the piece being constructed out of verse-refrain devices. The example discussed here occurs around the main climax of the work. At bar 151, after a passage where time seems almost ominously, expectantly to have been suspended, we hear four monumental, monolithic chords for full orchestra and solo piano, a kind of vastly expanded version of the chords which opened the work (returning to the same object from new perspectives, in itself a larger-scale verse-like organization). Each chord decays from loud to soft, and each entry is one dynamic softer than its predecessor (*ffff* → *fff* → *ff* → *f*). Each chord is followed by reiterated 'after shocks' on muted trombones. Just as generally in this work the tuned percussion act as a kind of sonic extension of the piano, at this particular moment it is as if the entire orchestra becomes an enormous piano. Then, beginning at bar 156, we are presented with a series of three soft piano verses, each interrupted by echoes of the monolithic chords as refrain. Here is an interesting role reversal where the orchestra takes on the characteristics of the piano (hard attack, fast decay) while the piano attempts to become a sustaining melody instrument, a role in which it is destined to be frustrated. These piano verses are immediately identifiable as such, bearing the familiar free, expressive, lyrical, cantus-like characteristics of so many of Birtwistle's verses. The third refrain (bars 173 ff.) is altered (bar form) by the introduction of a new cantus line in violins and high woodwind, and its ending is signalled both by the arrival of the orchestra on the pitch class E and by a four-element falling cadential gesture in the piano. This is a common situation in Birtwistle's music – similar cadences can be found, for example, at the ends of *Tragoedia*, *Melencolia I* and *Silbury Air*, and a clear pitch focus is a strong indicator of the presence of an important line. The Es mark the end of one section and the beginning of the next, as though the music were proceeding in waves (an interpretation in part prompted by the E-focus of the waves/tides in Act 3 of *The Mask of Orpheus*).

In the last of these three verses (Ex. 5.3) the piano has a two-

Ex. 5.3. *Antiphonies*, solo piano 'verse', bars 173–6.

voice melodic cantus. The upper voice (right hand) is a melody made up of a preponderance of Birtwistle's favourite three-note collections and ends (vertically) with his favourite four-note set (4–5). The lower voice (left hand) provides contrapuntal interest with an informal kind of organum, shadowing the upper voice mainly in tenths. This cantus is associated with a continuum in the cellos and basses which is more obviously concerned with rhythm and is built from a limited number of pitches: E–F–G♭–B♭ (also set 4–5) in cellos; D♭–D–E♭–G♭–G [+ E] (set 5–7, a superset of 4–5). Compare this with the discussion of 'background' and 'foreground' at the opening of *Secret Theatre* in Chapter 1. The only significant difference is that in the *Antiphonies* verse the cantus is built through repetition of interval set across the entire chromatic rather than, as in *Secret Theatre*, the repetition of specific pitch sets. What both examples have in common is the fact that the horizontal cantus and vertical continuum are held in a balanced opposition despite the fact that materials are shared between them. In *Antiphonies*, the role of such a local verse-refrain device is akin to the foreground presence of a building or regular patchwork of coloured squares in a Cézanne landscape; it punctuates the landscape without constituting its entirety.

> *One summer I was in the Italian town of Lucca, a medieval labyrinth of streets encircled by impressive walls. One of the churches even has a labyrinth carved on its façade, as if to reinforce the city's maze-like identity. My visit coincided with 'Festa', and a long procession of* tableaux vivants *snaked its way through the narrow streets. I became interested in the*

> *number of ways you could observe this event: as a bystander, watching each float pass by, each strikingly individual yet part of a whole; or you could wander through side alleys, hearing the parade a street away, glimpsing at a corner, meeting head on what a moment before you saw from behind. Each time the viewpoint was different, yet instantly identified as part of one body.*[11]

The 'antiphonies' in the title of the last work discussed refer – in part at least – to the alternating relationship between piano and orchestra. In a much earlier work whose structural premises are also emblazoned in its very title, the alternation of roles of cantus and continuum (long before the composer had adopted this pair of terms) is much more bold. In the first verse of *Verses* for clarinet and piano of 1965 there is just the same kind of role reversal as in *Antiphonies*, where the clarinet plays five times a note of fixed pitch (G), duration (dotted crotchet plus a semiquaver rest) and dynamic level (*pp*), while the piano utters a widely dispersed monody in a manner not dissimilar to the piano writing in *Antiphonies*. The piano attempts a song, while the clarinet is prevented from so doing. By the final verse, as Hall puts it, 'the relationship between clarinet and piano meets the demands of the recital situation without either of them sacrificing the characteristics assigned them.'[12] The change comes in verse 5 where the clarinet takes over the cantus material originally given to the piano (but here restricted to only six pitch classes) and the piano has the regular pulsations of the continuum.

The mutable status of piano and clarinet, of soloist and accompanist, is fully discussed by Hall. This relationship suggests interesting connections with Webern – see, for example, the continually changing relationship between violin and piano in the Op. 7 pieces.[13] Hall thinks of the work in dramatic terms, imposing on the overall shape of *Verses* an abstract organization derived from Greek tragedy in the manner of the work's immediate predecessor, *Tragoedia*. His argument springs from a reading of the etymology of the word *verses* as 'turning', and of *versus* as 'a furrow, a turning of the plough'. This he relates to the categories of *peripeteia* and *anagnorisis*, which he maps on to the instrumental role-play of the work:

> . . . the drama consists of how one character will affect the other, how their relative statuses will alter and how these will eventually lead to the canon of the sixth verse, where the two are on more or less equal terms. That will be a moment of recognition . . . Birtwistle's reversal comes in verse five. Until then the material had been growing more and more profusely. Suddenly the proliferations are cast away and only the bare bones remain.[14]

What Hall's analysis reveals is how all eight verses are, in essence, varied versions of each other, how Birtwistle works through the same material in different ways (once more, perhaps, an indication of the serial legacy). Here in microcosm is a clear illustration of the central issue of this chapter: Birtwistle's preoccupation with examining the same object from multiple perspectives, suggesting why verse forms are so important to him. But on to this sequence of verses is also superimposed the rhetoric of a verse-refrain structure through the alternation of piano and clarinet choruses/refrains (nos. 1, 3, 5, 6 and 8) and solo clarinet verses (nos. 2, 4 and 7) as is to be found in such models as responsorial psalmody (where the verse is sung by a solo cantor, and the response by the choir) and the verse anthem. Such a reading further reinforces the association of verse with the solo, lyrical, linear cantus.

> *It's like looking at an object: every view is unique but the object exists irrespective of the way it's viewed.*[15]

The title of *The World is Discovered* for double wind quintet, guitar and harp is derived from Isaak's canzona 'Der welte fundt' (*sic*), a detail of which makes a veiled appearance in the final section of the work. Like the formal directness of the canzona forms on which it is modelled, *The World is Discovered* – subtitled 'six instrumental movements after Heinrich Isaak' – has a bold overall shape of three verses alternating with three choruses. On the whole, it is the rhetorical differences between verse and refrain which are employed here, rather than anything more deeply structural. Each verse, like those at the centre of *Verses for Ensembles*, is characterized by a different solo wind voice (in turn, flute, oboe and clarinet) working with the guitar as continuo. The choruses employ the entire ensemble in more obviously homophonic writing. In practice, the guitar is more of an equal partner with the verse soloist, while both verse and chorus seem to proceed according to an increasingly elaborate kind of rhythmic unison; nonetheless, the functional distinctions between the two types still hold true. There are subtle links between each verse-chorus pair. Otherwise, these movements are more like a series of independent miniatures which process their different materials (albeit from a common late-fifteenth-century source) in similar ways than the more fully integrated verse forms of later works. This visual analogy is once again appropriate. Hall relates the story – no doubt transmitted directly from the composer – of how at the time of composition Birtwistle happened to encounter a series of Picasso pictures which explore details of Velasquez's *Las meninas*.[16] Birtwistle's attitude to his own found material is not only similarly Picassoesque but also plainly Stravinskian. A further clue to the work's compositional procedures might be suggested by its dedicatee, Peter Maxwell Davies, whose fascination with the parody and paraphrase techniques of medieval and renaissance music are echoed in *The World is Discovered*.

On another level, the pitch structures as well as the gestural language of these movements betray aspects of the dodecaphonic legacy. They also have something of the feel of late Stravinsky about them (faint shadows cast by *Threni*, perhaps?). Take verse 2 as an example which demonstrates Birtwistle's unique, non-serial approach to the deployment of the total chromatic. The pitches are exposed according to an informal wedge pattern of pitch classes (Fig. 5.1) without ever disallowing the possibility of repetitions and pitch focuses (see Ex. 5.4). This is typical of Birtwistle's (subversive) attitude in the late 1950s and early 1960s to twelve-note techniques. What is of interest here is how, from his earliest work, the 'developmental' possibilities of serial music are incorporated into 'non-development' verse-refrain forms. Just as Birtwistle was fascinated by the way in which in *Agon* Stravinsky transformed aspects both of serialism and of seventeenth-century French dance into something beautifully formalized, so in this work aspects of Isaak intertwine with aspects of dodecaphony to produce a series of rarefied, formalized portraits.

FIG. 5.1. 'Wedge pattern', *The World is Discovered*, verse 2 (bars 1–7)

```
D        E♭       E      F – F♯ – G – A♭
 \      / \      / \   /
  C – C♯    B – B♭    A
```

By repetition, you can assimilate the total object. [17]

The Mask of Orpheus, being essentially about time and memory, is predicated on the basis of repetition. Verse structures abound. The dominant example is the symbolic structure of the arches in Act 2 which embodies both the repetition of verses (the seventeen arches themselves) and the linear descent to and return from the underworld. Each arch corresponds to the seventeen verses of Orpheus's second 'Song of Magic' which he sings in order to overcome the various characters who oppose his (imaginary) journey, and each is of carefully calculated proportions which change subtly in relation to each other on each occasion (recognizable strophic repetitions which are nonetheless always slightly different). More specifically, each arch is formed of a series of dreams,

Ex. 5.4. *The World Is Discovered*, verse 2, bars 1–7.

nightmares and awakenings in which, as Zinovieff explains:

> . . . exact timings of these properties give rise to changes in the music and words. The duration of each arch is 3 seconds less than the previous one. The 1st arch lasts 2 minutes and 36 seconds. The 17th arch lasts 1 minute and 48 seconds. The proportion of nightmare to dream increases from the 1st to the 15th arches.

Musically each verse begins by building on the previous one, a perception reinforced by the electronic refrain (Apollo's signal) which articulates the beginning and ending of each verse (each signal is also varied slightly each time). But, as the composer has pointed out, there is 'a substructure which is not analogous with the text'.[18] The textual verses provide the 'superstructure', a basic framework across which the music moves. The orchestral 'substructure' gives the appearance of being through-composed; it certainly seems to direct itself across the strophic subdivisions by such means as an increasing rate of (rhythmic) activity, and by the progressively denser layering of ideas – variants of ideas already heard in previous verses and the superimposition and interjection of other recurrent materials (with such labels as 'Immortal Trio', 'Scream of Passion', 'Chorus of Awakening' and so on). The arrival at the climax at the end of the fifteenth arch is an appropriately shattering event and powerfully coincides with the end of the second scene, i.e. with the end of Orpheus's return, with his awakening, and with his realization that his journey had all been a dream (*peripeteia* and *anagnorisis*). By contrast, the third 'Song of Magic', which dominates the second half of Act 3, is much more obviously strophic on a musical level. The repetition of Orpheus's verses in his invented Orphic language are triggered by various 'responses', short orchestral refrains which represent symbolic objects lying on the beach and which are uncovered by the movement of the tides: 'Rockfall', 'Footprint', 'Fossil Shell', 'Oar', 'Bird Skull' and 'Fishing Net'. By the end of the work, attenuated exact repetitions of these refrains over the increasingly prominent electronic 'Aura' provide the sole orchestral material. It is almost as if, as was suggested by the composer's account of *Refrains and Choruses*, the refrains have taken on a new identity as verses (arguably, 'chorus'). Their very stability, their inability to do anything other than repeat, again makes it obvious why the verse structure is so well suited to the dramatic stasis being represented here, to an expression of a situation almost beyond time itself.

'[T]he new departures I've made in *Yan Tan Tethera* haven't arisen out of the blue, the seeds were planted some time back. They appear in the substructure of *The Mask of Orpheus*'.[19] At one level, *Yan Tan Tethera* of all Birtwistle's works is the one most heavily dependent on obvious patterns of repetition, symbolized by the continual ritual counting throughout the work – 'a simple tale about numbers', as Birtwistle puts it.[20] As in *Orpheus* (and, in general, unlike *Punch*) the many repetitions and strophic structures of the text do not necessarily receive corresponding musical treatment. A balance is struck between the repetitive and the progressive, between the circular and the linear: 'the repeats are not like ritornellos, they're not the same thing seen from a new perspective, they take context into account . . . The context of the moment is unique and must exert an influence, a strong influence.'[21] This represents a self-conscious change in attitude to repetition which he has continued to explore in a variety of ways in much of his subsequent music (see, for example, the discussion of *Gawain*'s 'fundamental line' in Chapter 7 below). It is an attitude which Hall, prompted by Birtwistle's own words, has called the necessity of recognizing the 'sanctity of the context'.[22] While still embroiled in the composition of *Yan Tan Tethera*, Birtwistle discussed this attitude. He gave as an example the section in which Hannah grieves for her twins, who have been taken by the Bad'Un, and which is given a strophic text to represent the rapidly accelerated passing of the years:

> . . . on one level the music repeats, but on another there's a long . . . organic, fugue-like texture in the orchestra which goes right through the section then blossoms into a chorale when the counting reaches the magic number seven. So I

> have a strophic superstructure as foreground and an organic substructure as background which are independent, or largely independent, of each other.[23]

Each of Hannah's verses interprets/extends the same set of ideas in different ways on each occasion, and the seven verses do not necessarily follow one another in an absolutely predictable succession (for example, an incantation of the 'Yan Tan Tethera' charm is inserted after the first and third verses). The chorus of Cheviot Sheep have a counting refrain that punctuates the end of each verse and whose music *does* repeat exactly, save for the progressive addition of an extra number each time. Underneath this, in keeping with Birtwistle's account, we find the corresponding 'verses' of the orchestral material have a structure built from certain elements that remain fixed, certain elements that are varied, and others that are entirely new (it bears interesting comparison with the processes identified in the Chapter 1 discussion of the 'Morals' from *Punch and Judy*), thus embodying the idea of simultaneous repetition and innovation, of 'stasis in progress'.

Verse structures also prevail in *Gawain*, and always for appropriate dramatic reasons. Each act is dominated by a large-scale repeating cycle: the Masque of the Seasons in Act 1 and the Hunt/Seduction sequence in Act 2. In both cases, the adoption of a (relatively static) verse structure at key moments in the drama reinforces their ceremonial/ritual dimensions. But each act interprets the idea of verse form differently. In Act 1, with the exception of the two 'Winter' verses which involve near-exact repetition, each verse is a distinct variation showing the same musical object from ever-changing perspectives just as changing seasonal light can transform the view of a (fixed) landscape. The 'turning' verses here are a musical metaphor for the turning world, though the sense of linear progression through the varied repetitions is also important in the context of Gawain's journey. The Act 2 sequence – three verses in total – involves a far higher degree of near-exact repetition as it is necessary for us to witness Gawain's ritual trial. The beginnings (Morgan le Fay's lullaby) and endings (the killing of the hunted animal and Gawain's trance) act as framing refrains, repeated virtually note for note, while the 'verses' in between are more freely varied (the second is compressed) but still follow each other closely. Elsewhere in *Gawain*, there are smaller-scale echoes of these verse-refrain structures. For example, the 'verses' of the opening duet between Lady de Hautdesert and Morgan le Fay are punctuated by a simple one-bar ritornello (it occurs five times, beginning just before fig. 7: 'The day darkens . . .'), giving a structure to the dialogue, even though the 'verses' themselves are through-composed across the divisions. At the other end of the opera 'the Court regains its original position and remains motionless' while, appropriately, Morgan sings two prophetic verses ('Look out of your window . . .'; 'Look in your mirror . . .'), punctuated by a varied instrumental refrain, before breaking free from the repetitions to launch herself through the door into the outside world and bring the opera to a close. In between, all manner of repetitions can be witnessed. One of the most significant for the unfolding of the drama are the threefold door knocks in Act 1, marked by exact and extensive musical repetitions; they do not create a verse structure as such (the third knock is too far separated from the first two for this to be the case) but such larger-scale recurrences clearly relate to the structural role played by verse forms; that is, they signal the viewing of one event from new perspectives. The point is that within the context of Birtwistle's ritual musical and dramatic concerns, verse structures and other related kinds of repetition play a central role. In *Gawain*, they are vital to the way in which the story is told and retold.

It was perhaps a reasonable expectation that similar verse-refrain techniques were going to be found in *The Second Mrs Kong*. In fact, as mentioned briefly in Chapter 3, we only overtly get one such verse structure in the first scene of Act 1 where the dead replay fragments of their remembered lives: Dollorama catches Inanna and Zumzum *in flagrante*, shoots the two of them, and is then himself shot by Inanna; Vermeer recalls Pearl's face, 'a face like music, partly now and partly remembered'; Orpheus and Eurydice mourn their mutual loss. Originally Paganini was also present here as an on-stage violinist; for various (non-musical) reasons his part was excised in advance of the first Glyndebourne performances, though the sound of his violin is still to be heard in the orchestra. There are four repetitions, four verses; on each occasion the music and text become more and more compressed, the drama moves ever more quickly, so that by the fourth verse it has degenerated into a kind of nonsensical pantomime. It is a very funny passage, not least because it seems to come across as a 'knowing' parody of Birtwistle's customary practices. The obvious formalism of overt repeating structures no longer has the same kind of power it once had for him, Birtwistle seems to be saying, even in a large-scale stage work. He has moved on from bold, ceremonial ritual (the almost static, highly predictable cycles of *Punch and Judy*) to a new, more continuous narrative which needs to demonstrate a greater awareness of the 'sanctity of the context'. This is not to say that verse structures have exhausted their usefulness; it is just that, as has been increasingly evident in the post-*Orpheus* works, they are now more fully integrated into much more fluid musical and musico-dramatic continuities.

> *There's one element that repeats, but when it repeats, it's never the same – it's always got an element missing. And then there's another one which is always the same, but it's never quite in the place you think it is . . . So there's this wild repetition going on, which is never what you think it is.*[24]

Birtwistle has long been fascinated by the 'frozen moment'. In *Punch and Judy*, Punch's 'Travel Music' at the beginning of each cycle of quests for Pretty Polly reveal him on his hobby-horse at specific times and seasons suspended between earth and heaven, between heaven and hell, and so on. In *The Mask of Orpheus*, the principal stage action, music and words, are interrupted and frozen for the mimed Passing Clouds of Abandon and Allegorical Flowers of Reason. In *Gawain*, time appears to be frozen at a number of key points, such as after Gawain raises the axe for the first time in Act 1, or for Gawain's trances in Act 2. *Exody* is located in 'the moment before time stops temporarily when 24:00

becomes 0:00'. The instruction to players to hold, to freeze their playing positions at important points, is frequently encountered. And everywhere, the notion of 'aria' for Birtwistle involves the suspension of the drama, 'the poetic flowering of the moment'.

More recently Birtwistle has coined the idea of the instrumental 'frieze', pre-eminently in *Slow Frieze* for piano and ensemble and in four of the quartet movements of *Pulse Shadows*. He enjoys the pun. But he also asserts that in a frieze on a wall, 'frozen' details are repeated to produce a new overall (and essentially endless) design. A kind of stasis is at the heart of both the 'frozen moment' and the 'frieze', a stasis habitually realized in Birtwistle through repetition. In *Slow Frieze* Birtwistle's 'images' are assembled like a collage of cinematic freeze frames resulting in a slow processional. What fascinates him in this work, as with verse structures generally, is that the local details of the repeating pattern may vary in all kinds of unpredictable ways yet the structure's large-scale logic is never placed in doubt. The Friezes in *Pulse Shadows* are of a different mood, being frenetic and wildly energetic, but they share the montage character of *Slow Frieze*. These Friezes are, in general, formed of a succession (a procession, even) of overlaid repeating objects whose identities are primarily rhythmic (varied ostinatos). The repetitions are always recognizably the same yet there is always something unpredictable about them (the opening of 'Frieze 1' is given in Ex. 5.5). Each Frieze is highly structured, a fact borne out by the extraordinary fourth Frieze, the 'Todesfuge', a textless realization of Paul Celan's poem which itself had developed anguished themes in a quasi-fugal manner. A fugue is a long way from the simple strophic structure of a song. But what this work reveals is just how far Birtwistle's lifelong preoccupation with certain basic formal and structural archetypes have been transformed in his recent music and absorbed into highly flexible compositional strategies. The Friezes in *Pulse Shadows* are no longer identifiable as verse-refrain structures *per se*, but they nonetheless continue to pursue from new perspectives the aesthetic principle embodied in such structures.

Ex. 5.5. *Pulse Shadows*, 'Frieze 1' (opening).

> . . . *forms of repetition, blocks of sound that are repeated from different angles but are never the same.*[25]

Repetition. Variation. Ritual. Birtwistle's obsessions are also basic to verse-refrain structures. It should hardly surprise us, therefore, that verse structures in one guise or another are ubiquitous in his music. Given Birtwistle's fascination with the formal situations presented by opera, it is natural that the structure of the strophic song should play such a significant role in his stage works. It signals key moments in the drama; through repetition, its essential stasis helps define the ritualized nature of his dramas. But the verse structure finds its way into his instrumental works too, where it plays similar roles and helps contribute to their 'secret theatres'. It is embodied in the very title of his very first published work and echoes through his most recent. Seen in this light, the idea of verses and refrains can be understood to be important not only in individual works, but also as a way of understanding Birtwistle's entire output. In each new work, though the idea, the ritualized function of the verse structure is retained, it is reinterpreted, it is realized in ever new ways, from ever new perspectives.

> *. . . I'm doing what I always do. An analogy would be wandering through a town with squares, various squares, some more important than others, a town with roads on which you go round and round, in through one square out through another. You then come back again and approach from another angle, and so on. In other words, various parts of the piece get repeated.*[26]

6 *Episodion IV* – A Pulse Sampler

Many of Birtwistle's works give the impression that they are born *ex nihilo*. Like a sculptor who begins with nothing but a block of stone, time and again Birtwistle begins his pieces with just the fundamentals of sound: a single pitch and a basic pulse. Unlike a sculptor, however, whose creative process – bar the occasional chisel mark – remains hidden and whose sculpture can only (usually) be viewed as a static end product, a composer can invite the listener almost to experience temporally the creative unfolding of a work. In Birtwistle's case, we are often given the sense that as listeners we are actually party to the act of creation, that we are observing how from the simplest materials a huge edifice is being built. The fact that Birtwistle always composes chronologically – that is, he begins at the beginning of a piece and works his way, bar by bar, through to the end – would seem to reinforce such an understanding.

This is symbolically represented at the start of *The Mask of Orpheus,* where we are presented with a kind of creation myth. The sun rises. We hear distant indeterminate sounds – the Aura of Summer, the noises of primal nature unspoiled by human intervention, the sounds heard by the prenatal child through the wall of the mother's womb. Out of this, voices emerge, uttering incoherent sounds and words, half-remembered events, half-formed sentences. Gradually, Orpheus discovers music and is able to sing his own name: he has found his identity; he has become conscious of himself, and the world around him begins to make sense.

It becomes clear why the subject matter of *Orpheus* was so appealing to Birtwistle – as it has been for opera composers over four centuries – despite his claims that the subject matter was in itself irrelevant. *The Mask of Orpheus* is fundamentally about time and music.

A new interest in the early 1970s in time and temporality manifested itself in two key works, *Chronometer* and *The Triumph of Time*, which provided the impetus Birtwistle needed to begin work on the composition of *The Mask of Orpheus*. Both these works are concerned with timeless time. Time passes and yet time appears to stand still. In *The Triumph of Time*, the seasons change endlessly. In *Chronometer*, the sound of ticking clocks articulates the passage of time and yet the end result is something dreamlike, almost static, seeming to exist out of time. In many ways, *Chronometer* illustrates perfectly the distinction explored by Stravinsky (and derived principally from Henri Bergson) between two kinds of music, 'one which evolves parallel to the process of ontological [clock] time', the other which 'runs ahead of, or counter to, this process', that is, 'psychological time'.[1] In *Chronometer*, ontological time *becomes* psychological time. These ideas were taken up in the later 1970s specifically in *Melencolia I* (after Dürer's engraving of the same name) which explores Günter Grass's notion of a 'stasis in progress'. Pulse became Birtwistle's principal preoccupation of the late 1970s and early 1980s, not least in the vast amount of music produced for the *Oresteia* production. And clocks have continued to echo through more recent works ('I'm very interested in pulse'), from his description of *Yan Tan Tethera* as 'like a big clock mechanism',[2] to the quasi-mechanical tickings of *Harrison's Clocks*, and in the frozen moment of *Exody*, with its subtitle '23:59:59', 'the second before midnight, the moment before time stops temporarily when 24:00 becomes 0:00, which carries increased significance and expectation on New Year's Eve at the turn of a century or millennium.'[3]

As its title might suggest, *Pulse Sampler* can usefully stand as an exemplar of Birtwistle's thinking about pulse. Written in the summer of 1981, it exists in relation to Act 3 of *The Mask of Orpheus*, the composition of which he returned to in the autumn of that year, in the same way that *Chronometer* and *The Triumph of Time* stand in relation to Acts 1 and 2. Scored for one oboe and a single pair of claves, the piece is pared down to the musical fundamentals of pulse and melody. *Chronometer* had already demonstrated that Birtwistle's idea of pulse is more complex than just a single stream of regular, unchanging aural stimuli. *Pulse Sampler* returns to the problem with which Birtwistle had had to grapple in the five hours of the *Oresteia*: namely, how to prevent a regular pulse, presented on one percussion instrument of fixed indeterminate pitch and timbre, from becoming predictable and hypnotic. In *Pulse Sampler*, the pulse is in a constant state of flux. This statement is not as contradictory as it might at first appear (a pulse is something which, by definition, remains constant). The pulse does, in fact, remain constant within each of the work's twenty-eight sections, but it changes between them, its acceleration or deceleration being determined according to a specific and audible proportional scheme. Furthermore, a 'home' pulse, a fixed point of temporal reference, is established at the start, to which (in all but a few cases) every new pulse returns. There are, in essence, only six different tempi in the piece, and each tempo is in a simple ratio with the home pulse (minim = 45/crotchet = 90). This can be represented according to the scheme in Fig. 6.1, what we might call (after *Silbury Air*) a 'pulse labyrinth'. Precedents for such operations can be found in Stravinsky's *Symphonies of Wind Instruments*, whose block structure has been strongly influential on Birtwistle. There, each block is identified with a specific tempo and the relationship between the work's three tempi are according to the simple ratio of 2:3:4. Such proportional tempi both articulate the discontinuity between

FIG. 6.1. 'Pulse labyrinth' for *Pulse Sampler*

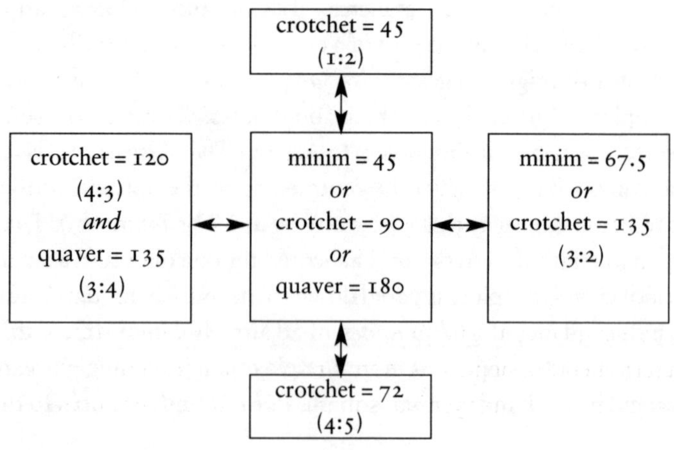

blocks and simultaneously express a relationship between them. This certainly seems to be the case in *Pulse Sampler*.

The post-World War II composer who has exploited such thinking most fully is Elliott Carter, for whom the notion of proportional tempi, or what he has coined 'metric modulation', is used 'both as a mode of proceeding smoothly or abruptly from one speed to another and as a formal device to isolate one section from another'.[4] The closest Birtwistle has come to such a procedure is in *Silbury Air* (discussed below), whose pulse labyrinth controls changes of both metre and tempo and ensures smooth metric modulation throughout. The opposite situation can be witnessed in *Silbury Air*'s companion piece from 1977, *Carmen Arcadiae Mechanicae Perpetuum*, in formal terms his work most overtly indebted to the *Symphonies of Wind Instruments*. Here, the successive opposition of pulses ('six musical mechanisms which are juxtaposed many times without any form of transition')[5] is reinforced by the (insignificant) ratio between the work's two main tempi (crotchet = 92:quaver = 168, i.e. 23:21) which denies immediately perceivable connections between blocks.

Pulse Sampler begins with the most basic of sonic materials: a single sustained E for the oboe (marked 'like a sine tone', the simplest and purest sonic entity) and a 'pulse mobile' for the claves which is in essence an evenly spaced pair of notes. The latter are elaborated into a 'model' of four rhythmic cells labelled A–D of one or two equal-length elements, and a 'variant' where each of the original cells is troped by the subdivision of one of its units into two of unequal duration (see Ex. 6.1). But in fact even cells B–D of the model can be understood as variants of A by means of displacement or subtraction – the same simple object is viewed from a number of slightly different perspectives. The claves player is free to choose which cells to play and how many times to play them, with the proviso that the ordering is preserved and that, because the claves always set the oboist's pulse, cell A commences each new section. The progress of the piece is to a large extent determined by the route taken through the pulse labyrinth. And just as the claves player has only a limited degree of flexibility to

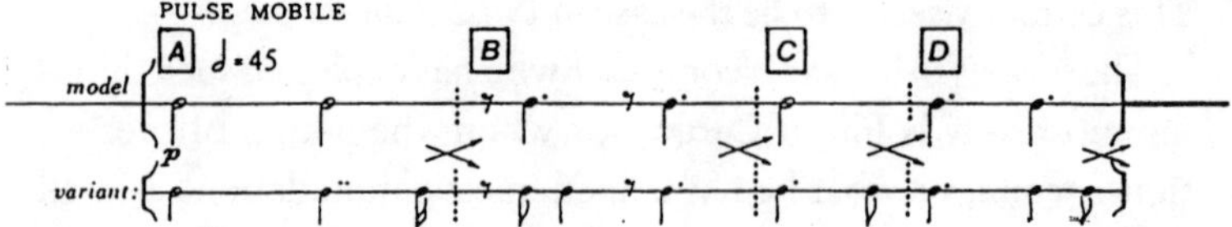

Ex. 6.1. *Pulse Sampler.*

move around the mobile within each section's given tempo, so the oboe presents a musical object in each section whose melodic materials are carefully limited; a sustained note signals that the oboe has, for the moment, exhausted its exploration of that material and prompts the claves to move on through the labyrinth, in turn signalling a change in the oboe's melodic material. Each section is like a little mechanism – a simplified form of those found in *Carmen Arcadiae* – a reading supported by the predominantly brittle (non-legato) sounds made by the oboe, matching those of the claves. Throughout, oboe and claves are both independent and interdependent. Their coming together at the climax in section 25 where for the only time the claves' rhythms are fully notated and are coordinated with those of the oboe (each playing in the others' rests to produce a composite stream of semiquavers) results in a return to the opening material. The pulse mobile is reinstated at its original tempo, the oboe again sustains an E (though now an octave higher than at the start), and thus a way out of the labyrinth is discovered: the entrance, it transpires, is also the exit. The end is signalled almost arbitrarily by a single, theatrical wood-block stroke. Though Birtwistle does not himself talk about *Pulse Sampler* in terms of a labyrinth, it is interesting that when he does use the word to attempt to explain the structure of *Exody*, it too is in the context of a music with 'only one way in and out' via the widely spaced Cs which begin and end the work.

But *Pulse Sampler* is not a machine. Despite the precision of the tempo relationships, despite the careful delimiting of musical materials, despite the relative simplicity of the musical form, Birtwistle is able to create something that is irregular and fascinating in its unpredictability. Its signal achievement is that from an element as basic as a pulse played on one pair of claves it produces a music which, as the composer intended, is in a permanent state of flux, a music that despite the fixed nature of its constituent sections seems to have an almost organic life of its own. And in performance there is also a clear sense of the ceremonial about this formalized relationship between oboe and claves. The role play of oboist and percussionist suggests we are witnesses to some kind of non-Western ritual. Certainly, its rarefied sound-world and the stylized movements of the clave player (silent beats; a 'long high slow-motion upbeat' to the final wood block stroke) bring to mind such ceremonial music as that of the Japanese Gagaku, the oboe taking on the character of the double-reeded *hichiriki*, though Hall has also suggested parallels with Indian music (a musical tradition of which Birtwistle confesses to know nothing). Closer to Birtwistle's own experience, the music of Messiaen may well have offered useful models, such as the Japanese-inspired *Sept haïkaï* (1962) which includes a transcription of a Gagaku piece and in which precisely calculated rhythmic schemes result in a highly irregular-sounding music.

An earlier work which is explicitly indebted to Japanese theatre is *Bow Down*. Written to be performed at the National Theatre, it anticipates techniques he was to adopt in the later music for the *Oresteia* – and in so doing brings to our attention the essential similarities between Greek tragedy and Noh drama (stylized presentation, central role of music, use of masks, all-male cast, etc.). Like a Noh drama whose four musicians (a bamboo-flute player and three drummers) and chorus are all in ceremonial dress and sit on the stage – their stylized entry, exit and hand movements being an integral part of the drama – so the four musicians of *Bow Down* are similarly seated within the acting space and form part of the chorus along with the five actors who, in their turn, sing, dance and play instruments. (The parallels with Brecht's ideals are also of interest here, as discussed in Chapter 2.) The music is pared down to the basics of pulse and interval. As in *Pulse Sampler*, the sparse sound-world of pulsed drumbeats and mournful oboe melodies suggests an ancient, hieratic ceremony.

A piece written just before *Bow Down*, but clearly also a product of Birtwistle's focus on musical fundamentals prompted by his work in the National Theatre, is *For O, for O, the Hobby-Horse is Forgot*. That a concern for pulse and ritual go hand-in-hand in Birtwistle's imagination is confirmed here by the work's subtitle: a ceremony for six percussionists. Indeed, this work is about little else other than pulse and limited ritual actions. Birtwistle had been working on a production of *Hamlet* at the National, and this work takes its title and starting-point from Hamlet's cry of 'For, O! for, O! the hobby-horse is forgot' which precedes the dumb-show, the play-within-the-play, in Act 3 scene 2. 'Enter a King and a Queen, very lovingly'. And so also begins Birtwistle's 'dumb-show': two of the percussionists play the roles of 'king' and 'queen' and they enter first, followed by the other four players, designated 'chorus'. Stylized stick positions and movements are specified by a diagram at the front of the score. The king and queen are the protagonists, with their own solo and episodic material, and it is they who cue the chorus, musically and gesturally. The chorus usually sets the pulse frame. For approximately the first half of the piece, these pulses are in crude multiples of 20, from crotchet = 40 up to crotchet = 200, allowing for audible relationships (metric modulations) to be established between boldly juxtaposed (and occasionally superimposed) blocks. In the second half, the situation is generally more complex: a greater fluctuation of pulse is achieved through the introduction of a range of new tempi as well as accelerandi and rallentandi, before the chorus restores order towards the end of the work with absolutely regular quaver pulsation. By the end, pulse and ceremony are united in that we perceive the continuing pulse only through the silent striking motion of the chorus. As in *Pulse Sampler*, a sophisticated structure is built from what are really very simple rhythmic components. Take, for example, the passage beginning at fig. 48 for unison chorus which we might describe as being constructed from another 'pulse mobile': five rhythmic cells, all closely related, each accenting the beat, are strung together in an apparently random order resulting

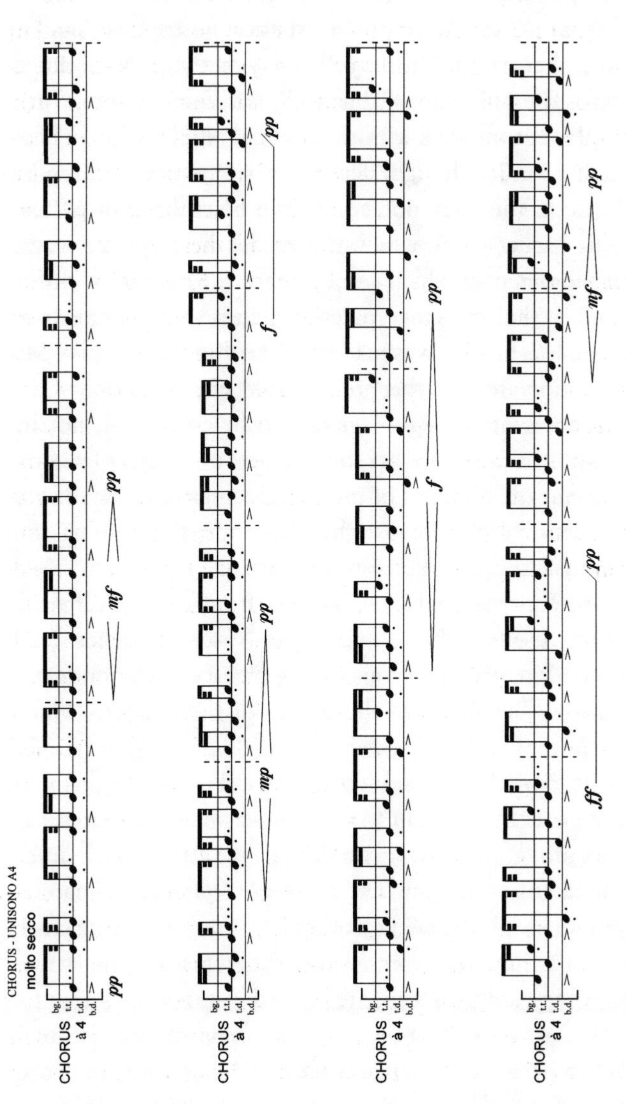

Ex. 6.2. *For O, for O, the Hobby-Horse Is Forgot*, fig. 48.

in an energetic music which combines an absolutely regular pulse with rhythmic patterns which are unpredictable, never quite the same twice (Ex. 6.2).

One passage early in *For O, for O* gives a glimpse of its origins in an earlier work. Ex. 6.3 shows a situation where it is possible for three members of the chorus to be playing the same repeated quaver material simultaneously but at three different tempi, while the fourth player continues with the original regular crotchet figure at crotchet = *c.*40 (though, depending on the signals given by king and queen, this may not necessarily be realized in performance). The earlier work which this recalls is Birtwistle's tape piece, *Chronometer*, in which can be heard the ticking of clocks manipulated so that the same material sounds simultaneously at different speeds. The tape was made by Peter Zinovieff at his EMS studio in London and – in this pre-IRCAM era – was one of the earliest examples of *musique concrète* to be composed, not by splicing lengths of tape together, but, rather, by means of a computer to analyse the hundred or more recordings of clock sounds and to regenerate them on to eight-track tape, the graphic and numerical music score being reinterpreted using a program called MUSYS. As Zinovieff tells us, sounds from widely differing sources were used: 'for instance, the Natural Science [*sic*] Museum, London, provided some of the oldest clock sounds still available, while Big Ben was the source of the ostinato which dominates the piece'.[6] It is with this sound of Big Ben, slowed right down to little more than a distant throb, that the work begins, and it remains a virtually constant (often almost subliminal) presence as the piece unfolds above it, very much like the atmospheric auras which were later to underpin *The Mask of Orpheus*. All manner of ticks and tocks, punctuated by other occasional whirring clock mechanisms ('a number of very dense, short, fast-moving structures with complex dynamics'), are layered in a rich contrapuntal texture. There are also 'three 2-minute interludes of very fast complex sounds where every change is preceded by a short pure signal',[7] for which all other activity is suspended, frozen, just as is the case with the Passing Clouds and Allegorical Flowers of *Orpheus*.

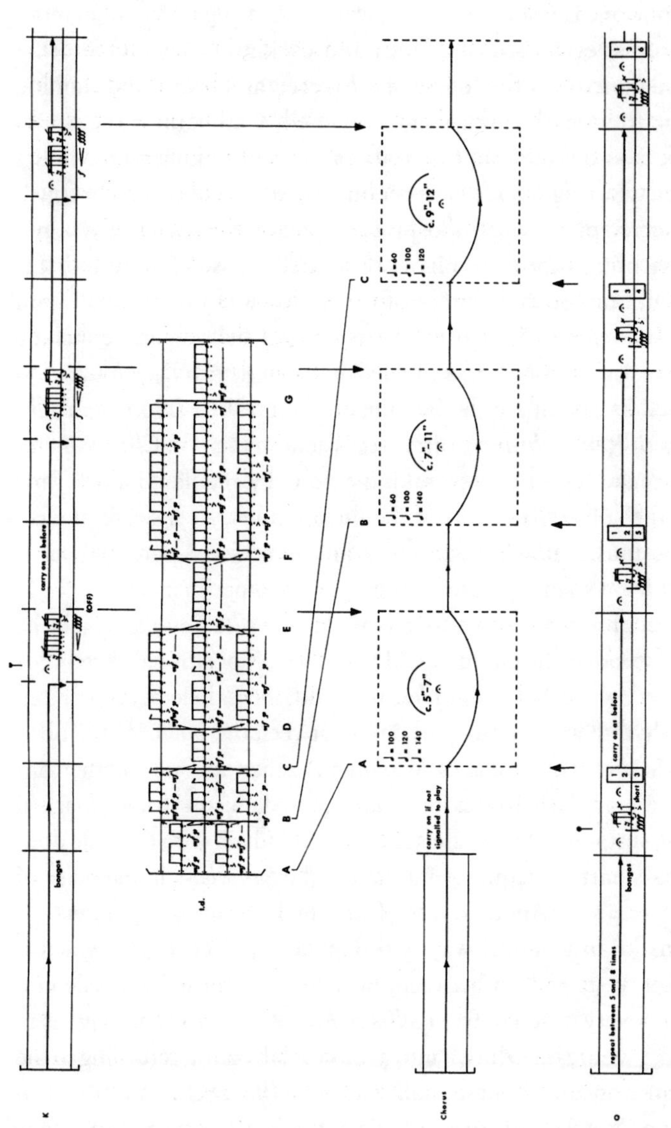

Ex. 6.3. *For O, for O, the Hobby-Horse Is Forgot.*

The overall result is an extraordinarily surreal soundscape in which the 'natural' sounds are so transformed that one begins to imagine one is hearing gurgling water, a beating heart, all manner of drums, even croaking frogs and cackling crows. One other sound punctuates the course of the piece: the striking and chiming of the fourteenth-century clock at Wells Cathedral. (The actual clock is also wonderfully 'theatrical' in its marking of the hours with a whirring wooden jouster on a horse – a lovely secular touch in a sacred place which, like other comical medieval gargoyles and misericords, appeals to Birtwistle's earthy sense of humour.) It is the full, unmodified chimes of the Wells clock which finally call *Chronometer* to its close, like the ritual bells which conclude Stravinsky's *Les Noces*, and recall his own *Ring a Dumb Carillon* as well as anticipate the bell imagery central to *La Plage: Eight Arias of Remembrance*. Birtwistle's achievement in *Chronometer* is to make time timeless, taking externally regulated clock time into the subjective realm of the unconscious. As a work of electronic music, its clear structure and expressive potential set it apart from so many lesser contemporary experiments.

Though written some four years later, *Pulse Sampler* might be understood as the paradigm, almost the compositional sketch, for *Silbury Air*. In *Pulse Sampler*, the fundamental elements of pitch and rhythm are teased apart, split between the *melos* of the oboe and the *tactus* of the claves; in *Silbury Air* they operate together. *Silbury Air* similarly begins *ex nihilo* – muted unison strings, marked *pppp*, sustaining Birtwistle's favourite middle E with only the double bass harmonic quietly intimating the *Sampler*'s home pulse of crotchet = 90. (Another work from the late 1970s, . . . *agm* . . ., begins in an identical way with regularly pulsed Es, to which it returns at its end. In between, however, the music proceeds in a manner very different from *Silbury Air*.) As in *Pulse Sampler*, as in *Exody*, we are here drawn into a musical labyrinth, returning to the entrance once at about the half-way point (fig. 28, but now the 4/16 bar is at crotchet = 120) and again at the very end where we realize the entrance is also the exit (fig. 39, where the 4/16 bar is at crotchet = 80). Instead of turning back into the maze, an arbitrary halt is called by four chords on the harp, precisely paralleling the woodblock stroke which signals the end of *Pulse Sampler*. A generally familiar punctuating object in Birtwistle's musical landscapes (look, for example, at the recurrent cadential figure for harp which punctuates and closes *Tragoedia*), this particular device is in fact an exact quotation of the harp chords which had ended *Melencolia I*. The two works are, on the surface, very different, the one concerned with melody, the other with pulse, though we come to realize that melody is a feature of both when the Silbury 'air' (a woodwind melody) emerges out of the network of pulses and asserts itself as an independent element in the second half of the work. So why the quotation? Birtwistle's 'subtitle' to *Silbury Air* might help explain, a subtitle not only taken from Klee but which also refers to an earlier work of the same name:

> I have often alluded to my music of landscape presenting musical ideas through the juxtaposition of 'static blocks' or, preferable for my terminology, objects. These objects themselves being subjected to a vigorous invented logic via modes of juxtaposition, modes of repetition, modes of change.
>
> The sum total of these processes being a compound artificial landscape or 'imaginary landscape', to use Paul Klee's title.[8]

This construction of a landscape through an invented logic is also key to understanding *Melencolia I*, which takes over the title of an engraving of 1514 by Dürer. Erwin Panofsky's interpretation of the various objects which litter Dürer's picture – an hour-glass, a pair of scales, a magic square, a pair of compasses, a turned sphere of wood, a 'truncated rhombohedron of stone' – is that they are symbols or emblems of 'the fact that the terrestrial craftsman, like the "Architect of the Universe", applies in his work the rules of mathematics . . . In fact, the whole array of implements in the engraving can be summed up under the heading "Typus Geometriae"' where, specifically, the magic square (of Saturn, once again denoting geometry), the hour-glass with bell and the scales stand for measurement in time and space.[9] Silbury Hill is man-made, 'an artificial but organic intruder of the landscape', and it is this balance of artifice and nature, of geometry and art, that Birtwistle sets out to recreate in *Silbury Air*. The final harp chords serve to remind us of Melancholy as Geometry. *Silbury Air* is a work which involves the very careful measurement of time and space; though the 'intrusion' of a seemingly organic melody in the latter part of the piece perhaps begins to point in a different direction, the harp, calling out from *Melencolia I*, exhorts us to remember the artificial dimensions of this landscape.

The geometrical aspect of *Silbury Air* is, unusually for Birtwistle, writ large for all to see at the front of the score (unusual because he is usually quite private about the technical aspects of the compositional process). This is the 'pulse labyrinth', four charts of time signatures and metronome markings which – in the abstract – govern the progress of the work (Ex. 6.4). Like a physical labyrinth, it remains fixed while the 'music' moves through it; like an individual in a maze who can never fully grasp from the ground the design of the whole, so in the piece itself we never see the labyrinth complete but progressively build up a picture of its structure as we move from one object to the next, one moment to the next. The pulse labyrinth is in practice a precisely calculated matrix for ensuring smooth metric modulation so that, as in *Pulse Sampler*, the piece is an exploration of pulse that appears to be in a constant state of flux. The rules of operation (as far as they can be discerned through their practice) require that movement through any one of the four tables must be between neighbouring squares and can only be horizontal or vertical, with the exception of movement between those identical metronome values connected by double-headed arrows (the 'knight's move', if you like). As Michael Hall has pointed out, the ratio between horizontal values (when they are not equal) is a constant 15:16,[10] a gearing mechanism which guarantees that both a change of time signature (i.e. bar length) and a change of metronome mark can be brought about comparatively smoothly. The rest of Hall's account is, however, a little misleading. (For example, he discusses the beginning of the work which moves through table III but confusingly reproduces only table IV.)

Fig. 6.2 shows all the metric shifts of the first section of the

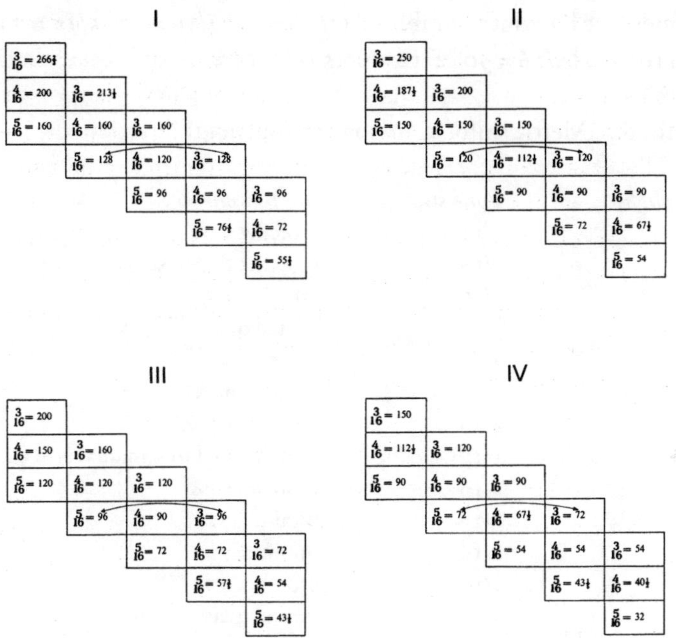

Ex. 6.4. *Silbury Air*, 'pulse labyrinth'.

work. It can be seen that the 'metric modulations' are brought about by means of movement through table III of the pulse labyrinth, though even in this relatively short passage there is one principal anomaly and a few other notational inconsistencies (inconsistencies nonetheless 'consistent' with Birtwistle's desire to corrupt for his own musical purposes systems he perceives as being too academic or restrictive). What Fig. 6.2 does not show is the entry at fig. 4 of an independent ostinato for double bass which continues until the end of the section at a strict crotchet = 108 (i.e. in a ratio of 3:2 within the prevailing tempo of crotchet = 72) and anticipates the first 'free' interpolation at that tempo between figs. 5 and 6. The parenthetical status of these bars (they remain outside the strict control of the pulse labyrinth) is articulated by framing pauses at either end and punctuated by chords on the piano, harp and marimba. The regular pulsation resumes at fig. 6 (at 2/4, later 4/16, crotchet = 150) and at fig. 8 the music enters the labyrinth of table IV (5/16 = 90 | 4/16 = 90 | 5/16 = 72 | 4/16 = 90 | 3/16 = 90 | 4/16 = 67.5 | etc.).

FIG. 6.2. Metric shifts in *Silbury Air* (opening)

Reh. fig	*Time sig.*	*Metronome*
	4/16	crotchet = 90
	5/16	crotchet tied to semiquaver = 72
	4/16	crotchet = 90
	3/16	dotted quaver = 120
1	4/16	crotchet = 120
	3/16	dotted quaver = 160*
	4/16	crotchet = 120
	5/16	crotchet tied to semiquaver = 96
2	4/16	crotchet = 96†
3	8/16	minim = 72‡
4	8/16	minim = 72
	4/16	crotchet = 72§
	3/16	dotted quaver = 96
	5/16	crotchet tied to semiquaver = 96
	4/16	crotchet = 120
5	*pause*	

* In the score, Birtwistle does not change the metronome mark of crotchet = 120 with the change of time signature; to be consistent, however, I show here a value for the length of a 3/16 bar (which then also fits with the corresponding value in table III of the pulse labyrinth).

† An anomaly – Birtwistle overrides the fact that table III here gives a value of 4/16 = 90; this would be 'correct' only if he were in table I.

‡ There is no time signature change away from 4/16 here, despite the fact the music is written in bars of 8/16 at crotchet = 144; once again, to be consistent both with what follows and with the pulse labyrinth, I show a value here for the length of an 8/16 bar. As we see at reh. fig. 4, an 8/16 bar at minim = 72 is equivalent to a 4/16 bar at crotchet = 72.

§ This is merely a notational change – a halving both of note values and metronome mark makes no audible difference.

But there are other aspects of the organization of pulse here which are not governed by the matrices. The unit of pulsation is freely determined so that even when the time signature and tempo are fixed, a number of different but related pulses can be heard to be operating simultaneously. Even, for example, by the end of the first page of the score (5/16 = 72) we see a sustained E in brass and double bass (i.e. no pulse); a semiquaver pulse in piano, harp and marimba; a bar-long pulse in the remaining strings (i.e. a five-semiquaver unit); and crotchet pulse in the woodwind. Thus, the E is interpreted in four ways simultaneously resulting in an effect rather like the turning of three different-sized cogs of ratio 1:4:5 in the presence of a separate cog which remains motionless (Ex. 6.5). Note how the metric modulation between blocks is brought about here: the underlying semiquaver unit remains at a constant speed and though, when the time signature changes, the bar-long pulsation in the strings changes from a four-semiquaver unit (at the start) to a five-semiquaver unit length, the four-semiquaver pulse is transferred to the woodwind, cutting across the new metre. The change from 4/16 to 5/16 is smooth because at least one of the old elements remains in the new (though this is not

Ex. 6.5. *Silbury Air.*

always the case). Another feature which contributes a pulse at a higher metric level is the grouping of bars within any given block, indicated in the score by an additional integer to the immediate right of the time signature – what one might call the music's hypermetre. The opening 4/16 and 5/16 blocks, for example, are grouped in units of three bars.

Thus, the aural impression – certainly in the first half of the piece – is of a continually changing kaleidoscope of different pulses, slowing down and speeding up, successively and simultaneously, and operating on a number of structural levels. In this sense it is quite obviously the direct successor to *Chronometer*. In the boldness of some of its oppositions it recalls similar procedures in earlier works – compare, for instance, the rapid juxtaposition of blocks (each of which consists of the simple repetition of a single event or alternating pair of events) between figs. 8 and 14 with the passages between figs. 18 and 26 and 58 and 66 in *Verses for Ensembles*, or similar procedures in *An Imaginary Landscape*. It also suggests – to my ears at least – interesting parallels with the layers of ticking clocks to be found in the contemporary works of Ligeti, or the fantastic mathematical mechanisms constructed by Nancarrow in his studies for player piano. And, as so often, many of the objects we encounter in Birtwistle's landscape have a distinctly Stravinskian feel, whether in the very fact of their block construction, or in their rhythmic layering, or in the contained repetitive character of their melodic lines, or in aspects of their scoring. Certainly the typical Stravinsky-derived process of viewing the same musical objects from different perspectives is here formalized to an extent not found in any other work by Birtwistle: this is the 'vigorous invented logic via modes of juxtaposition, modes of repetition, modes of change'.

If such an account suggests a mechanical piece of artifice, a merely academic exercise in splicing together music generated by the pulse matrices, then nothing could be further from the truth. Not only is movement through the pulse labyrinth free and undetermined – based to a large extent on the composer's whim – resulting in a music whose progress is inevitable yet unpredictable, but also the 'air' when it emerges after the first return of the opening music is rhythmically free, decidedly unconcerned with the repetitive pulsations of the music which has preceded it, and contrastingly lyrical (legato, cantabile) in character. The melody first emerges clearly in the flute at fig. 29 (see Ex. 6.6) and is later shared among the four woodwind instruments, first soloistically, then heterophonically. The flute melody (cantus) rides seemingly independently over the top of the rest of the ensemble (continuum), whose pulsations on this occasion work their way through table I of the pulse labyrinth. While pulse remains an underlying feature of the remainder of the work, the melody nonetheless comes to dominate and almost seems to undermine the reassuring regularity of the pulsed voices. The melody itself is somewhat restricted, in keeping with the (Stravinsky-like) pitch restrictions of the musical materials explored up to this point. Ex. 6.6 shows the flute exploring a segment of the total chromatic, making a feature of octave displacements; in this respect, it can be compared with the style of melodic writing of *Secret Theatre*, though it never takes full flight like the cantus in that work. In some senses, *Silbury Air* might be understood to have paved the way for *Secret Theatre* (indeed, *Silbury Air*, *Carmen Arcadiae* and *Secret Theatre* seem to form a trilogy in more senses than simply being written for virtually the same ensemble and premièred by the London Sinfonietta: the exploration of the relationship between the fixed and the free, between melody and pulse, are shared concerns of all three works). The rather two-dimensional opposition here between linear melody and repetitive, circular 'accompaniment' takes on a much more elaborate and flexible perspective in the continually changing relationship between cantus and continuum in *Secret Theatre*. But then *Silbury Air*'s primary preoccupation is with pulse: its simple premise of exploring the rich compositional possibilities of something as musically basic as pulse in a permanent state of flux is fully realized.

Brief mention should also be made here of the work concerned with pulse which was written immediately after *Silbury Air*. *Pulse Field (Frames, Pulses and Interruptions)* is a ballet score and was

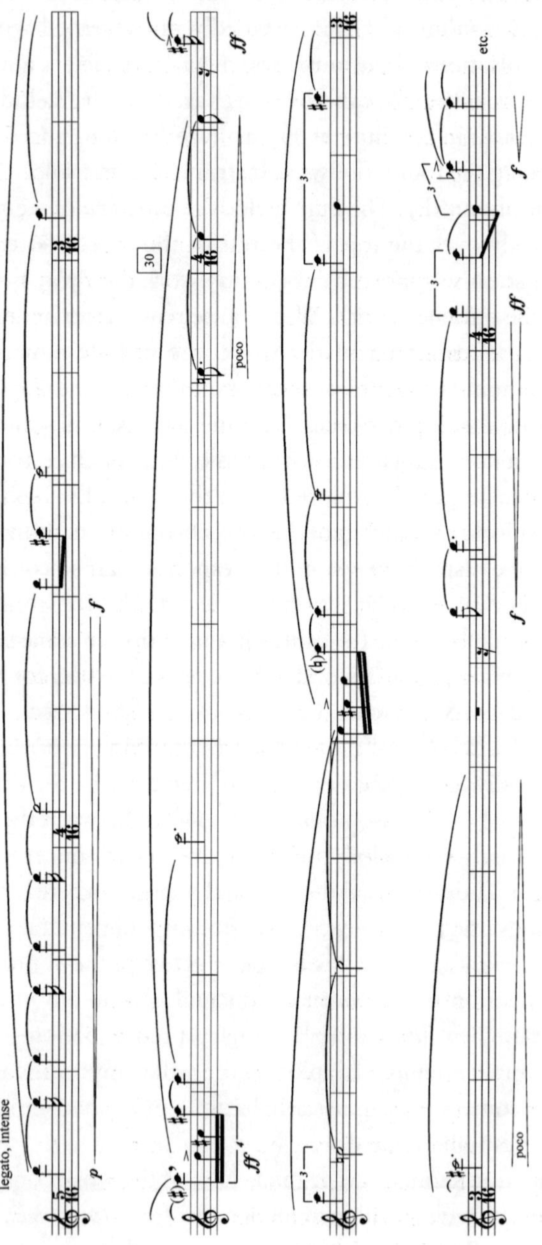

Ex. 6.6. *Silbury Air*, fig. 29, flute 'air'.

commissioned by the Ballet Rambert and premièred at the 1977 Aldeburgh Festival. Despite Birtwistle's interest in the stylization of dance, and the incorporation of important danced and mimed elements into a number of his works including *The Mask of Orpheus* and *Gawain*, his involvement with purely danced pieces has not been a particularly successful experience. Debra Craine, writing in the *Times*, claimed 'Birtwistle and dance are not natural partners',[11] but that is plainly nonsense; it is Birtwistle and choreographers who are not natural partners. The reasons for the 'failure' of his dance projects have more to do with the practicalities of collaboration (the relationship is one of which composers, on the whole, have less experience than that other fraught and unequal relationship between composer and librettist) than any innate inability to understand or respond to the nature of dance. At the 1996 'Secret Theatres' Festival on the South Bank, London, the choreographer Richard Alston was commissioned to create dances to *Secret Theatre* and *Nenia: the Death of Orpheus* plus a new work in collaboration with Birtwistle, *Bach Measures* (arrangements of eight of Bach's *Orgelbüchlein* chorale preludes). In general, the critics and – by all accounts – the composer, too, were not happy with the results, principally because the danced dimension seemed redundant. There was little evidence of collaboration: the very different theatres of Alston and Birtwistle did not fuse. Two decades earlier, the Rambert company had approached Birtwistle to work with the choreographer Jaap Flier on a new work. Hall has documented the disagreements and misunderstandings on that occasion between composer and choreographer.[12] *Pulse Field* attempts to explore the relationship between musicians and dancers and in order to achieve this (as the *Oresteia* would do for musicians and actors) Birtwistle felt it necessary to pare down his music to the basics of pulse and drone. As in other contemporary pieces such as *For O, for O* and *Bow Down*, the musicians are on the stage and partake of the theatre, signalling cues to each other and to the dancers, such that the movements of both musicians and dancers echo one another. The result is a musical–theatrical experience which, as Hall has observed, evokes once again the sparseness and stylization of Japanese theatre. The structure devised by Flier and Birtwistle is one of a succession of frames of slow pulses which are occasionally interrupted ('freeze frames', anticipating similar situations found in later works). The pulse does change between frames, but each frame is in itself relatively 'empty', needing to be 'filled' by the players in performance.

Since the *Oresteia*, Birtwistle has never again worked with pulse in such an obsessive way. This is not to say that a concern for pulse disappears; far from it: 'I'm very interested in pulse – more and more. I'm thinking about it a lot at the moment.' Rather, having explored the musical and gestural possibilities of pulse in these works of the 1970s, regular pulsation, rhythmic ostinatos and the like have been more fully absorbed into his musical vocabulary, offering formal contexts rather than exclusive focus. Arguably the one exception to this is *Harrison's Clocks*, but even here, despite the presence of the many pianistic ticks and tocks, and despite the work's preoccupation with all kinds of repetition, an unchanging, regularly pulsed musical object is difficult to find. The last movement, the *moto perpetuo*, is the only one where an obsessive semiquaver pulse is literally present throughout (note how this, like *Pulse Sampler*, begins with an unpulsed, sustained E before the clock mechanism gets going) but because of its unchanging nature, this is not the focus of the movement: it is the rhythmic structures which emerge at a higher level through the use of accents, as well as the movement away from and towards particular pitch focuses, which attract our attention.

Pulse and repetition as dramatic devices were fundamental to *The Mask of Orpheus*, a work concerned in almost its every aspect with the nature of time, and such techniques echo across more recent stage works too. The monumental 'Turning of the Seasons' Masque which constitutes the final section of Act 1 of *Gawain*, for example, is clearly concerned with the (ritualized) passage of time: from night to day, and from season to season (from one winter through 'twelve months and a day' to the next).

As the off-stage choir sings in the 1991 version:

> Moment by moment, sunrise by sunrise,
> season by season, and so the world turns.

Each of the seasons is represented (winter twice over) in this turning of an enormous wheel, during which Gawain is ceremonially washed and armed for his journey. But within each season we also see represented the smaller wheels, as it were, of night and day. Day seems to symbolize the transition from one season to the next, during which the female chorus sings a text of invented pagan language; during the night the male chorus intones the Latin words of the Mass for the Dead while the knights prepare Gawain mentally for his journey and bless him. Day turns faster than night, but in a clearly defined relationship (day is at crotchet = *c*.72, night is at crotchet = *c*.48; that is, a tempo ratio of 3:2); furthermore, day seems to stand as the refrain to the verses of the night. The sense of 'ritual' time, as opposed to 'real' time, during the day is symbolized musically by an absolutely regular quaver pulse throughout and the presence of regularly repeating 'objects' in the orchestra; by contrast, the night sections give the impression of being more freely linear, dominated by falling tuba lines. Each season is a clear and appropriate musical variant of the first Winter (the wheel remains the same but, in turning, reveals new and more complex perspectives) with the exception of the second Winter which – other than the text – is a virtually exact repetition of the first (the wheel has now turned full circle).[13] The context may be rather different from the works of the 1970s, but the construction of an 'imaginary landscape' through the careful and proportional organization of pulse is similarly undertaken for ritual ends.

Pulse Shadows is not the study in pulse its title might suggest. Indeed, it is important to remember that the title was coined by Birtwistle after the work's completion to bind together the (intentionally) loose amalgam of two cycles – the *9 Settings of Celan* and *9 Movements for String Quartet* – composed independently over a period of some eight years. Nevertheless, it offers a fascinating study in the ways in which he has absorbed the concerns for a flexible pulse explored in earlier works. Sometimes this manifests itself as overt moments of ostinato, such as those which close 'Thread Suns' and 'Tenebrae', reminding one of similar uses of ostinato in music from much earlier in the century – as in such aphoristic atonal works as Berg's *Altenberg Lieder* or Webern's Six Pieces for Orchestra, Op. 6. Sometimes this manifests itself as an absolutely regular pulse on the surface, as in the repeated semiquavers shared between the two clarinets in 'With Letter and Clock'. (This movement is an interesting study in how extremely simple fixed musical objects can be extended in time. In essence, the clarinets, cello and bass present throughout just two alternating fifths [A–E and G–D] chromatically and rhythmically elaborated. The voice begins in similar fashion moving chromatically either side of the initial E, but slowly encompasses the entire chromatic as the movement unfolds, shadowed in part by the viola high in its register. Three times this is interrupted/punctuated by a short refrain: 'swimming light'. In other words, the movement presents the familiar situation of the balanced opposition of a limited continuum of fifth drones and pulses, and a linear cantus which works with but remains independent of the continuum's materials, contained with a verse-refrain structure.) Sometimes this manifests itself as an independent repeating 'pulse mobile', such as the viola line from bar 60 to the end of 'White and Light' whose four variants are strongly reminiscent of the claves' mobile from *Pulse Sampler*, and which serve to summarize the flexibly pulsed, symmetrically elaborated D drone which is a virtually continuous presence in the viola throughout the movement (Ex. 6.7). Drone and pulse are thus again combined. Or sometimes this manifests itself as a series of pulse objects creating, as in 'Frieze 2', another kind of imaginary landscape. This movement begins with the E in violin 2 and proceeds to unfold a partial chromatic 'wedge' at an even quaver pulse; then the line migrates up to violin 1 (to a new chromatic subset) and the pulse modulates to even triplet quavers; and so on. As the movement progresses, the idea of this pulse in flux becomes more elaborate, more complex, but as the music appears to move from one kind of subdivision of

Ex. 6.7. *Pulse Shadows*, 'White and Light' (ending).

the bar to another, and from one repeating musical object to the next, the procedure is in essence little different from the model offered by *Pulse Sampler*. Repeating musical objects are, to a greater or lesser extent, a feature of all four of the 'Friezes' in *Pulse Shadows*. The analogy with the visual frieze is thus an appropriate one in that Birtwistle's friezes, too, are usually a horizontal (temporal) succession of fixed, repeated or decoratively varied objects and whose beginnings and endings are – to a degree – arbitrary (that is, the repetitions are potentially infinite, and are merely 'torn off' when their usefulness has been exhausted). Like the architectural frieze, Birtwistle's friezes, while independent, do not stand alone but have to be understood in relation to the objects either side. Moreover, Birtwistle puns on the word in that his friezes are also 'freeze-frames'; that is, the refrain as a frozen moment.

The organization of pulses in *Earth Dances* is altogether more complex. There *are* passages controlled by a dominant, regular pulse, such as the insistent demi-semiquavers driving the music inexorably towards its final climax (around fig. 77) – a passage that strongly calls to mind the rhythmic energy of Stravinsky's 'Danse sacrale'. But equally there are passages where different pulses are layered on top of one another, musical layers that combine and recombine in many ways throughout the piece, dancing, continually shifting like the very strata of the earth's crust. Each stratum has its own registral, intervallic and instrumental characteristics. But it is perhaps through their rhythms that they are most clearly differentiated. Take, by way of example, the section that begins at fig. 32. Once again, a sustained cantus in the violins gradually unfolds outwards from an E in irregular rhythms while another stratum (continuum) in low wind and strings punctuates with highly regular patterns. This latter then turns itself into an ostinato, while other strata are superimposed, such as the mechanical repeating blocks in brass and percussion at fig. 34. From moment to moment, the music is always changing, its layered pulses always shifting unpredictably. Yet the forward progress of the music is never in any doubt. Though achieved quite differently from *Silbury Air* and *Pulse Sampler*, *Earth Dances* reveals a further fascinating interpretation of the idea of the pulse in flux.

What is revealed through this wide-ranging examination of pulse in Birtwistle's music is just how essential it is to his musical thinking. Though it became especially transparent in a number of important works of the 1970s and 1980s, it should be apparent that a deep concern for pulse was present in earlier works (*Refrains and Choruses* emerges from the gentle pulsation of a single pitch) and continues into the music of the 1990s. While the contrapuntal and rhythmic complexity of *Pulse Shadows* may seem a long way from the relatively blunt techniques of layering pulses found in *Chronometer* or the simple pulse mobile and metric modulations of *Pulse Sampler*, the differences are only a matter of degree, not of substance. Pulse and repetition, as the fundamentals of all music, primitive and modern, underlie all Birtwistle's works. Pulse may be presented merely as a means of measuring clock time, it may be elaborated into all kinds of sophisticated temporal structures, it may even (and often does) take on a ritual significance; but, in essence, in every new work Birtwistle appears to begin again, to compose *ex nihilo* with the basic musical building blocks of a single pulse and a single pitch. To recognize this is to recognize something of the rawness, the fundamental simplicity, and the immense primitive power of so much of his music, from the pure, almost child-like pulsations of 'Urlar', the first of his flute *Duets for Storab*, to the monumental, elemental rhythms of *Earth Dances*.

7 *Episodion V* – 'On Stasis in Progress': Line, Melody, Tonality

Gawain, Birtwistle has declared, is built on a fundamental melodic line. In the light of this assertion, Rhian Samuel has claimed that 'Wagner's spirit (particularly as expressed in *Parsifal*) has entered the work; a new emphasis on drama in its naturalistic sense, and a new relationship between linear, narrative flow and closed forms has transported *Gawain* to new territory.'[1] There is no doubting that *Gawain* represents a refocusing of Birtwistle's musical and dramatic concerns where much more overt precedence is given to narrative. Despite its typically stylized text, and despite the presence of the ritual, repeating cycles which dominate both acts of the work, it nonetheless 'tells a story' in linear fashion, unprecedented in any of his previous stage works. It is notable that *Gawain* was the first work Birtwistle designated 'opera' (with all the narrative and expressive associations the nineteenth-century usage of that term carries), a title he employed also for his next stage work, *The Second Mrs Kong*, which shares with *Gawain* a clear narrative impulse. And yet the closer one looks at Birtwistle's music, the more one comes to recognize that an interest in line has been present from the start of his composing career. The simple essentials of this interest were explored in Chapter 1 and can be summarized in Klee's formulation of 'taking a line for a walk'. Samuel reports a conversation with the composer in which he drew simple geometric patterns to elucidate the linear progress of the opera: 'This line could multiply into several simultaneous lines (a kind of organum) or be subjected to ornamentation, but it was one line. He drew the line on a brown paper envelope – it spiralled around a circle . . . And he drew the repeated sections as rectangles on this circle.'[2] If this is compared with Klee's account of his line accompanied by various forms which reflect its motion, taking the shape of complementary ideas, secondary lines or even by the line circumscribing itself, and, moreover, if we recall the long-standing influence of Klee's writings on Birtwistle, then it rapidly becomes apparent that *Gawain*'s line represents not new thinking in his music, merely a shift in emphasis. From *Monody for Corpus Christi* through the obviously linear 'processionals' of the 1970s to the cantus of *Secret Theatre* and *An Interrupted Endless Melody*, line has remained at the heart of Birtwistle's musical thinking.

But – prompted by Birtwistle's *ad hoc* sketches and his adoption of Klee-like rhetoric – though we talk of line as a geometric feature, it has temporal implications for his music too. Line implies continuity, directedness, temporal as well as geographical points of arrival and departure, and this in turn invites us to consider the nature of 'tonality' – for want of a better term – in Birtwistle's music, its pitch focuses which centre a sense of line. Indeed, even to talk of a fundamental melodic line, as Birtwistle readily does in relation to *Gawain*, is to invoke the notion of the Fundamental Line (the *Urlinie*) as expressed in Schenkerian theory. This is not, for one moment, to suggest that linearity in Birtwistle's music is achieved through directed tonal means that can be demonstrated in Schenkerian terms. But it is interesting to note that the composer did make a study of Schenkerian analytical methodology during his time as a Harkness Fellow at the University of Colorado at Boulder in 1967. Like his study of integral serial compositional methods with Milton Babbitt during his time as visiting fellow at Princeton University the previous year, it was something Birtwistle declares – somewhat disingenuously – it was necessary to undertake in order for him then to reject it. He claims to have learnt nothing at Princeton and Boulder other than the personal discovery that these methods had nothing to do with his own creative ambitions and techniques. Yet while Birtwistle is not a serial composer, serial thought has had a far-reaching impact on his work, and the rigour of Babbitt's 'constructivist' approach has clearly left its mark in many different ways. Similarly with Schenker. Though the theory itself has little directly to offer Birtwistle, Schenker's understanding of linear directed motion and continuity in tonal music, of the way in which a line unfolds in time, of the structural relationship between music's horizontal and vertical dimensions, and even his theory of levels (Birtwistle is fond of using the terms 'foreground' and 'background' to distinguish between functions in his music – see, for example, his notes on *Secret Theatre*), these have at the very least helped to contextualize the composer's attitude towards the linear aspects of his music. It is interesting to note that his orchestral work *Nomos*, with its long, continuous melody for four amplified flutes, clarinet, horn and bassoon, was composed while he was at Boulder.

In tonal music, the *Urlinie* descends in a dynamic, directed fashion to its conclusion, signalling the closure of the musical structure. Musical time, as Schenker represents it, is linear and unidirectional. Birtwistle's music constructs a very different kind of temporality. This is expressed at its most complex in *The Mask of Orpheus*, with its many time shifts and reversals, its attempts to allow past and future to exist simultaneously in the present. Written in 1976, *Melencolia I* was Birtwistle's first major work to be written following the collapse of the original commission for *Orpheus* and the suspension of his work on the composition of Act 2. Birtwistle borrowed the title and aspects of the subject matter of Dürer's engraving for his own melancholic work, composed in memory of Tony Wright who had been responsible for promoting Birtwistle's music at Universal Edition. The writings of both Erwin Panofsky and Günter Grass also became important to him during the composition of the piece. Grass's essay 'On stasis in progress: variations on Albrecht Dürer's engraving *Melencolia I*' forms the concluding section to his partly autobiographical 1972 novel, *From the Diary of a Snail*, and the title of the essay could well stand for Birtwistle's attitude to musical time in general. His music is always in motion, is in a constant state of flux, and yet it rarely arrives fully at a definitive destination. The image of the frozen moment is an apt one: motion within the context of something essentially static. As in Stravinsky's music, the notion of progress does not necessarily carry with it the sense of a linear *development*: Raymond Williams reminds us that the early uses of the word progress implied 'a physical march, journey or procession, then of a developing series of events. There is no necessary ideological implication in this sense of a forward movement or developing series.'[3] Such are Birtwistle's processionals – 'a freeze-frame, only a sample of an event already in motion . . . a procession made up of a (necessarily) linked chain of material objects which have no necessary connection with each other'[4] – and thus is expressed 'stasis in progress'.

How does this manifest itself musically in *Melencolia I*? As in *Gawain*, there is a fundamental line at the heart of the work. It begins from a single point, a gently throbbing, sustained A on the solo clarinet. This line weaves its way through the work, though its progress is rarely straightforward – moving on, then stopping, turning back on itself, before meandering forward again. In characteristic fashion, the line emerges from the initial A by (non-symmetrical) motion either side of it, first down a tone to G and on to F♯, then up a tone to B and B♭, then slowly and gradually filling out the restricted chromatic space between F and B, before pausing on a sustained F, and then moving on again . . . E, E♭, D, C, C♯. Whittall writes of 'the clarinet's slowly unfolding style of lyric melancholy' and of 'Birtwistle's method of generating an extended line in slow motion as we listen',[5] while Griffiths comments that this 'conception of melody as continuing growth, rather than as completed statement, is one of the sources of Birtwistle's continuity, and of the strong sense in each piece that it is creating itself out of the rudiments of sound.'[6] We might legitimately here take over the term Birtwistle adopted for the continuously present line in *Secret Theatre*: cantus. Like the image of the procession in *The Triumph of Time*, the clarinet is (at least at the start) in the foreground; the background (continuum, 'recurrent procedures') is formed by punctuating chords from the muted low instruments of the two string orchestras whose pitch classes (but not actual pitches) are generated initially by symmetrical movement around the clarinet's A (G♯–A♯) and then open out into another chromatic collection. The harp takes the role of a continuo instrument (a familiar role in Birtwistle: compare, for example, the roles of the harp in *Tragoedia*, the cimbalom in *Gawain* and the accordion in *The Second Mrs Kong*) and acts as a kind of intermediary, at one moment echoing, supporting and cajoling the clarinet, at the next joining in with the continuum. Having begun by suggesting a direction the clarinet might (and indeed does) take – A–G – the harp then further suggests the clarinet's *modus operandi* by revolving round a restricted chromatic set contained between B♯ and F♭ but in a rhythmically less fluid and fluent manner than the clarinet will eventually adopt (the harp's utterances are spasmodic, unlike the clarinet's sustained cantus).

The fundamental line is, explicitly or implicitly, present throughout the work. As the piece proceeds, the continuum from time to time attempts to speak in the clarinet's voice, taking over its linear characteristic; as the line migrates to the continuum, so the clarinet (as at fig. K, for instance, once again supported by the harp) responds by adopting a more fragmentary character, with wide leaps, trying to make itself heard. From here on, the relationship between the clarinet and the strings is continually fluctuating: at times the strings attempt to halt the flow of the line with aggressive interjections; at other times (as, for example, at the chorale-like fig. R) a greater equilibrium is attained. This is followed by a now familiar moment of 'aria' for clarinet, accompanied by harp ostinato and sustained strings (see Ex. 7.1), which stands as a foil to the work's denouement which begins at fig. S: a sequence of wide and dense chords for multiple subdivided strings, through which the clarinet screeches, fragmentedly, for attention. For the one and only time in the work, the clarinet is silenced. The strings' music splinters into tiny shards: freely rotating superimposed ostinatos (a rare moment of Lutoslawski-style aleatoricism), whose resulting kaleidoscope perfectly expresses the idea of individual progress in the context of overall stasis. Out of this emerges the clarinet, now only able to express the same idea in its own accent by stumbling through a final, rhythmically awkward, five-note ostinato. The harp calls the proceedings to a sudden halt.

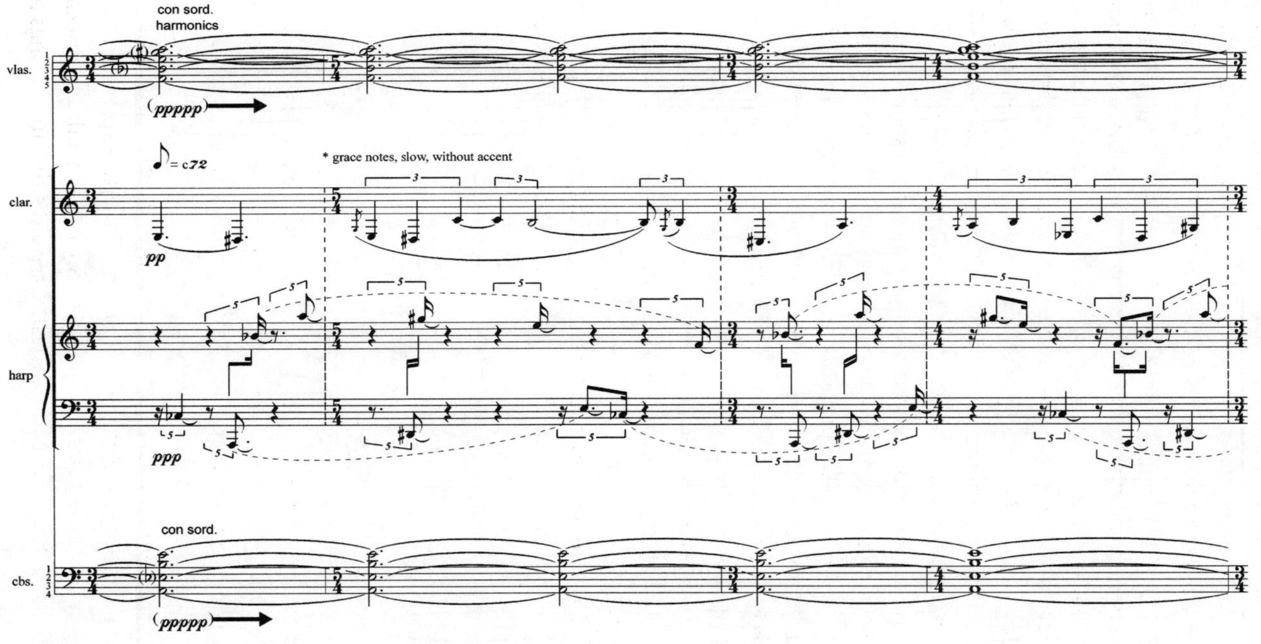

Ex. 7.1. *Melencolia I* (before reh. letter S).

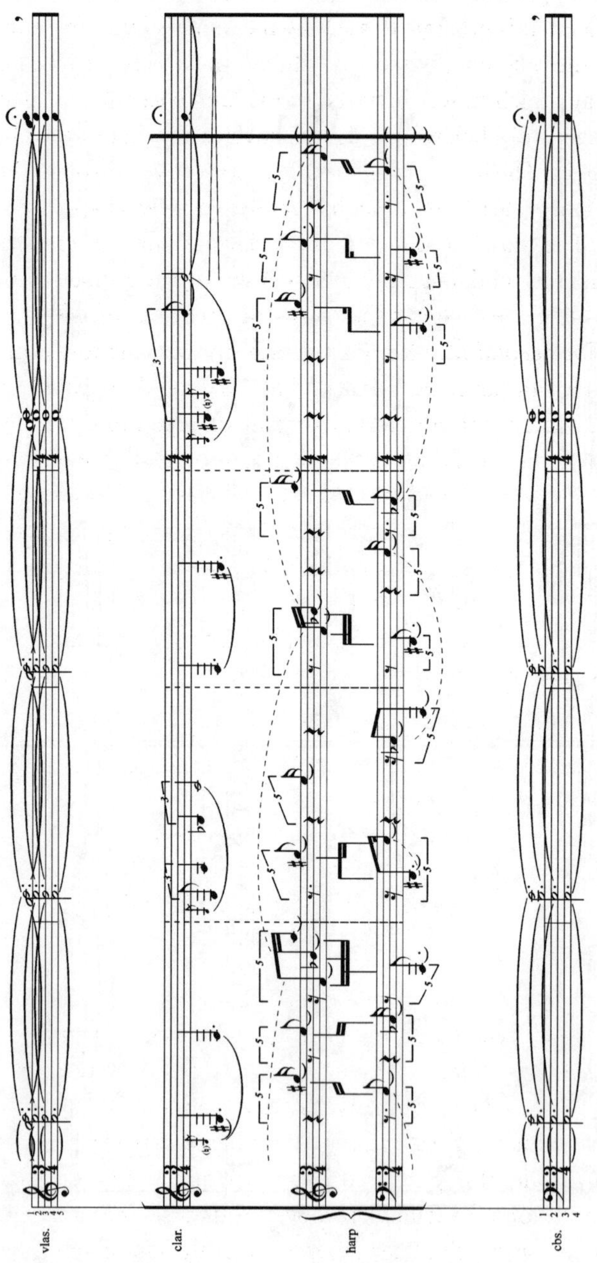

Ex. 7.1 (cont'd).

Such an apparently 'narrative' account of *Melencolia I* is not unintentional. It is possible to see how the work is built on a fundamental melodic line, a narrative thread on which the piece is hung, a line which moves between soloist and ensemble as their roles change, and a line whose identity subtly shifts in response to these changes. The line's progress (that is, its journey through the piece) is always clear even though it ends up merely as a series of ostinatos. The 'stasis in progress' of the clarinet's final utterances (see Ex. 1.5) is fundamentally melancholic because it seems to embody – like the melancholic 'stasis in progress' of the final scene of *The Second Mrs Kong* – the idea of a striving for something which can never be fulfilled. The line could continue *ad infinitum*, locked into an eternal present of repetitions, fading away into nothingness ('out of the silence, into the silence returning', as Swami Zumzum sings at the end of *Mrs Kong*); or else it could be forced into silence, which is the role of the harp here. Birtwistle confronts us with, as Grass expresses it, 'the dark side of utopia'; his creative commentary on Dürer's picture could equally well stand for the melancholic character of much of Birtwistle's music:

> Phases displaced individually and in relation to each other. Progress overtaken. Inactive amid instruments. As though geometry had outmeasured itself. As though the latest knowledge had bogged down in doubt after its first attempts to walk. As though science had canceled itself out. As though beauty were an empty fiction. As though only mythology would endure.[7]

Such words could certainly be taken to apply to *Linoi*, an earlier work which seems to anticipate, in more modest form, the concerns of *Melencolia I*. Originally written for a 1968 Pierrot Players concert and premièred by the *Verses* duo of Alan Hacker and Stephen Pruslin, it was first scored for basset clarinet in A and piano; Birtwistle also produced two subsequent versions, one with the addition of a Zinovieff tape and dancer, the other for clarinet, piano and cello. Being a lament (for the musician Linus, brother of Orpheus), it shares the melancholic mood of *Melencolia I* as well as the colour and linearity of that work's solo voice. *Linoi* consists in essence of a single musical line for the clarinet, albeit a somewhat fragmentary one that never really blossoms into fully fledged melody. Starting in typical fashion from a single reiterated pitch, on three occasions the clarinet attempts to build a sustained line, and on three occasions fails, finally falling to its very lowest note, and to silence. The pianist functions as 'chorus' with sounds produced exclusively from inside the piano, evoking among other things Linus's lyre – the very lyre indeed that was used to kill him. (Given Pruslin's association with both this work and *Punch and Judy*, it is tempting to draw parallels with the murder of Choregos who was sawn to death in that opera by the bow of a bass viol.) Like the harp in *Melencolia I*, the plucked piano here both punctuates and engages directly with the clarinet. At the work's climax, three loud chords (the piano strings are struck with timpani sticks) are heard, which, again anticipating *Melencolia I*'s climax, form the moment of *peripeteia* and bring about an irreversible change in the clarinet. Linus is killed by the lyre. And such, too, was to be the fate of Orpheus in *The Mask of Orpheus* who is ultimately silenced by his own (electronic) lyre. Both Linus and Orpheus commited hubris by challenging Apollo; both paid the ultimate price.

The sad song of Melencolia resurfaces in the rather different guise of the solo tuba in *The Cry of Anubis*, Birtwistle's 'spin-off' piece from *The Second Mrs Kong*. It is not, however, another *Gawain's Journey* – a confection from the parent opera – but an independent work. Just as his string piece *Still Movement* took a new route through material presented in the opera *Yan Tan Tethera*, so *The Cry of Anubis* takes a subsidiary character from the opera, places him centre stage, and begins a new compositional journey. Anubis in the opera is the ominous ferryman: 'In my black boat coming and going, bringer of souls to this world of shadows'. As we saw in Chapter 3, Anubis feeds off the passions and dreams of the dead. Here, it is an orchestral 'chorus of the dead' which begins the work, that is, the collective, background continuum playing regular ostinatos, out of which a lone, mournful voice is heard (viola) and from which, in turn, the tuba (cantus) line emerges – feeding, as it were, directly off the chorus. The tuba's character throughout is essentially lyrical, its journey through the musical landscape perhaps less troubled than that of the clarinet in *Melencolia I* – that is, the soloist's engagement with the orchestra is less obviously confrontational: protagonist and chorus move towards and away from one another with a far greater degree of fluidity. One significant point of contact is the note D, the work's focal centre – I hesitate to describe it as a 'tonal centre' but it is an unusually clear gravitational point towards which the music is pulled at key moments during the course of the work. For the first third of the piece, every one of the tuba's phrases either starts from or finishes on the note D, culminating at the first major point of structural articulation with reiterated Ds. Other instrumental lines move in and out of the tuba's ambit, though the orchestra's music here is predominantly constructed from a variety of ostinatos. Thus, though tuba and orchestra interact in intriguing ways, their independence is nonetheless maintained by means of this cantus–continuum opposition. Interesting relationships are forged along the way: one particularly fruitful connection is with harp and percussion who help to define the tuba's main cadences, and which results in a curious duet for tuba and timpani just before the work's final close on D. The principal internal climax at the halfway point is again focused on D. This is perhaps the moment of closest contact with opera: the tuba's heartfelt cry (Ex. 7.2) over a D pedal clearly reminds us of Anubis's operatic alter-ego, Death of Kong, whose killing in Act 2 is accompanied by four loud, sustained, descending gong strokes. This is the opera's moment of *peripeteia*: nothing can be the same again. And this is true for *The Cry of Anubis*, too: the remainder of the work explores the consequences of Anubis's cry, the tuba's motif echoing through all subsequent material.

In keeping with Anubis's Egyptian identity as the god of the necropolis, the melancholic character of *The Cry of Anubis* suggests some sort of funeral procession, with the tuba at its head.

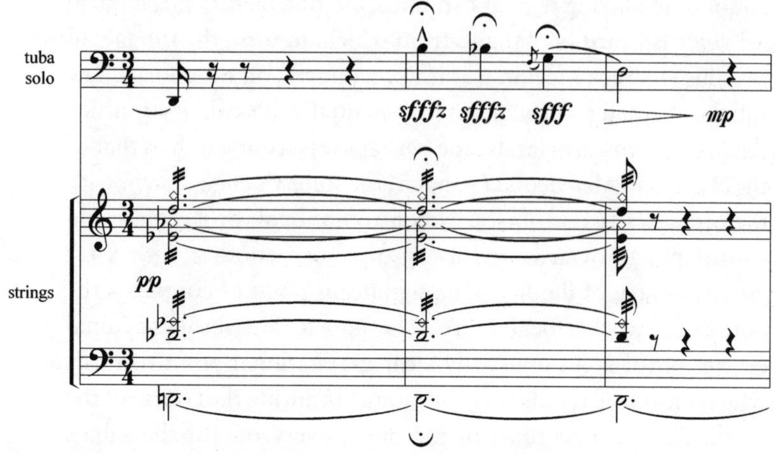

Ex. 7.2. *The Cry of Anubis*, bars 119–21.

The nature of the line here is distinctly different from the line in *Melencolia I* (after all, almost twenty years separate their composition) but their shared linearity nevertheless makes for a fruitful comparison. In *Melencolia I*, the line's identity is asserted in part through its attempts to maintain its presence in the face of the many external challenges: to adopt Grass's terms, the line has a Utopian vision (progress), a desire for forward movement, for change, but which is in tension with a melancholic resignation to the fact that 'nothing can be changed, that all human effort is vain, that an imponderable fate rules: human existence as doom. Only order, a universally respected system, offers security [stasis].'[8] The line's fate, then, is to be locked into endless repetition of its closing ostinato. Like the clarinet in *Melencolia I*, the tuba sings virtually continuously throughout *The Cry of Anubis*, but there is a far greater inevitability about this journey: Birtwistle's description of the progress of the line in *Gawain* spiralling around a basically circular path[9] is appropriate here too. The recurring Ds are a sign of this 'static progress': the line cannot escape its destiny to keep returning to this focus, even if the D is viewed somewhat differently on each new occasion.

Such an account suggests that *The Cry of Anubis* has an earlier companion piece: *Endless Parade* for solo trumpet, vibraphone and string orchestra (written for the Swedish virtuoso, Håkan Hardenberger). It is, in fact, the very complement of the later tuba work: bright, light, positive, confident, extrovert. Both are in a sense 'endless parades', but whereas *The Cry of Anubis* is a sombre funeral procession, *Endless Parade* is a joyful carnival celebration (echoed in the choice of solo instrument and the vivacious character of its writing). Its origins lie in a very real carnival procession Birtwistle had witnessed winding its way through the narrow medieval streets of the Italian walled town of Lucca: 'I became interested in the number of ways in which you could observe this event . . . Each time the view point was different, yet instantly identified as part of one body.'[10] In the actual musical work the carnival translates into a procession of musical ideas which we continually re-encounter, sometimes as unchanging objects, sometimes viewed from new perspectives – such as the trumpet's opening motif (Ex. 7.3) whose recurrence punctuates the course of the procession and indicates the progress of the musical line on its basically spiral path. Like the gravitational Ds to which the line of *The Cry of Anubis* is constantly being pulled back, the return of the trumpet's motif suggests a continual 'beginning again', a process which is literally 'endless':

> Pieces don't really start: they're part of a continuous process. There are certain things thrown up in the course of composition. Arriving at a certain place I can see another point that I might try to get to, but I'll never get there.[11]

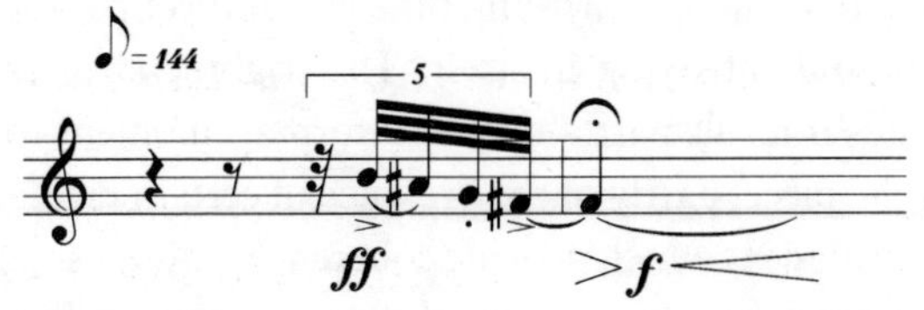

Ex. 7.3. *Endless Parade*, trumpet motif.

Once again, we encounter stasis in progress, that striving for something which can never be reached, which links *Melencolia I* to *The Second Mrs Kong* – though in *Endless Parade* the melancholic aspect of such a world-view is tempered by the temporary pleasure that can be derived from revelling in the sensuous moment (a necessary consequence of the work's self-indulgent virtuosity . . . and virtuosity as an end in itself is a rare commodity indeed in Birtwistle). In fact, *Melencolia I* and *Endless Parade* seem to represent opposite sides of the same coin: processional works for solo wind instrument and string orchestra with a continuo player (harp and vibraphone respectively) mediating between cantus and continuum, between protagonist and chorus, in which Self (soloist) is constantly being challenged to reassess itself in relation to Other (orchestra). One almost gets the feeling (especially from *Melencolia I*'s clarinet, Birtwistle's own instrument) that the composing subject is himself embodied in and speaking out from these lugubrious solo instruments.

The exemplar of Birtwistle's processionals is *The Triumph of Time*. Like *Melencolia I*, it takes on the aspect of a slow-moving yet unstoppable funeral procession, 'a huge *Adagio* of Mahlerian proportions', as Hall describes it,[12] a movement whose overall inevitability is as certain as its local unpredictability. Like so many of Birtwistle's large-scale works (the most notable and successful examples being *Secret Theatre* and *Earth Dances*), the total form is extremely difficult to describe, and yet there is a 'rightness' about the way it unfolds. The work achieves the extraordinary result of both suggesting it is a fragment of something much larger, infinite even ('parts of the procession must already have gone by, others are surely to come'), something timeless, and yet paradoxically is complete and satisfying in itself. The 'rightness' of the work's structure is a result partly of the (informal) moment-to-moment logic of the piece, partly of the presence of certain regularly recurring musical ideas which provide coherence without suggesting an inappropriately synthetic unity, and partly of the skilful timing of events whereby the movement towards and away from climactic points seems almost unavoidable.

I cannot listen to *The Triumph of Time* in the same way that I listen to the other processionals discussed so far in this chapter. It is (intentionally) a much more fractured work. Though it is still just possible to talk of a 'line' which threads its way through the piece, its journey is more complex, the line multiplies itself and moves in a number of different directions, it is not always simply or directly articulated. Whereas I suggested above that in *Melencolia I* and *The Cry of Anubis* the listener might choose to identify the solo instrument with the voice of the composer himself, speaking out of the music, in *The Triumph of Time* Birtwistle has suggested that the composer's relationship to the music is a more objective one – like that of someone looking at a picture. In this particular case he has a specific picture in mind: Pieter Bruegel the Elder's etching of 1574 which gave the musical composition its title and which Birtwistle encountered only once his ideas for the piece had begun to crystallize. The etching is not directly represented in the music; nonetheless, it suggested to Birtwistle that 'the position of the spectator [is] identical with the composer's during composition'. I would go further and equate the listener here with the spectator/composer: we listen passively as the musical procession passes in front of us.

In Bruegel's allegory, the procession is in the foreground, a motley and frightening crew led by Time (as destroyer) pulled on a cart by two horses representing night and day, followed by Death on a sickly horse, and winged Fame on the back of an elephant, blowing his own trumpet. Scattered beneath their feet are the ephemeral accoutrements of earthly life – tools and weapons, symbols of authority, musical instruments, even the artist's palette and brushes – trampled unforgivingly by the passing procession. The artist, the composer, we all are victims of Time's triumph – though it is intriguing to note that, as Margaret Sullivan points out, Fame lives on.[13] In the background are those aspects of life which are eternally if intermittently present, what Birtwistle describes as 'recurrent procedures': the wind, the tides, peasants dancing round a maypole careless of the fact that they are to be overtaken by time and death. The attraction of such a picture to Birtwistle should be obvious: it presents in allegorical form the distinction between foreground and background, between a linear procession (cantus) and circular repetition (continuum). But the cantus in this case is not a single line. The composer reflects on the fact that Bruegel's procession is 'made up of a (necessarily) linked chain of material objects which have no necessary connexion with each other' and proposes his 'piece of music as the sum of musical objects, unrelated to each other, apart from one's decision to juxtapose them in time and space.'

The work begins with the background: a series of layered ostinatos, soft, low, slow-moving, repetitious, portentous. The first foreground event to be superimposed on this, the first 'material object' in the processional chain, is the cor anglais melody which appears at fig. 2 and which recurs twice more in the same form at about the mid-point (after fig. 19) and again at the very end (fig. 40) (Ex. 7.4). But, though the melody remains virtually the same, its context (continuum) is changed on each occasion: it moves, as it were, to different positions in the landscape. The actual structure of this melody – dependent on repetitions which are never exact – suggests something simultaneously timeless and progressive (stasis in progress) and raises interesting questions about the differences in the nature of the repetitions of foreground and background, of cantus and continuum. Writing about ideas in relation to the later *Secret Theatre*, Birtwistle mused:

> *Question* – at what point does an ostinato cease to function as such, due to the number of notes present in it? or the amount of time for it to register as a repeat – Why mention this? – Ostinato into melody perhaps . . .[14]

Take the final statement of the cor anglais melody. Here, the free cycling round a limited number of pitches (seven) draws attention to the fact that the melody shares something of the stasis of the background (regular ostinatos) which frames and contextualizes it, and yet its very unpredictability enables that stasis to be transcended, to point forward to a goal which remains in the infinite distance. There are fascinating parallels with the ending of *Melencolia I*.

Ex. 7.4. *The Triumph of Time*, fig. 2, cor anglais melody.

The seemingly isolated appearances of this melodic object are, to some degree, connected by related cantus-like material, such as that initiated by the cor anglais at fig. 6. Another 'object' which occurs more frequently is a three-note motif (E♭–G–D) for amplified soprano saxophone. The first of its appearances is made just after the first statement of the cor anglais melody (before fig. 3) and thereafter regularly punctuates the progress of the procession. This is not a line in itself, though it does point indexically to the existence of some sort of thread running through the piece, and it too spawns cantus-like lines such as the horn melody which begins at fig. 11. It is almost as if this motif is searching for its own linearity because, towards the end of the piece, it fractures and takes on a fuller melodic identity (see fig. 26), eventually proliferating outwards into all the woodwind at fig. 28 who loudly proclaim a climactic, heterophonous version of this melody (in Birtwistle's words it 'explodes . . . blossoming into a gigantic unison'). It is tempting to read the amplified saxophone as representing Fame with his trumpet in Bruegel's picture, though this would be to map Birtwistle's work too literally on to the engraving. Equally attractive is Hall's reading: 'Time the destroyer is revealed in all his terrible ruthlessness'.[15] And Samuel's commentary on *Gawain* is apposite here too: such 'isolated melodies and non-refrain motifs with independent significance emphasize the linear, developmental, non-ritualistic aspects' of the work.[16]

Other 'objects' which are carried along by the procession include literal quotations of Birtwistle's own music: most notably the brief *Chorale from a Toy-Shop* (after fig. 15) and the striking opening of *The Fields of Sorrow* whose octave Es are rescored with resounding bell-like clarity for harps, piano and metallic tuned percussion (fig. 21). It is an extraordinary moment. It is as if the procession has reached its closest point to the observer and comes fleetingly into full focus, before moving on again. The Es are quickly clouded, other elements intrude; the progress of the line is unstoppable. The line of *The Triumph of Time* is articulated in quite a different way from the essentially singular way in which it is presented in *Melencolia I* and *The Cry of Anubis*. Like the individual members of a procession, the components of this line are varied and often unrelated, but they share a common purpose, a common direction. The result is far from a mere collage of disparate fragments; the music's linear dimension sweeps all before it (the very triumph of time) not as a unifying force as such but as a common strand to which the different components of the cantus variously relate.

And so to the fundamental line in *Gawain*. Despite the simplicity and directness of Birtwistle's statements on this matter, it should not be assumed that a single melodic line can be traced weaving its way through the entire work. Nonetheless, there is a far more overt concern for narrative continuity in this work than in his earlier works for the stage – though we have also seen that Birtwistle has been exploring this linear impulse in many of his instrumental pieces – which manifests itself as cantus, broadly defined. In *Gawain*, true to the origins of the word, cantus becomes song. One of the most striking aspects of this opera is its ability to present subtle characterizations through the vocal lines: the 'objective' chorus-like commentaries of Morgan Le Fay and Lady de Hautdesert in Act 1 (strangely awkward in places, such as the recurrent 'This is the hour of legacy or loss' or the oddly garbled 'Now I shall test his strength with mine'); the wise but somewhat world-weary Arthur; the courteous, noble yet naïve Gawain who develops in Act 2 into a richly rounded character ('I'm not that hero'); the self-assured authority of the Green Knight. Indeed, it would seem that the techniques of characterization are much more conventionally (nineteenth-century) operatic than we have formerly encountered in Birtwistle. For example, the very first words of the Green Knight in Act 1 stamp his authority on the opera (Ex. 7.5a – 'Which of you is King?'), a falling figure with a complex of associations surrounding the Green Knight and courtly bravery throughout the work (compare with the recurring motif 'Who's brave?' first sung by Arthur early in Act 1 and reiterated by the Green Knight in setting out his challenge – Ex. 7.5b). It is linked to the very opening of the opera with its low falling line for trombones and tubas, and with the music accompanying the

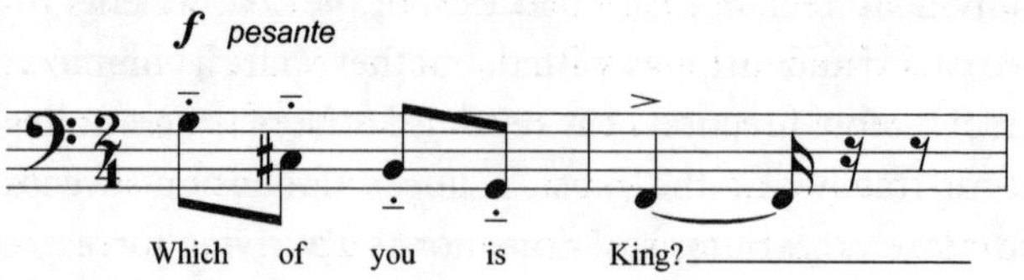

Ex. 7.5a. *Gawain*, Act 1, fig. 43 (Green Knight).

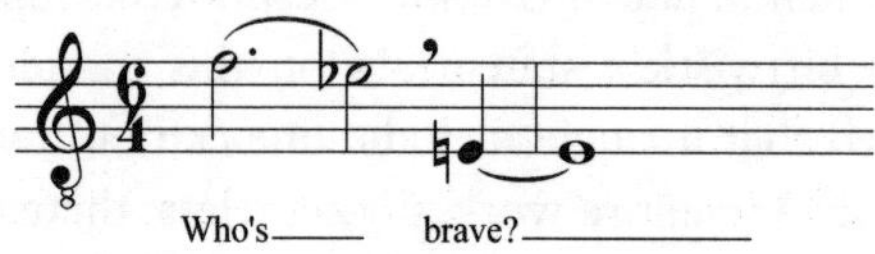

Ex. 7.5b. *Gawain*, Act 1, fig. 12 (Arthur).

opening of the door. There is no doubting the import of the first entry of the Knight on his horse: despite the pantomime aspect to some of this music (the sounds of trombone horse whinnies and 'coconut-shell' hooves), it has an immense dramatic force and sets the scene for what is to come (though achieved very differently, in dramatic effect this instrumental moment parallels the similarly rhythmic, highly charged music that signals and supports the arrival of Klytemnestra in Birtwistle's music for *Agamemnon* at the National Theatre).

The Green Knight's first major 'aria' (beginning 'Do you talk of victories') moves almost seamlessly from agitated parlando (quasi-recitative) through arioso to the declamatory – a climax of almost Bergian intensity. The beginning evinces the familiar cantus–continuum opposition where the orchestra (pizzicato low strings/brass/untuned percussion) has a kind of irregular ostinato while the voice exposes a line built from chromatic segments (G–A–B♭–A♭–B | E–D–E♭–C–D♭–D | etc.) and which follows the contour and rhythms of the words. The end of each vocal phrase is punctuated by a repeating triplet-semiquaver figure for tuned percussion and high violins. But there is also a single line doubled on wind instruments which counterpoints the voice, and which seems to stand somewhere between cantus and continuum. In its very linearity and the free way in which it cycles round its pitches it belongs with the cantus and provides continuity and a certain forward momentum; but the far greater restriction of its pitches and register suggest an affinity also with the continuum (recall Birtwistle's comments above on 'ostinato into melody'). The arioso passage ('I came here looking for a man whose courage shone . . .') again has a vocal line with a conventionally expressive profile but now supported by ominous low pedal notes and a line characterized by fourths and fifths which, like the earlier orchestral line, suggests an underlying continuity. The music moves to a D focus as the Knight declaims 'I know these songs; I know they make you hot; they leave me cold.' Low pedal notes again hint at a linear continuity which is temporarily suspended at the word 'cold' by brightly coloured repeating chimes and which is then picked up again by a new sustained instrumental line which supports the Knight's impassioned return to arioso with 'I came to find a man whose courage shone . . .'

What this description reveals is that, even in such a short section of the opera concerned essentially with 'song', there is not a single melodic line but a variety of kinds of cantus which generate a sense of continuity, and other sustained events (pedals, pitch focuses) which similarly suggest an essential linearity (the fundamental line). In *The Cry of Anubis* moments of tonal focus (D in the case of that work) are important in structuring the progress of the line. The music of *Panic* flows towards and away from particular pitch centres. And E dominates the closing scene of *The Second Mrs Kong*, in relation to which Birtwistle has also discussed an underlying line, a 'musical journey, . . . a sort of perpetual melody'.[17] In *Gawain*, too, the linearity of the music is made clear by the general movement towards and away from tonal focuses. One such important pitch is G, which is the first note of many of the Green Knight's lines and also relates, as Samuel has suggested, to the character of Gawain whose name is marked at significant points by the pitches G–B♭–G♭.[18] A prominent instance can be heard just before the commencement of Gawain's journey in Act 2: the boldly presented Gs support Gawain's cry, 'Cross of Christ,

Save me', and like the Knight's lines, this G then initiates an orchestral cantus (G–B♭–A♭–A–C–B♭–D♭–B, etc.). In Chapter 3, we saw Stravinsky's *Oedipus Rex* as a possible model for so many of Birtwistle's works, and while – despite the many formalized aspects of its structure – *Gawain*'s narrative impulse seems to share little with *Oedipus* as such, its use of 'tonal centres' bears useful comparison with Stephen Walsh's account (after Wilfred Mellers) of tonality in Stravinsky's work:

> Stravinsky still treats keys, as he treated modes in his Russian works, as static entities, rather than organic elements of grammar. Each of these tonalities . . . has a certain weight and a dramatic location comparable to the fixed position of each of the dramatis personae on the stage . . . Behind such writing lies the idea of tonality as the opposition of colours, rather than a system of relationships. But it also has to do with the importance Stravinsky attached to 'the musical interval'.[19]

Tonal focuses in *Gawain*, too, are not part of a functional grammar, and they most definitely carry a dramatic weight, though they are never so explicitly identified with characters or situations as in *Oedipus*. They signal key dramatic moments and draw attention to the movement of the 'line' towards and away from them. But to an extent (notwithstanding the importance of G as already discussed) the precise pitch of such centres can seem arbitrary. Birtwistle has admitted as much in relation to *Exody*. The composer recognizes the structural significance of the moment of the arrival on G towards the end of that work (bar 487), signalled by the tonal clarity, but the actual choice of pitch centre, he claims, was not premeditated and was arrived at merely as a consequence of working with the music which immediately preceded that moment.[20] What this suggests, once more, is that pitch focus (even a very generalized notion of tonality) is important to Birtwistle and is closely connected with the ideas of line and journey, but a journey whose origin is murky and whose destination is never reached ('Arriving at a certain place, I can see another point that I might try to get to, but I'll never get there'). Like Gawain's journey to the Green Chapel, his arrival is not a final destination but he discovers there things about himself that compel him to begin a new journey. The opera ends with an almost exact repetition of Morgan's words and music which had heralded Gawain's journey at the start of Act 2: 'Then with a single step your journey starts'. Despite its fundamental line, *Gawain* is essentially circular – a musical and dramatic web of repetitions and variations. And in relation to *The Second Mrs Kong* Birtwistle talked in Klee-like terms of a music that 'is always looping itself'.[21]

One of the clearest examples of the movement from one pitch focus to another is to be found in *The Fields of Sorrow*. In customary fashion, Birtwistle moves outwards symmetrically from opening octave Es, first to F and D♯, then gradually – but in no way predictably – filling out the entire chromatic space. The music becomes more dense, as new lines are generated (usually ostinatos) and are layered on top of one another, while other lines are doubled by a kind of organum technique (see for example the entry of the first soprano soloist doubling a fourth above the second soprano at letter C – though this is sometimes altered into a smaller interval). At the same time, solo wind instruments follow their rhetorically related but musically and temporally independent paths (cantus, perhaps?). Throughout, the E is virtually continuously present in the chorus. Just before letter D, the texture clears and the opening piano Es are regained, a process not altogether dissimilar to that found in the 'Introduction' to Stravinsky's *The Rite of Spring*. The music then follows a somewhat different course from the same starting-point, a new cantus emerging as a unison/octave line for horn and vibraphone. The Es in pianos and chorus are now expanded to the interval E–G♯, expressed both as an ascending third and a descending sixth. This is a much more compressed section than the first, and once the horn/vibraphone line has exposed the twelfth note of the chromatic (appropriately, an A♭ at 2 bars before letter F), it swiftly leads us to the next and final section in which the focus shifts to D.

The procedures of the opening section are now reviewed from the perspective of this new pitch centre, though by the end – despite the omnipresent Ds – the lowest notes of the pianos are reminding us of the E–G♯ from the second section. The shift of focus from E to D has a 'rightness' about it, partly because we are effectively led to it by what comes immediately before it, partly because D has in any case been in melodic proximity to E for much of the piece. The internal elements of the procession thus determine, to a degree, the logic of its own progress. But there is no *necessary* reason why we should arrive on D at letter F, any more than why the piece should finish when it does. What the pitch centres achieve is to point to the essential linearity of this music and provide a context for the emergence of other complementary lines. As in *Gawain*, one might argue that the music is here predicated on the idea of a single line but which manifests itself in multiple but related forms. What is also of interest here, as also in *Nomos* which preceded it, is that a distinction is suggested between two kinds of musical function: cantus and continuum. The desire of the cantus wind lines to escape the hegemony of the main ensemble clearly anticipates the physical movement of *Secret Theatre*'s cantus players away from the continuum.

So we see in *The Fields of Sorrow* Birtwistle, like Stravinsky in *Oedipus Rex*, treating pitch centres ('keys') 'as static entities, rather than organic elements of grammar'. Such single points of focus are clearly important to Birtwistle's music, though he has regularly claimed in recent years that his music is not principally about pitch, but interval.[22] Walsh's statement quoted above regarding the importance Stravinsky attached to 'the musical interval' is supported by a quotation from the *Conversations* where Stravinsky told Robert Craft that 'when I compose an interval I am aware of it as an object'.[23] This idea was also developed in the *Poetics* where Stravinsky asserts that 'our chief concern is not so much what is known as tonality as what one might term the polar attraction of sound, of an interval, or even of a complex of tones'.[24] There is strong evidence to suggest that Birtwistle, too, thinks in terms of intervals as 'objects' – or, we might say, motifs. The characteristic rising major third and falling perfect fourth of the recurrent saxophone motif in *The Triumph of Time* is an obvious case in point, an idea which the composer specifically identifies as a 'musical object'. Still more striking is the recurrence of particular intervals as objects across a number of his works employed as important structural signals. Perhaps the most prominent of these is the D–F motif which begins, ends and punctuates the linear course of *Secret Theatre*:

> . . . for *Secret Theatre* I drew up a lot of pre-compositional ideas about how things could progress, how they could get from point to point; I constructed a whole map, as it were. But then in the process of composition, in the journey, I went in other ways, so those original journeys are still there. I'm now writing an orchestral piece [*Earth Dances*] which will be a different facet of the same thing.[25]

Like the above account of the pitch focuses in *The Fields of Sorrow*, the D–F dyad is a kind of trace of Birtwistle's 'original journeys' to which the music keeps returning as the starting point for new journeys – one such becoming an entirely different piece, *Earth Dances*. The D–F object is certainly prominent in *Earth Dances* (especially at the final climax) and also recurs prominently in *Ritual Fragment* and even *Gawain*. In the case of the latter, Samuel identifies one important motif which she labels the 'axe' motif – because it occurs at the beheading of the Green Knight in Act 1 (fig. 81) and at the point in Act 2 where the Knight reciprocally swings the axe and grazes Gawain's neck (fig. 125). This has four pitches, D–F–D♭–E, the first two being in exactly the same register as the D–F motif in *Secret Theatre*. Samuel considers such independent motifs significant because they emphasize the linear, developmental, non-ritualistic aspects of the work. The connection between pitch focus ('tonality') and recurrent intervallic/motivic objects in both Stravinsky and Birtwistle is thus made clear: both techniques point to the presence of a 'fundamental' line in so many of Birtwistle's works, a line which is concerned with arrival and departure, a line on a 'journey', a line which in *Earth*

Dances becomes – to borrow Arnold Whittall's phrase – a '"tragedy" in which a feeling of "gravity" asserted, reasserted and finally lost is crucial'. Indeed, Whittall proposes *Earth Dances* almost as a sequel to *Melencolia I*; in part as a result of their shared exploration of time as stasis in progress, 'an anatomy of (human) melancholy which achieves a brief climax of assertion before sinking back into oneness with the natural world'.[26]

Birtwistle's recent references to film suggest interesting analogies with his idea of line. On the surface, his fascination with popular television and Hollywood blockbusters, both of which make a fetish of attempting to achieve an ever-greater naturalism, would seem to stand in sharp contrast to his own concerns with stylization and ritual. But he is also interested in art-house films and continually refers to the work and writings of Eisenstein.[27] He has also recently claimed that he would like to make a film, indeed that he would like to have been a film-maker. What interests him is the *process* of film-making whereby unrelated events can be shot out of sequence and then later edited and reassembled according to a governing narrative. For Birtwistle, the musical paradigm for such a technique is to be found in Stravinsky's *Symphonies of Wind Instruments* where – to use Edward T. Cone's celebrated terms – events are locally 'stratified' (that is, interrupted and juxtaposed in a mosaic-like manner) yet are made to 'interlock' on the larger scale (that is, a narrative is constructed which cuts across the local discontinuities).[28] In relation to *Yan Tan Tethera*, Birtwistle has talked in similar terms of a 'strophic superstructure as foreground and an organic substructure as background which are independent, or largely independent, of each other.'[29] And in relation to *Gawain* he has specifically suggested a comparison with film: 'He drew [a] line on a brown paper envelope – it spiralled around a circle . . . And he drew the repeated sections as rectangles on this circle . . .' ('like snapshots, or stills in a film').[30]

In fact, Birtwistle has, on one occasion, produced music for a film: Sidney Lumet's *The Offence* of 1973. He has spoken of writing the music independently of the film and then chopping it up

(Stravinksy fashion) into lengths to fit the cinematic sequences as required by the director. In one other obvious instance, Birtwistle has also engaged directly with film. He claims that the film sequences shown in *The Second Mrs Kong* are completely separate from the rest of the opera. On one level, and in all but one case, this is true – the exception being the showing of the sequence (in Act 2) where the celluloid Kong is shot at by aeroplanes and then topples from the Empire State Building, to which the orchestra provides its own 'soundtrack' replete with wood-block machine-gun fire and a mimetic descending figure passing through the wind as Kong falls. In all other cases, the orchestra falls silent, or sustains a single chord, as the film/video sequences are shown. In this sense, they are rather like the Passing Clouds and Allegorical Flowers from *The Mask of Orpheus*, whose appearance similarly brings about the suspension of activity elsewhere on the stage and in the orchestra pit. But to say that the film sequences are unconnected to what surrounds them is not strictly true: what seems to interest Birtwistle is the way in which he can mediate between two very different media, how he can form a transition between two seemingly opposed kinds of material.

The idea of transition has long fascinated him. In certain works one finds transitional material taking on a greater significance as the music proceeds. One bold example is the transitional sections in *Carmen Arcadiae Mechanicae Perpetuum* which both separate and mediate between the juxtaposed blocks of musical material. Cone's term for such passages as they occur in Stravinsky's *Symphonies* is a 'bridge', a device for 'mitigating the starkness of the opposition between strata . . . an area with a life of its own . . . Although acting as a bridge in the immediate context, it reaches forward to its next appearance in the interlocking pattern.'[31] In *Carmen*, the 'bridge' signals the start of the piece as a simple sustained pitch (E in the horn) and a sharp, punctuating chord on marimba and piano; by the end of the piece it has grown into lengthy series of sustained and punctuating chords, becoming almost another section or 'mechanism' to add to the six Birtwistle identifies. Indeed, the irony is that successive statements of the bridge (refrain) interlock across the work to form a stratum which is seemingly far more continuous than any other in the piece, engendering a sense of continuity, a 'line' even. The problem for Birtwistle in *Mrs Kong* was a similar one: how to build a bridge between film soundtrack and orchestral music which mitigates the starkness of the opposition without undermining the necessity of that opposition (that is, without destroying the artifice of the narrative-within-the-narrative). Uncharacteristically, Birtwistle has talked of a *musical* work that provides a model for understanding his thinking: he is intrigued by the way in which Brahms gets from the theme to the first variation in the *Variations on a Theme of Haydn* – a 'seamless transition' as he describes it – interestingly, a pulse on a single note.[32] The solution in *Mrs Kong* was a very simple one: create a sustained chord for the orchestra from a pitch or pitches of the soundtrack, bring in that pitch/chord almost imperceptibly while the film is playing so that the audience only slowly becomes aware of its presence and then use it to lead back into the 'opera proper', often forming the basis for new musical departures. The starkness of the contrast is successfully mitigated, a transition is effected, yet the differences between the 'film' and 'opera' worlds remain – a fact made plain by what the stage characters subsequently sing. For instance, after the first film interpolation (Act 1, fig. 98), Kong sings, 'I'm not the giant head, the giant hand, the little puppet moving on the screen . . . there never was a giant ape!'; and after the second (Act 1, fig. 115), Pearl sings, 'Is this the Kong who never was? This is not the one whose voice I heard!' The effect is somewhat akin to a fade (as opposed to a sharp cut) between two distinctly different film scenes which are nonetheless held together by some underlying narrative thread.

A slightly different example of the way in which a transition grows in structural significance can be found in the beautifully poignant Passion Chorales from *Punch and Judy*. Pruslin provided Birtwistle with a formalized text of seven lines where the length of each line, Dylan Thomas-like, is successively reduced by one syllable on each occasion as follows:

Passion Chorale I

Day murdered fame one game lost
Dreamer dread flaming lust
Deforming lameness
Deaf or nameless
Demon dared
Dam-ned
Dumb

Birtwistle is not interested in just slavishly following the structure provided by the librettist. Throughout the work, music and text complement rather than reinforce one another, just as themes of balanced opposition dominate the text itself ('the sweetness of this moment is unendurably bitter', etc.). The vertical, homophonic setting here of the text for the chorus is counterbalanced by the linear trumpet figure which connects successive lines; that is, which provides the musical transition one might find, say, in a chorale prelude. The trumpet connects the first two lines with a three-note figure (C♯–F–D); between the second and third lines, two more notes are added to this (C♯–F–D–C–G); between the third and fourth, a further note (C♯–F–D–C–G–F♯); and so on, until by the time the chorus has just one syllable to sing ('Dumb', appropriately), the trumpet's melody has grown to fourteen notes employing ten different pitch classes. What began as transition has, by the end, become the primary musical idea. Striking parallels with Klee's thinking present themselves here. In the first part of the *Pedagogical Sketchbook*, Klee discusses what he calls 'productive and receptive movement' where a work can be produced by either an additive or a subtractive method, both processes being 'time-bound'. Importantly, Klee here recognizes the significance of 'counter-movement'.[33] This is precisely the situation as it occurs in the Passion Chorales. A similar situation can be encountered in Zinovieff's libretto for the arches structure of Act 2 of *The Mask of Orpheus* where, for each arch (each of which corresponds to a verse of the Second Song of Magic) the temporal proportion of 'nightmare' to 'dream' increases progressively and systematically.[34]

Such discussion of lines and bridges in Birtwistle might suggest parallels with Wagner's notions of 'endless melody' and the 'art of transition'. Many of Birtwistle's projects can be (superficially at least) evaluated in Wagnerian terms, from the epic *Gesamtkunstwerk* that is *The Mask of Orpheus* (even, like *The Ring*, down to the gap in its composition between Acts 2 and 3 resulting, as in *Siegfried*, in a significant reassessment of musical priorities), to the *Parsifal*-like nature of *Gawain*. Concerns with myth and Greek theatre, with retelling, with 'strophic superstructure as foreground and an organic substructure as background' are common to both composers. Wagner's name has cropped up with increasing frequency in Birtwistle's public utterances of recent years. In reality, what fascinates him most in Wagner, it would seem, is the orchestral interludes in *The Ring* which he has described as Wagner's 'arias', by which he means the 'flowering of the musical moment'.[35] But presumably these interludes must also impress him as musico-dramatic devices of transition, whether taking us, for example, from the shattered world of the Wanderer to the realm of the sleeping Brünnhilde in Act 3 of *Siegfried*, or Siegfried's Funeral March in Act 3 of *Götterdämmerung*, or even the magical transformation between scenes 1 and 2 of Act 1 of *Parsifal* where, through music alone, Parsifal is led by Gurnemanz into the hall of the Knights of the Grail. Birtwistle's music is never like this, though one can quickly identify moments in his operas – such as the final act of *The Mask of Orpheus* or the final scene of *The Second Mrs Kong* – where one experiences a parallel musical flowering. It soon becomes apparent that Birtwistle's notion of a fundamental melodic line is neither endless melody nor permanent transition but rather something more elusive, a substructure which underpins the music, an idea which is constantly being alluded to but which is not literally present in the music at all times.

At least, not in the case of a work of the proportions of *Gawain*. But in some smaller-scale pieces the fundamental melodic line is absolutely clear and omnipresent. Take, for example, the simple but effective pieces for two flutes called *Duets for Storab* written in

1983 while Birtwistle was still living on the remote island of Raasay, close to the Isle of Skye, off the north-west coast of Scotland. The directness of these pieces is, in part at least, a consequence of Birtwistle's close adoption of aspects of a significant vernacular musical tradition, namely the *piobaireachd*, that most highly developed of musical forms for the Highland bagpipes with its characteristic modality, drones, decorative figurations and variation structure (a direct tribute, indeed, to his island: until 1858 the Mackays of Raasay were a notable piping family). Essentially a form of theme and variations, the *piobaireachd* is based on a single-line melodic theme or ground known as the *urlar*. Birtwistle follows this pattern, naming his first piece 'Urlar' which presents the material to be explored and elaborated in the subsequent five 'variations' (though he does not designate them as such) entitled 'Stark pastoral', 'Fanfare with birds', 'White pastoral', 'From the Church of Lies' and 'Crunluath'. The fundamental melodic line of 'Urlar', focused on the note D and decorated with grace-note-like figurations typical of a native *urlar*, forms the paradigm for the 'variations'.[36] It is typical of Birtwistle that, once again, he should choose to work with a formal device which allows him to explore multiple aspects of his material (variations) on many levels, both within and across individual movements – yet a further instance of viewing the same object from ever-changing perspectives. That such procedures relate to the larger scale is immediately apparent if one examines the composer's claims for *Gawain* (as mediated via Rhian Samuel) and compares them with the procedures just outlined for *Duets for Storab*:

> The composer explains that *Gawain* is built on a fundamental melodic line whose progress he describes visually in three dimensions – it spirals around a basically circular path . . . Embellishment of this line is a prime means of generating material, though organum-like, almost-parallel voices are also added.[37]

Such spiralling and embellishment can be seen clearly in 'White pastoral' (Ex. 7.6). Its materials are severely limited: each flute

Ex. 7.6. *Duets for Storab*, 'White pastoral'.

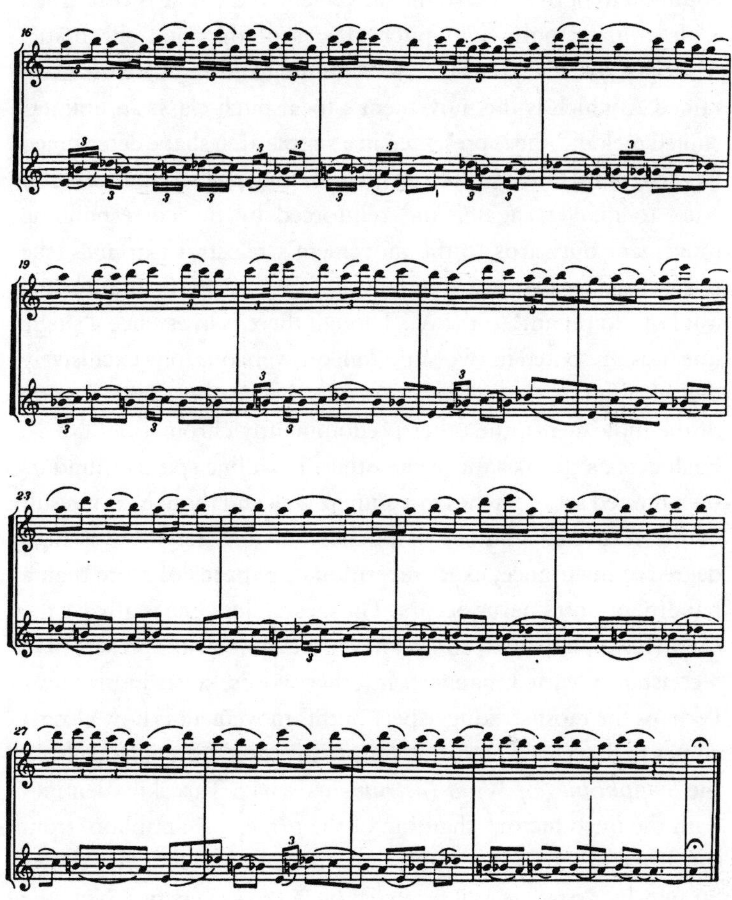
16
19
23
27

has only six pitches whose register is fixed; four pitch classes are common to both flutes, so the movement as a whole is concerned with utilizing only eight pitch classes of the total chromatic, namely A, B♭, B, C, D♭, D, E, G. Beginning and ending with a sustained A which is the movement's focal pitch class, an uninterrupted melodic line is presented in a simple arch shape determined by the general movement from quavers to triplet semiquavers and back to quavers again, and reinforced by the corresponding movement outwards to the movement's registral extremes (the pitch class E – first heard in bars 12–13 – acting as an informal kind of 'dominant' to the A). Though there is in essence a single line, it is presented in two simultaneous versions, one exclusively diatonic (flute 1 uses 'white' notes only, hence – possibly – the title of the movement), the other predominantly chromatic (flute 2). Each acts as the variant of the other. Each line spirals round its own limited set of pitches in a similar way and though, as a result of the restricted number of pitches and register there is high degree of invariance, exact repetition of patterns of more than a handful of notes never occurs. Thus, each flute line is always the same (fixed pitch field) and yet never the same twice (presented in a constantly varied manner). In other words, stasis in progress. Perhaps the most striking aspect of this movement is how close it comes to Stravinsky, most obviously the three-flute episode from the *Symphonies of Wind Instruments* which Taruskin identifies with the introductory chanting of the *pripev* or 'antiphon' from the Russian Orthodox Office of the Dead.[38] Ex. 7.7 shows Stravinsky's passage as it occurs at fig. 6 (1947 version). Note the diatonic melody – G♭, A♭, B♭, C♭, D♭ – with its chromatic accompaniment – C♭, C, D♭, D, E♭, F♭ – and also the manner in which the basic quaver motion of the melody is decorated by triplet semiquavers. Taruskin emphasizes the 'points of contact between the *Symphonies* and Stravinsky's earlier work as well as his Russian heritage';[39] likewise, the points of contact between Birtwistle's 'White pastoral' and *piobaireachd* are significant. Both composers have chosen to work with 'found' materials and techniques which are absolutely appropriate to their own compositional prac-

Ex. 7.7. Stravinsky, *Symphonies of Wind Instruments*, figs 6–8 (1947 version).

tices. One final point worth noting about *Duets for Storab* which anticipates procedures we have already identified in *Gawain* and elsewhere is the important role played by particular focal pitches in indicating the presence of the line. In the outer movements this is D. 'Crunluath' is a close recomposition of 'Urlar', an almost improvisatory trope or commentary on the original theme (my allusion to Boulez-like terminology here is not without good reason); the continual presence of the D is a strong indicator of this music's essential linearity.

Examples of similar procedures can be found in many of Birtwistle's works from the earliest to the most recent. Though Michael Hall rather overstates this matter by elevating the idea of 'melody' to an over-generalized principle – 'all Birtwistle's music, no matter how dense and rich it may be, is essentially monody'[40]

– such a view would certainly seem to be true of one of the earliest examples, as its very title suggests. The *Monody for Corpus Christi* was only Birtwistle's second published work. It begins in the simplest manner with a soprano monody which exposes a five-note chromatic set (F♯, G, G♯, A, B♭), widely distributed, the horn's entry on B extending this set and providing a focal pitch as pedal point (see Ex. 7.8a). In general terms, this sets the pattern for the rest of this twelve-minute piece: the 'monody' unfolds throughout the work, while the instrumental lines proliferate outwards from it, at times taking on a life of their own (the second movement is for the three instrumentalists alone). B remains the primary (not the only) pitch focus throughout. Look, for instance, at the closing bars of the first movement where the voice exposes the entire chromatic in smaller chromatic segments starting from B/F♯ and returning to B for a setting of the crucial words 'Corpus Christi', itself a reworking of the opening phrase (bars 95–110, see Ex. 7.8b). The flute accompanies with an elaborate kind of organum.

Ex. 7.8a. *Monody for Corpus Christi* (opening).

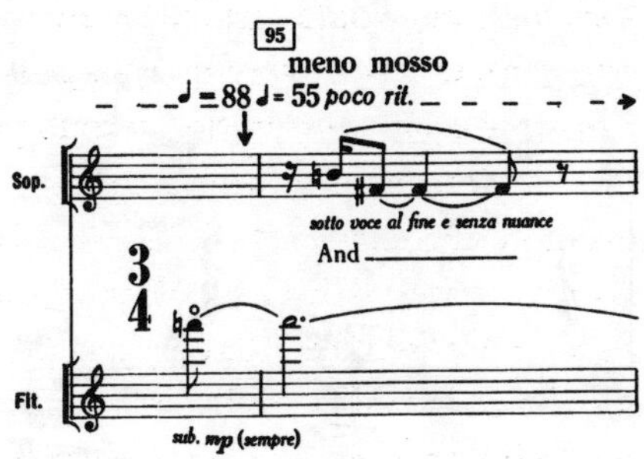

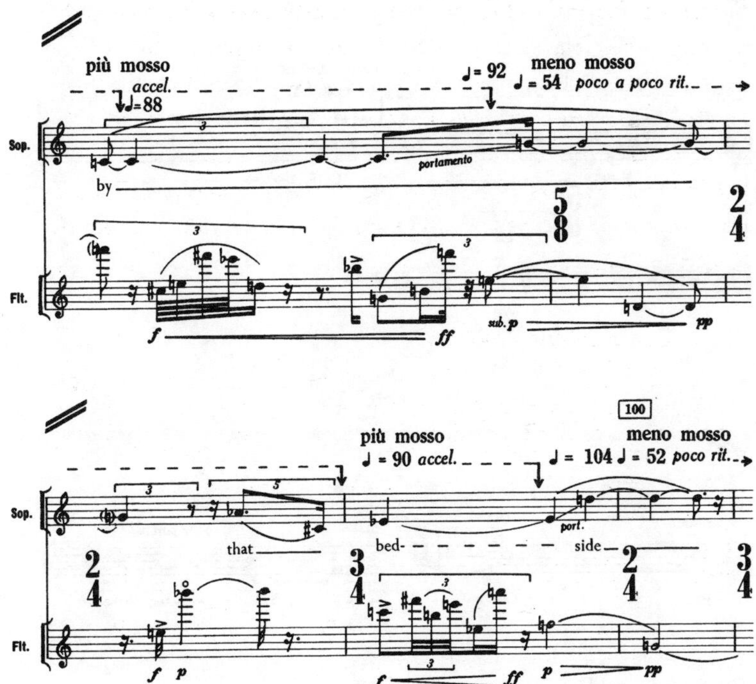

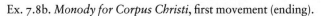

Ex. 7.8b. *Monody for Corpus Christi*, first movement (ending).

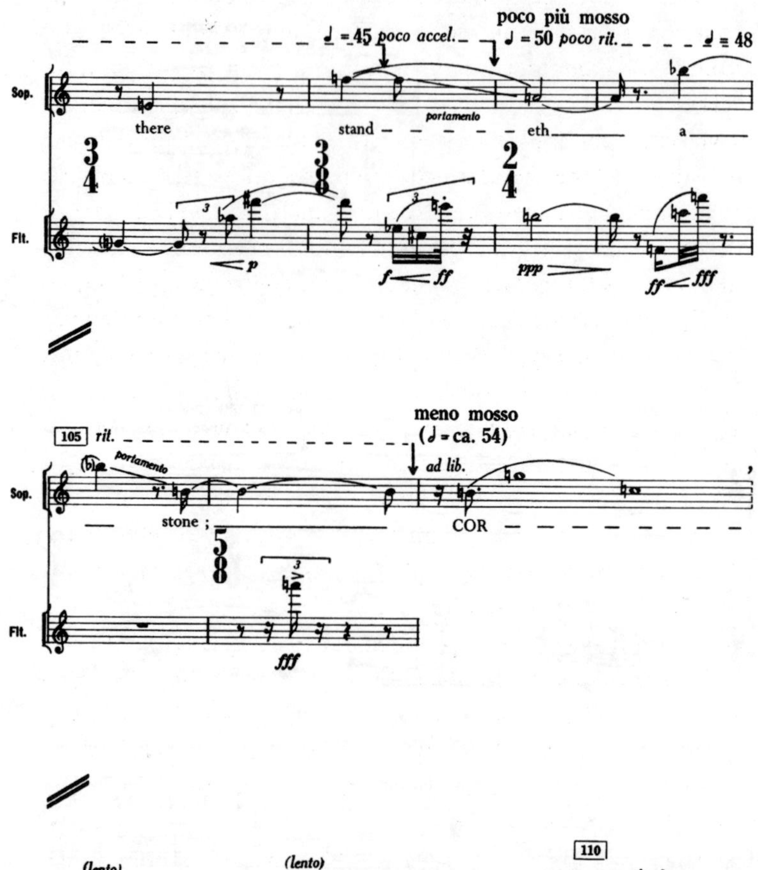
poco più mosso
♩ = 45 poco accel.
♩ = 50 poco rit.
♩ = 48
Sop.
Flt.
there
stand
portamento
eth
a
105 rit.
meno mosso
(𝅗𝅥 = ca. 54)
ad lib.
portamento
stone ;
COR
(lento)
(lento)
110
quasi parlando
PUS
CHRI
portamento
STI
writ–ten there on.
attacca

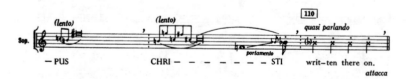

Ex. 7.8b (cont'd).

Much more recently, the (elaborated) D drone that is a virtually continuous presence in the viola throughout 'White and Light' from *Pulse Shadows* is again an indicator of an important musical linearity. As in *Monody*, the basic idea is extremely simple. Two heterophonous lines stand either side of the central drone: the voice and the two clarinets above, the cello and bass below, almost acting as melody and bass in counterpoint. (The origins of the manner in which the clarinets 'echo' the vocal line probably stem back as far as early twentieth-century Viennese techniques of *Klangfarbenmelodie*, and is certainly familiar from similar effects found in, say, Berio and Boulez – see, for example, Berio's *O King* of 1968 and Boulez's . . . *explosante-fixe* . . . begun in 1971 *in memoriam* Stravinsky.) The process by which the melody unfolds is a familiar one, namely the progressive exposure of chromatic segments (E, D, F, D♭, E♭ at the start, for example). It is interesting that the prominent E of the opening melody, taken with the D drone and the C in cello and bass suggests the possibility of a controlling background symmetry, but one that is not actually realized on the musical surface.

An Interrupted Endless Melody exaggerates the opposed characteristics we have come to identify with cantus and continuum. The eponymous melody for oboe is a flexible, freely flowing line, while each of the three alternative piano accompaniments is, in essence, a sequence of varied ostinatos (mobiles), restricted in pitch and rhythm (note the familiar scotch snaps in the first of the three). The melody is endless because it is looped – the 'end' leads back to the 'beginning'. The player can choose to start at any of three (identical) points and finishes when the piano part is completed. The interruptions are brought about by giving the player the option to leapfrog certain passages in the melody. Multiple views are in-built by inviting the player to decide at various points between one of two alternative routes, each a variant of the other. A performance can consist either of the melody with one accompaniment only, or of all three forming a three-movement work, or of interspersing movements between other pieces in a programme. The melody perfectly encapsulates Birtwistle's interpretation of stasis in progress: the linear and the circular collapse into each other.

Whether we take Birtwistle's declaration about the fundamental melodic line in *Gawain* at face value as, for example, Hall's understanding of the composer's essentially monodic structures would suggest, and as is realized in such pieces as *Monody for Corpus Christi*, *Nomos* and *Linoi*, or whether we treat the notion of line more loosely as in Klee's celebrated formulation, or whether we take into account the more sophisticated opposition of Grass's notion of stasis in progress as explored in *Melencolia I* and elsewhere – not least in the balance of the linear/progressive and the circular/ritualized in *Gawain* – what is clear is that line is at the heart of Birtwistle's musical thinking, manifesting itself variously as monody and cantus, processional and narrative. Increasingly, the use of clear pitch focuses have been used to emphasize the linear in his music, to signal the presence of a line, a line which – like tonality itself – is concerned with departure and arrival. Pevsner claimed that 'line, not body' was the fundamental characteristic of English art and architecture; the line in Birtwistle might suggest a deep-lying (English) lyrical impulse which has been heard with growing clarity in his recent works. Line in becoming cantus literally becomes song.

8 *Exodos* – Futures

Orpheus invented music for himself and recognized its immense power. With only his own song and to the accompaniment of a lyre, he won the love of Euridice, and was able to charm his way even into the underworld. He lost his lover twice, once to a serpent's venom, once to his own weakness. On both occasions he consoled himself in song, lamenting his grievous loss:

> . . . He himself
> Sought with his lyre of hollow tortoiseshell
> To soothe his love-sick heart, and you, sweet wife,
> You on the desolate shore alone he sang,
> You at return, you at decline of day.[1]

Orpheus's love songs and Orpheus's laments resound throughout the music of Birtwistle. These are his 'Love Cries'. Like Orpheus, Birtwistle has discovered music for himself. Like Orpheus, he recognizes its boundless expressive power. For Birtwistle, music is primitive, music is passionate. In every one of his works he explores musical and human fundamentals in such a way that it seems as if every piece is beginning again out of nothing. It is a music that is both utterly modern and utterly ancient. Every work is the same, yet none is ever the same. Birtwistle always challenges; he always offers new perspectives.

Birtwistle's newest opera, *The Last Supper*, will be premièred in 2000, first in Germany, then by Glyndebourne Touring Opera in Britain. As far as one can tell at this stage in its composition (at the time of writing, Birtwistle has completed only half of the opera),[2] the work represents a return to the world of *Gawain*. (It inevitably conjures up associations with *Parsifal*.) Robin Blaser's text appears more like Harsent's than Hoban's highly self-conscious libretto for *The Second Mrs Kong*: it has a more 'poetic' character; it is less 'busy'. (This parallel between Harsent and Blaser is in part borne out by the fact that Birtwistle recently interrupted the composition of the opera to write *The Woman and the Hare*, a setting of a specially commissioned text by David Harsent for soprano, narrator and ensemble, premièred in March 1999. He has also asked Harsent to write the libretto for his Covent Garden opera, *The Minotaur*.) This seems to have resulted in a greater attention to the words than has often been the case in Birtwistle, a desire to allow the words to be heard, and a consequent sparseness of musical texture, which contrasts with the density of a number of his more recent pieces, most notably *Exody*. It is also a much more stylized work, less concerned with the sort of narrative issues that were important in *Mrs Kong*. This is confirmed by the important role played by the chorus, as commentator and as intermediary with the audience. The chorus sings in Latin, thus differentiating itself from the solo disciples, who sing in the vernacular (Latin being both the language of the Christian liturgy and the objectivizing, 'dead' language of Stravinsky's *Oedipus Rex*).

It is the theatrical, ritual and dramatic possibilities of the situation and story of the Last Supper that, as always, seem to have prompted so many of Birtwistle's musical ideas here. He seems anxious that he should create a continuum between stage and audience. One of the ways in which this will be achieved is through the use of two raised platforms at the far left and right extremes of the orchestra pit. At key dramatic moments, at moments of important structural articulation, pairs of solo instrumentalists will take up their positions on these daises so that they will be in full view of the audience. At the start, two trumpets will ring out fanfare figures: a Monteverdian call-to-order, echoing the start of *Punch and Judy*, as well as the two trumpets calling from their platforms at the front of the stage at the start and close of *Verses for Ensembles*. At other moments, Birtwistle's characteristic, darkly coloured soloists will mount these stages-within-the-stage – the precise instruments are as yet undecided, but they will probably be taken from pairs of cor anglais, violas, alto flutes, clarinets.

One duet has already been written: that for a pair of trombones, instruments with a strong (pre-classical) ceremonial pedigree. They hocket in quasi-medieval fashion across the pit while the soloists are singing Blaser's new English translation of the Lord's Prayer (continuous chant), and the chorus are doing the same but in Latin ('Pater noster', more fragmentary). This is doubled by an electronic 'chorus resonans', a transformed version of the stage chorus on tape, fed back into the auditorium, and has the function of creating a sense of space through resonance – compare this with the techniques Birtwistle employed in *The Mask of Orpheus* (the voice and signals of Apollo), *The Second Mrs Kong* (the Mirror) and *Antiphonies* (piano plus percussion). But it also further serves to weave a thread between stage and audience. This moment is preceded by a very interesting passage of pseudo-Palestrina polyphony – the appropriate musical topic for the drama, Birtwistle asserts, but with the composition of which he struggled for some time. The Lord's Prayer/'Pater noster' concludes with the word 'Amen', sung by Judas, who has entered unnoticed. Immediately, the music changes, and the musico-dramatic argument moves in an entirely new direction (most likely this will prove to be another significant moment of *anagnorisis* and *peripeteia*). As so often before, Birtwistle finds his strongest musical response to strongly defined dramatic events.

The Last Supper is no 'source opera'. Nonetheless, Birtwistle's fascination with stylized musical forms from the past continues to resonate through this work. Bach's Passions were one of the models for *Punch and Judy*, and here too the ceremonial of their choruses, their arias of poetic reflection, their carefully articulated dramatic turning-points, are all alluded to. Consciously or unconsciously, Birtwistle's violas echo the poignancy of the pair of viole d'amore which support the tenor's bitter-sweet aria, 'Erwäge, wie sein blutgefärbter Rücken', or the terrible stillness, the sorrowful joy of the viola da gamba in the aria 'Es ist vollbracht, from the *St John Passion*. The laments of Bach and Birtwistle have much in common. Their shared formality, their musical and dramatic stylization, their deeply melancholic expressivity belong to the same world. Like Bach's tellings of the passion story, Birtwistle recognizes that in choosing the Last Supper, he is dealing with 'a big subject'. '"Drink this in remembrance of me" . . . It's the initiation of something completely new. It's a beginning – an ending and a beginning. There are loads of musical and formal possibilities.'[3]

Each of the disciples will be individually musically characterized. But, like the obligato orchestral instruments, the disciples will enter in pairs too, each (as the composer conceives it) at the back of the stage, slowly moving forward towards the audience. This reinforces an understanding of the work more as a tableau than an opera – an 'opera-oratorio', perhaps, to use Stravinsky's designation. Ritual is brought to the fore. And at three moments during the course of the work the main action will be suspended (reminiscent of *Orpheus*'s Passing Clouds) for the presentation of punctuating, contrasting, stylized tableaux which look backwards and forwards: to the crowing of the cock at Peter's denial, to the crucifixion, and to the garden. Time and its representation are again central concerns.

The next major work that Birtwistle will write after the completion of *The Last Supper* will also be an opera, at present named *The Minotaur*, to a scenario by the late Friedrich Dürrenmatt. It contains all those themes which appeal to Birtwistle: it is a well-known myth; it is centred on another 'satyr', in this case a creature with a man's body but a bull's head, a wild creature who, like Kong, dances with a girl; it takes place in a labyrinth; it is concerned with mirrors and reflections; time is again cyclic, a story of birth and death. In Birtwistle's account of the scenario, as related to Hall, he characteristically teases out its formal possibilities as well as the familiar theme of retelling: 'The whole piece is a series of duets . . . Moving between text and dance must be done in a properly constructed way . . . And because you're doing things by means of mirrors, you could make the second act a mirror of the first, a different representation of the same story.'[4] Picasso, too, was fascinated by the Minotaur. It became the dominant recurrent image of his later work, partly an aspect of self-portrait perhaps, but an archetypal symbol nonetheless of deep, earthy violent emotions and urges, most powerfully transposed into a representation of man's animalistic inhumanity to man in his 1937 *Guernica* picture. What is also fascinating is that Picasso went through a period of painting canvas after canvas of Minotaurs, each new picture looking at the same essential theme from a slightly different perspective. It remains to be seen how Birtwistle chooses to represent his Minotaur. But in a sense we already know, because the same mythical creature – half human, half animal – has already manifested itself many times: as Punch, as Kong, as Anubis, even, one might argue, as the part-man, part-god Orpheus. He himself recognizes *The Minotaur*'s strong parallels with *The Mask of Orpheus*: 'It seemed to be a genuine extension of the Orpheus idea. But of course you can't repeat Orpheus. It'll be very different form Orpheus and yet belong to a similar type of theatricality.'[5]

That Birtwistle is highly likely to continue to explore the same body of ideas and techniques into the future is clearly suggested by one of his most recent and simplest of pieces. The *Three Niedecker Verses* were commissioned and published by the journal *Tempo* to celebrate the ninetieth birthday of Elliott Carter in 1998.[6] Birtwistle's composition occupies just two pages of the journal and is a setting of texts by Lorine Niedecker for soprano and cello. The texts are typical for Birtwistle in their pastoral imagery of river, tree and flowers, of time, of death and life. The three verses are organized into an informal ABA shape, with the outer verses exploring similar musical materials in similar ways, the second verse offering a slightly different perspective (only in the second verse are voice and cello vertically coordinated). All three verses share a related melancholic *Affekt* achieved in part through the obsessive way in which pitch and duration are treated. The second verse is given as Ex. 8.1. The manner of the expansion of the vocal line outwards registrally from its initial pitch to reach its highest and longest note on the final word, 'sun',

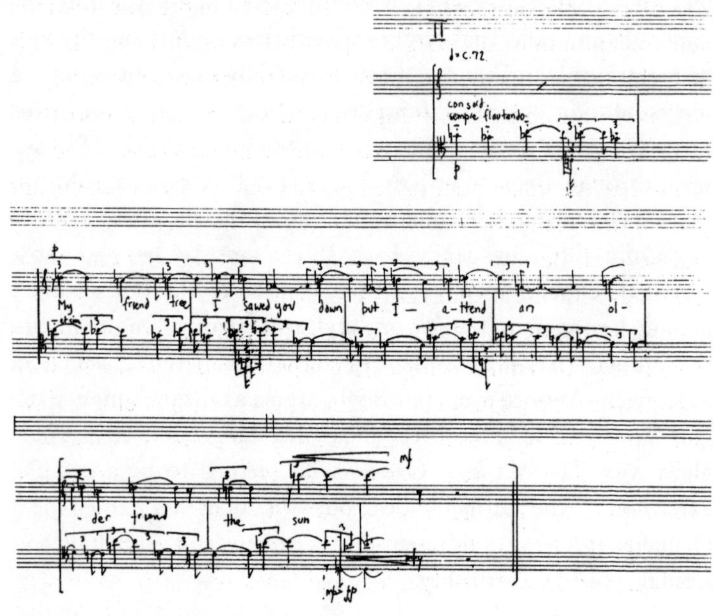

Ex. 8.1. *Three Niedecker Verses*, II.

is a familiar rhetorical device. The gravitation of this line around the initial D is also familiar from more recent works (not least the Celan settings), and is echoed in the registrally distinct D of the cello, its lowest and shortest note. The pitches of both lines are drawn from two symmetrically organized sets of pitch classes:

SOPRANO: C D♭ D E♭ – G♭ – A♭ A B♭ B
CELLO: F G♭ G A♭ A – B C D♭ D E♭

though this symmetry is not formally evident in their actual registral placement. Both lines follow the same kinds of contour but in independent ways. All these structural issues and expressive concerns were evident in Birtwistle's first published work, *Refrains and Choruses*; though continually reinterpreted as appropriate to new contexts and a new age, they remain essentially unchanged in his most recent works.

*

The place of the music of Harrison Birtwistle in the culture of the new millennium is, of course, impossible to predict. But there is little doubt that his music will continue to inspire and enrich, as well as irritate and infuriate, as it has already done for more than forty years. Performers and promoters, musicologists and informed critics have guaranteed Birtwistle's work a significant place in the history of European music of the twentieth century and beyond. But it is also interesting to chart the fact that as his standing with the cognoscenti has grown, so there has been a counterbalancing popular force in the opposite direction, identifying Birtwistle's music with all that is perceived to be wrong with twentieth-century musical modernism: inaccessible, élitist, difficult, noisy, incomprehensible. A letter written to the *Guardian* newspaper on 20 March 1999 from an ordinary music lover and amateur musician is typical of its kind: the writer complained that he was 'sick of being lectured so patronisingly by musical snobs who sneer at those of us who like real tunes and melodies in preference to the tinnitus-inducing cacophony of, say, Harrison Birtwhistle [*sic*]'. Such attitudes to modernism are strongly entrenched in the British culture, especially given the fact that progressive continental modernism was a comparatively late arrival. The most widely publicized and best received première of a new British work in recent decades was, ironically, Anthony Payne's 1998 completion of Elgar's Third Symphony, commissioned by the BBC in 1932 and left unfinished at the composer's death two years later. Despite the extraordinary achievements of Birtwistle and his contemporaries in the 1960s and 1970s in opening up British musical culture to rich and diverse influences from around the world, the success of Elgar's Third evinces a popular desire for a return to earlier (tonal) values and a deeply rooted antagonism towards the new – a reactionism supported, even driven, by the commercial forces of the likes of the classical music radio station, Classic FM. Modernism has still not been fully accepted in 1990s Britain.

The clearest evidence of the way in which Birtwistle's music has become a battleground for the conflicting views of his supporters and detractors was witnessed in the reactions to the 1995 Proms première of *Panic*. Of course, placing anything new, let alone a raucous concerto for saxophone and drum-kit, among the conventional pot-pourri of nationalistic 'Last Night' confectionery was guaranteed to upset the traditionalists. But what was unprecedented was the extreme way in which different sectors of the British press used the occasion to claim Birtwistle for their cause. For the tabloid and right-of-centre press (the popular voice of ordinary working people) he was caricatured as the bogeyman of élitist culture: *Panic* was the 'Last Fright of the Proms' (*Today*), 'unmitigated rubbish' (*Daily Express*), an 'atrocity of epic proportions' (*The Spectator*). For the broadsheet newspapers (representatives of the bourgeoisie) he became the lone hero of contemporary British art: *Panic* offered 'brief, magical breaths' (*The Times*), it 'revealed wonders only Birtwistle could have found' (*Daily Telegraph*), it was 'utterly, utterly marvellous' (*Observer*). The debate was unhelpfully polarized and it is probably true to say that Birtwistle's reputation – for good and for bad – has never fully recovered.

Birtwistle does not try to court controversy. He asks for neither paeans nor brickbats. He merely does what he does in the only way he knows how, and will continue to do so. 'There are no choices any more: I know exactly where I want to go. One thing suggests the next . . . I can only do one thing, and there is nothing else.'[7] It must be hurtful when his sincerely and carefully conceived efforts are described by a correspondent to the weekly *Radio Times* following the *Panic* première as 'a complete cacophony of unrhythmic, unmelodious and unmusical sounds'. This is blatant nonsense. But equally he is highly impatient with sycophants, with critics who claim an exaggerated status for his work. For him, his music is essentially very simple, because it is concerned with the fundamentals of musical structure, with pulse, melody, repetition and variation, and with the quest after appropriate contexts that can give shape to deep feelings and ideas – hence his ongoing preoccupations with myth and ritual, with formal theatre and stylized drama.

For me, the power of Birtwistle's music lies neither in one position nor the other, but in its skilful balancing of the progressive and the traditional. It is on those aspects of his music that most clearly align him with radical twentieth-century modernism – its fragmentation, its instrumental extremes, its expressionism, its temporal multiplicity, its apparently complex organization of pitch and rhythm, and so on – that his supporters and his detractors alike have so often focused. But equally his music is preoccupied with much older formal and expressive values which manifest themselves in the subject matter with which he chooses to work, in his music's essentially simple linearity, in its use of verse-refrain forms, of recitative and aria, of chorus, in its adoption of conventional topics of lament and celebration. His is, in the broadest sense, a tragic art that attempts to contain the primordial impulses of Dionysus within the rational forms of Apollo. And he continues to explore the deep, primeval aspects of the human psyche, to articulate through music those truths which language is incapable of expressing. Whatever the future may hold for Harrison Birtwistle and his music, and in whatever ways his work will be received and understood by future generations, we can at the end of the twentieth century say with confidence that his unique vision has changed for good the music of our own age, and has given us all – listeners, performers, composers, musicologists – the opportunity to look afresh at ourselves, to see anew the reality around us. What more could one possibly ask of any art?

Notes

Prologue – Preface and Acknowledgements

1 Birtwistle in conversation with Paul Griffiths, *New Sounds, New Personalities: British Composers of the 1980s* (London: Faber Music/Faber and Faber, 1985), p. 188
2 'Harrison Birtwistle', in Lewis Foreman, ed., *British Music Now* (London: Elik, 1975), p. 60
3 See Friedrich Nietzsche, *The Birth of Tragedy* (1872)

1 *Parados* – Origins, Contexts, Models

1 Niklaus Pevsner, *The Englishness of English Art* (Harmondsworth: Penguin/Peregrine, 1964; 1st pub. 1956), p. 136
2 Ibid., pp. 153, 137, 177
3 See Michael Hall, *Harrison Birtwistle* (London: Robson, 1984), p. 5
4 *The Englishness of English Art*, p. 71
5 Daniel Albright, *Stravinsky: the Music Box and the Nightingale* (New York: Gordon and Breach, 1989), p. 4
6 D. H.Lawrence, *Sons and Lovers* (Harmondsworth: Penguin, 1981; 1st pub. 1913), p. 35
7 *The Englishness of English Art*, p. 179
8 See Birtwistle in conversation with Paul Griffiths, in *New Sounds, New Personalities*, p. 186
9 See Jonathan Cross, *The Stravinsky Legacy* (Cambridge: Cambridge University Press, 1998), pp. 113–18
10 Birtwistle, quoted in Norman Lebrecht, 'Knights at the opera', *Independent Magazine* (18 May 1991), p. 58
11 *New Sounds, New Personalities*, p. 191
12 Ibid.
13 Birtwistle, in conversation with Michael Hall, in *Harrison Birtwistle*, pp. 151–2
14 *New Sounds, New Personalities*, pp. 186–7
15 See 'Manchester years', in Alexander Goehr, *Finding the Key:*

Selected Writings of Alexander Goehr, ed. D. Puffett (London: Faber and Faber, 1998), pp. 27–41

16 *Hymnos*, CC0019 (London: Clarinet Classics, 1998)

17 *Harrison Birtwistle*, pp. 9–11 and *passim*

18 I have written elsewhere of Stravinsky's medievalism, and of the coincidence of many of the aesthetic concerns of the medieval and the modern: see *The Stravinsky Legacy*, pp. 83–4

19 *Finding the Key*, p. 28

20 Ibid., pp. 30, 31

21 *New Sounds, New Personalities*, p. 186

22 *Finding the Key*, p. 31

23 Benjamin Britten, 'Britten Looking Back', *Sunday Telegraph* (17 November 1963), quoted in Humphrey Carpenter, *Benjamin Britten: a Biography* (London: Faber and Faber, 1992), p. 52

24 Birtwistle in conversation with Ross Lorraine, 'Territorial rites 1', *Musical Times*, 138/10 (October 1997), p. 8

25 Stravinsky and Robert Craft, *Dialogues* [and a Diary] (London: Faber Music/Faber and Faber, 1982), p. 24

26 A view expressed in a private conversation with the author, 25 August 1998. In Matisse, he argues, form is used to describe colour; in Picasso and Cézanne, it's the other way round.

27 Birtwistle in a talk to the Friends of English National Opera, Royal Academy of Music, 21 April 1986

28 P. M. Doran, ed., *Conversations avec Cézanne* (Paris: Collection Macula, 1981), p. 109; quoted in Joyce Medina, *Cézanne and Modernism: the Poetics of Painting* (Albany, NY: State University of New York Press, 1995), p. 97

29 Igor Stravinsky, *An Autobiography (1903–1934)* (London: Marion Boyars, 1975), p. 53

30 'Quelques confidences sur la musique', in Eric Walter White, *Stravinsky: the Composer and his Works* (London: Faber and Faber, 2nd edn, 1979), p.585. 'Why not love it [music] for itself? Why not love it as one loves a picture, for its fine colour, its fine drawing, its fine composition? . . . It is sufficient in itself' (my translation)

31 Stravinsky and Craft, *Expositions and Developments* (London: Faber Music/Faber and Faber, 1981), p. 101

32 Quoted in Ulrike Becks-Malorny, *Paul Cézanne 1839–1906: Pioneer of Modernism* (Cologne: Taschen, 1995), p. 74

33 Ibid., p. 73

34 *New Sounds, New Personalities*, p. 191
35 Birtwistle's preface to the score
36 Medina, *Cézanne and Modernism*, p. 101
37 Giulio Carlo Argan, preface to Jürg Spiller, ed., *Paul Klee Notebooks. Vol. 1: The Thinking Eye* (London: Perry Lund, 1961)
38 Klee, 'Creative Credo, in ibid., p. 76. First printed in Kasimir Edschmid, ed., *Tribüne der Kunst und Zeit*, vol. xiii (Berlin: Erich Reiss, 1920)
39 Klee, *Pedagogical Sketchbook*, tr. and intr. Sibyl Moholy-Nagy (London: Faber and Faber, 1953), p. 16
40 *Harrison Birtwistle*, p. 26
41 See *The Music of Edgard Varèse* (New Haven: Yale University Press, 1987), esp. ch. 1
42 For a fuller discussion of these matters, see Jonathan Cross, 'Analytical issues in Birtwistle's *Four Songs of Autumn*', in M. Finnissy and R. Wright, eds, *New Music '89* (Oxford: Oxford University Press, 1989), pp. 16–23
43 Composer's note on the work, reproduced in Hall, *Harrison Birtwistle*, p. 175
44 'Territorial rites 1', p. 4
45 A story narrated by Dava Sobel in *Longitude* (London: Fourth Estate, 1996)
46 Ibid., p. 146
47 See Michael Nyman, 'Two new works by Birtwistle', *Tempo*, 88 (1969), pp. 47–50
48 Birtwistle in interview with David Freeman, in ENO programme book for *The Mask of Orpheus*, ed. Nicholas John (London: ENO, 1986)
49 See Peter Zinovieff, libretto to *The Mask of Orpheus* (London: Universal Edition, 1986)
50 Birtwistle, quoted in Hall, *Harrison Birtwistle*, p. 151
51 Klee, 'Creative Credo, p. 76
52 Sibyl Moholy-Nagy, introduction to the *Pedagogical Sketchbook*, p. 7
53 Norbert Lynton, *Klee* (London: Hamlyn, 2nd edn, 1975), p. 61
54 Birtwistle, quoted by Andrew Clements in his note on the work, in 'Endless Parade' [programme book to accompany the BBC Birtwistle Festival] (London: BBC, 1988), pp. 52–3
55 A review of the work by Peter Heyworth, *Observer* (17 January 1988)
56 Review of Hall, *Harrison Birtwistle*, in *Soundings*, 12 (1985), pp. 75–8

57 Composer's note accompanying the recording of the work (London: Argo, 1967), ZRG 759
58 Ibid.
59 Max Paddison, *Adorno, Modernism and Mass Culture: Essays on Critical Theory and Music* (London: Kahn and Averill, 1996), p. 52
60 Andrew Clements, 'Harrison Birtwistle: a progress report at 50', *Musical Times*, 129/1 (January 1988), p. 139
61 Birtwistle, 'Territorial rites 1', p. 4
62 Birtwistle in conversation with Ross Lorraine, 'Territorial rites 2', *Musical Times*, 138/11 (November 1997), p. 14
63 John Golding, 'Cubism', in *Concepts of Modern Art: from Fauvism to Postmodernism* (London: Thames and Hudson, 3rd edn, 1994), p. 77
64 Glenn Watkins, *Pyramids at the Louvre: Music, Culture, and Collage from Stravinsky to the Postmodernists* (Cambridge, MA: Belknap Press, 1994)
65 Richard Taruskin, *Stravinsky and the Russian Traditions: a Biography of the Works through Mavra* (Oxford: Oxford University Press, 1996), p. 1452
66 For a fuller discussion, see *The Stravinsky Legacy*, esp. pp. 19–23
67 Birtwistle in public conversation with the author, 'Birtwistle's Secret Theatres' Festival, Royal Festival Hall, London (2 May 1996)
68 Edgard Varèse, 'The liberation of sound' [1936], in Elliott Schwarz and Barney Childs, eds, *Contemporary Composers on Contemporary Music* (New York: Holt, Reinhart and Winston, 1967), p. 197
69 Ibid.
70 Golding, 'Cubism', p. 77
71 Michael Tippett, *Those Twentieth Century Blues: an Autobiography* (London: Hutchinson, 1991), p. 226
72 Stephen Walsh, *The Music of Stravinsky* (Oxford: Clarendon Press, 1993), p. 233
73 Pruslin, in his note on the work, in *54th Cheltenham Festival Programme Book* (1998), p. 21
74 For a fuller discussion, see Jonathan Cross, 'Lines and circles: on Birtwistle's *Punch and Judy* and *Secret Theatre*', *Music Analysis*, 13/2–3 (1994), pp. 203–25
75 Goehr, *Finding the Key*, p. 29
76 Ibid., p. 36
77 For a fuller discussion, see Jonathan Cross, 'The challenge of mod-

ern music: Birtwistle's *Refrains and Choruses*', in Anthony Pople, ed., *Theory, Analysis and Meaning in Music* (Cambridge: Cambridge University Press, 1994), pp. 184–94

78 *The Music of Stravinsky*, p. 223

79 See Allen Forte, *The Structure of Atonal Music* (New Haven: Yale University Press, 1973)

80 The published score contains many inaccuracies. According to Hall (*Harrison Birtwistle*, p. 155), Peter Maxwell Davies owns a corrected copy. New solutions to the score's anomalies were found by Stephen Pruslin, in consultation with Birtwistle, in the preparation of his recent recording (CC0019, 1998).

81 In a private conversation with the author, 25 August 1998

82 In conversation with Hall, *Harrison Birtwistle*, p. 147

83 David Beard, 'Birtwistle and serialism: *Three Sonatas for Nine Instruments*', an unpublished paper first given at the Society for Music Analysis 'TAGS' Day, University of Oxford Music Faculty, 21 May 1998

84 *Harrison Birtwistle*, p. 21

85 In a private conversation with the author, 25 August 1998

86 For a fuller account, see Cross, 'Lines and circles'

87 Reproduced in the London Sinfonietta 'Response' Programme Book (1987), p. 19

88 Constant Lambert, *Music Ho! a Study of Music in Decline* (London: Faber, 1934), p. 90

89 Programme note for the première of the complete version of *Harrison's Clocks*, in *54th Cheltenham Festival Programme Book* (1998), p. 88

90 Goehr, *Finding the Key*, p. 35

91 Quoted in Karl H. Wörner, *Stockhausen: Life and Work* , tr., ed. and intr. Bill Hopkins (Berkeley: University of California Press, p/b edn, 1976), p. 61

92 Birtwistle, quoted by Huib Emmer in his liner note for the CD recording (Amsterdam: Etcetera, 1992), KTC 1130

93 Composer's note on the work, in Hall, *Harrison Birtwistle*, p. 173

94 Though one might wish to identify a number of younger British composers whose ambit comes close to that of Birtwistle's: for example, Simon Holt, Colin Matthews, Mark-Anthony Turnage, John Woolrich

95 *The Music of Edgard Varèse*, p. xix

96 The composer in conversation with Stephen Pruslin, Michael Tippett Centre, Bath, 20 January 1999

2 *Episodion I* – Theatres

1 Nicholas Snowman, 'Birtwistle the dramatist: some reflections', in the Royal Opera House programme book for *Gawain* (May 1991)
2 Peter Brook, *The Empty Space* (London: Pelican, 1972; 1st pub. McGibbon and Kee, 1968), p. 44
3 Ibid., p. 40
4 Friedrich Nietzsche, *The Birth of Tragedy*, tr. Walter Kaufmann (New York: Vintage, 1967), p. 58
5 See Glenn Watkins, *Pyramids at the Louvre*, especially 'Masquerades', pp. 277–374; Stephen Walsh, *The Music of Stravinsky*, pp. 67–9; also Walsh, *Stravinsky: Oedipus Rex* (Cambridge: Cambridge University Press, 1993), especially 'Of masks, masses and magic', pp. 11–22
6 Antonin Artaud, *The Theatre and its Double*, tr. Victor Corti (London: Calder, 1993), p. 74
7 Ibid., p. 68
8 Ibid., pp. 44, 42
9 Samuel Beckett, *Waiting for Godot* (London: Faber and Faber, 2nd edn, 1965), p. 41
10 Martin Esslin, *The Theatre of the Absurd* (Harmondsworth: Penguin, 3rd edn, 1980), p. 400
11 Bertolt Brecht, 'About the singing of songs', from 'Notes to *The Threepenny Opera*', tr. and ed. Ralph Manheim and John Willett (London: Methuen, 1979), p. 95
12 Birtwistle, in a talk on *The Mask of Orpheus* to the Friends of English National Opera at the Royal Academy of Music, London, 21 April 1986.
13 Aristotle, 'On the art of poetry', in *Classical Literary Criticism*, tr. T. S. Dorsch (Harmondsworth: Penguin, 1965), p. 39
14 Ibid., p. 40
15 *54th Cheltenham Festival Programme Book* (1998), p. 21
16 Aristotle, 'On the art of poetry', p. 40
17 Ibid., p. 47
18 Quoted in Pruslin's note on the work, *54th Cheltenham Festival Programme*
19 'On the art of poetry', p. 40
20 Ibid., p. 46
21 All quotations taken from Terence Cave, *Recognitions: a Study in Poetics* (Oxford: Clarendon Press, 1988), pp. 1–2

22 Ibid., p. 233
23 For the full text and stage instructions, see Tony Harrison, *Theatre Works 1973–1985* (Harmondsworth: Penguin, 1986)
24 Virgil, *The Georgics*, tr. L. P. Wilkinson (Harmondsworth: Penguin, 1982), p. 141
25 Cave, *Recognitions*, pp. 3, 184; quoting F. L. Lucas, *Tragedy: Serious Drama in Relation to Aristotle's Poetics* (London: Chatto & Windus, rev. 1981; 1st pub. 1928)
26 Cave, *Recognitions*, p. 3
27 Ibid. My emphasis
28 *Harrison Birtwistle*, p. 34
29 *Recognitions*, p. 263
30 Ibid., p. 262
31 Edward T. Cone, 'Stravinsky: the progress of a method', *Perspectives of New Music*, 1/1 (1962), pp. 19–20
32 Pieter C. van den Toorn, *The Music of Igor Stravinsky* (New Haven: Yale University Press, 1983), p. 342
33 Hall, *Harrison Birtwistle*, p. 25
34 A more detailed analytical account – from which the discussion here is derived – is to be found in Cross, 'Birtwistle's Secret Theatres'
35 'Two new works by Birtwistle', p. 50
36 Robert Graves, 'Secret theatre', in *Collected Poems 1975* (London: Cassell, 1975), p. 402
37 Arnold Whittall, 'The geometry of comedy', *Musical Times*, 134/1 (January 1993), p. 17
38 Ibid., p. 19

3 *Episodion II* – Myth and Ritual

1 James Drever, *The Penguin Dictionary of Psychology* (Harmondsworth: Penguin, rev. 1964, p. 180
2 'The structural study of myth', in *Structural Anthropologies*, tr. C. Jacobson (Harmondsworth: Penguin, 1968), pp. 206–31
3 Ibid., p. 217
4 Frieda Fordham, *An Introduction to Jung's Psychology* (Harmondsworth: Penguin, 3rd edn, 1966), p. 26
5 Ibid., p. 23
6 Ibid., p. 26
7 Ibid., pp. 50, 51–2

8 Russell Hoban, *The Moment Under the Moment* (London: Picador, 1993), p. 245
9 Ibid.
10 Ibid., p. ix
11 Birtwistle in public conversation with the author at a pre-performance talk, Glyndebourne, October 1994
12 Friedrich Nietzsche, *The Birth of Tragedy*, tr. W. Kaufmann (New York: Vintage, 1967), p. 35
13 Ibid., p. 36
14 Ibid., p. 37
15 Ibid., p. 107
16 Aristotle, 'On the art of poetry', p. 39
17 *The Birth of Tragedy*, p. 61
18 The source of these lines is the opening of 'A Musical Instrument' by Elizabeth Barrett Browning; Birtwistle, however, seems to have forgotten this, and instead appends the following: 'something I remember from school but can't remember by whom (A. Noyes maybe?!)' The full poem can be found in Francis T. Palgrave's *The Golden Treasury*, originally published in 1861. The third edition has a drawing of Pan on the title page.
19 For a fuller discussion, see David Bruce, 'Challenging the system', *Musical Times*, 137/4 (April 1996), pp. 11–16
20 *The Birth of Tragedy*, p. 60
21 See *Philosophy of Modern Music*, tr. Anne G. Mitchell and Wesley V. Blomster (London: Seabury Press, 1973), and also my discussion of Adorno's arguments in *The Stravinsky Legacy*
22 Dominic Muldowney in conversation with Paul Griffiths, in *New Sounds, New Personalities*, pp. 161–2
23 Note on the work, in *54th Cheltenham Festival Programme Book* (1998), p. 21
24 Lévi-Strauss, *Structural Anthropology*, p. 232
25 Birtwistle's programme note on the work, reproduced in Hall, *Harrison Birtwistle*, pp. 173–4
26 See Jonathan Kramer, 'Discontinuity and proportion in the music of Stravinsky', in Jann Pasler, ed., *Confronting Stravinsky: Man, Musician, and Modernist* (Berkeley: University of California Press, 1986), pp. 174–94
27 Igor Stravinsky, *An Autobiography*, p. 95
28 See Richard Taruskin, *Stravinsky and the Russian Traditions*, pp. 1486–99

29 Stravinsky, *An Autobiography*, p. 128

30 At least, this is true for British audiences, but may actually be an obstacle to a wider reception of the works. Birtwistle's operas, for one reason or another, have not travelled too well. By 1999, only *Punch and Judy* and *The Second Mrs Kong* had had productions outside the United Kingdom.

31 Hall, *Harrison Birtwistle*, p. 57

32 Ibid., p. 147

33 The experimentalism of *Medusa*'s first version extended as far as the construction of a new instrument (built by the composer Hugh Davies) for the ensemble's pianist to play (Stephen Pruslin at the first performance). Tiny objects, each with its own contact microphone, were housed in the cover of a book – the last volume (SHO–ZYG) of an encyclopaedia, hence the name invented for the instrument, shozyg. In the second version, the shozyg was replaced by a synthesizer.

34 D'Arcy Wentworth Thompson, *On Growth and Form* (Cambridge: Cambridge University Press, abridged edn, 1961). First published in 1917.

35 Note on the work, *Cheltenham Festival Programme*, p. 21

36 This discussion is based on the original complete version of the work as presented in the Universal Edition score. At the first performances at English National Opera in 1986, and again for the semi-staged performance at the Royal Festival Hall in 1996 (recorded by the BBC and released by NMC recordings NMC D050, 1997), Acts 1 and 3 were substantially cut. The cuts do not affect the telling of the story but they do, inevitably, affect our understanding of the structure of the whole.

37 Stephen Walsh, *The Music of Stravinsky*, p. 137

4 *Episodion III* – Pastoral

1 See Hall, *Harrison Birtwistle*, p. 69

2 Erwin Panofsky, '*Et in Arcadia Ego*: Poussin and the Elegiac Tradition', in *Meaning and the Visual Arts* (Harmondsworth: Peregrine, 1970), p. 342

3 Ibid.

4 Harrison Birtwistle, text by Michael Nyman, *Down by the Greenwood Side* (London: Universal Edition, 1971)

5 Panofsky, '*Et in Arcadia Ego*', pp. 362, 359

6 Ibid., p. 346
7 William Empson, *Some Versions of Pastoral* (Harmondsworth: Penguin, 1966; 1st pub. 1935), pp. 31, 40–1
8 Ibid., p. 50
9 Ibid., p. 29
10 Geoffrey Chew, 'Pastoral', in Stanley Sadie, ed., *New Grove Dictionary of Opera*, vol. 3 (London: Macmillan, 1992), p. 913
11 'Territorial Rites 1', pp. 4–5
12 Empson, p. 17
13 Ibid., p. 18
14 Ibid., p. 25
15 C. G. Jung, quoted in Frieda Fordham, *An Introduction to Jung's Psychology*, p. 24. The role of archetypes in the collective unconscious is discussed by Jung in 'Instinct and the unconscious'.
16 Virgil, *The Pastoral Poems*, tr. E. V. Rieu (Harmondsworth: Penguin, 1949), pp. 61, 67
17 Empson, p. 39
18 For a fuller discussion, see Jonathan Cross, 'Birtwistle's secret theatres', in C. Ayrey and M. Everist, eds, *Analytical Strategies*, pp. 207–25
19 Preface to the score
20 Birtwistle, 'Territorial Rites 1', p. 8
21 L. P. Wilkinson, in his general introduction to Virgil, *The Georgics*, tr. L. P. Wilkinson (Harmondsworth: Penguin, 1982), p. 40
22 Ibid., p. 41
23 Empson, pp. 40–1
24 Ibid., pp. 31–2
25 Birtwistle in conversation with Paul Griffiths, *New Sounds, New Personalities*, p. 191
26 'Territorial Rites 2', p. 12
27 Geoffrey Chew, 'Pastoral and neoclassicism: a reinterpretation of Auden's and Stravinsky's *Rake's Progress*', *Cambridge Opera Journal*, 5/3 (1993), pp. 261–2. Emphasis added.

5 *Stasimon* – Verses and Refrains

1 Birtwistle in conversation with Paul Griffiths, *New Sounds, New Personalities*, p. 191
2 Aristotle, 'On the art of poetry', p. 47
3 Hall, *Harrison Birtwistle*, p. 150

4 I discuss this in 'Birtwistle's secret theatres', esp. pp. 210–17. See also the discussion in Chapter 2.
5 Birtwistle's note on *Tragoedia*, reproduced in Hall, *Harrison Birtwistle*, p. 174
6 'Territorial rites 1', p. 8
7 Reproduced in Hall, *Harrison Birtwistle*, p. 173
8 Quoted by Huib Emmer in liner note for CD recording of *Refrains and Choruses* (Amsterdam: Etcetera, 1992), KTC 1130
9 'Territorial rites 2', p. 13
10 The title is actually taken from a collection of poems by Robin Blaser that Birtwistle was reading in the early stages of planning *The Last Supper*: 'Exody' (1990–3), to be found in *The Holy Forest* (Toronto: Coach House Press, 1993), pp. 345–71. The perpetual 'beginning again' of so many of Birtwistle's structures has, in a strange way, a parallel in Blaser's curious habit of using only the left-hand (opening) parenthesis without its corresponding right-hand form in the titles (and elsewhere) of many of his works, most notably the ongoing series of 'Image-Nation' poems which are, in his words, 'folded in' to the collection, and which have punctuated his creative output, e.g. 'Image–Nation 1 (the fold'; 'Image–Nation 2 (roaming'. In his note that prefaces *The Holy Forest*, Blaser writes in distinctly Birtwistle-like tones of the arrangement of the poems following 'a principle of *randonnée* – the random and the given of the hunt, the game, the tour'.
11 From the composer's note on *Endless Parade*, reproduced in the programme to accompany a performance of the work by the London Philharmonic Orchestra, QEH, London, 16 January 1995
12 Hall, *Harrison Birtwistle*, p. 46
13 For a discussion of the alternation of 'sustaining' and 'punctuating' roles in Webern's Op. 7, No. 3, see Arnold Whittall's illuminating discussion in 'Webern and atonality: the path from the old aesthetic', *Musical Times*, 124/12 (December 1983), pp. 733–7
14 *Harrison Birtwistle*, p. 35
15 Birtwistle in conversation with Griffiths, *New Sounds, New Personalities*, p. 191
16 Hall, *Harrison Birtwistle*, p. 23
17 From a talk given to the Friends of English National Opera, Royal Academy of Music, London, 21 April 1986
18 Birtwistle in conversation with Hall, *Harrison Birtwistle*, p. 145
19 Ibid., p. 147

20 Ibid., p. 143
21 Ibid., pp. 144, 146
22 Michael Hall, 'The sanctity of the context: Birtwistle's recent music', *Musical Times*, 129/1 (January 1988), pp. 14–16
23 *Harrison Birtwistle*, p. 145
24 On the 'friezes' in *Pulse Shadows*, 'Territorial rites 2', p. 15
25 Quoted in Norman Lebrecht, 'The music of a lone explorer', *Sunday Times Magazine*, 18 May 1986, p. 53
26 Birtwistle in conversation with Hall, *Harrison Birtwistle*, p. 144

6 *Episodion IV* – A Pulse Sampler

1 See 'The phenomenon of music', in Igor Stravinsky, *Poetics of Music in the Form of Six Lessons*, tr. Arthur Knodel and Ingolf Dahl (Cambridge, MA: Harvard University Press, 1942; 5th printing 1979), pp. 21–43. It is important to note that much of the work on this book was undertaken by Stravinsky's close friend, Pierre Souvtchinsky, who had been strongly influenced by Bergson.
2 Birtwistle in conversation with Hall, *Harrison Birtwistle*, p. 144
3 Composer's note, preface to the score
4 Elliott Carter, *The Writings of Elliott Carter*, ed. Else and Kurt Stone (Bloomington: Indiana University Press, 1977), p. 356
5 Composer's note on the work, in Hall, *Harrison Birtwistle*, p. 177
6 Zinovieff's note to accompany the recording, ZRG 790 (London: Argo, 1974). Zinovieff is referring to the collection of timekeepers at the Science Museum in South Kensington, London
7 Ibid.
8 Preface to the score
9 Erwin Panofsky, *The Life and Art of Albrecht Dürer* (Princeton NJ: Princeton University Press, 4th edn 1955), pp. 157, 161. Birtwistle read this book during the composition of *Melencolia I*
10 Hall, *Harrison Birtwistle*, p. 108
11 'Mysterious measures', *Times* (7 May 1996)
12 *Harrison Birtwistle*, pp. 110–12
13 This account of the musical structure relates to the revised 1994 version of *Gawain*. Substantial cuts were made to the original 1991 version for the revival at Covent Garden in 1994, the Seasons Masque being subject to the most extensive excisions and rewriting. Such revisions are highly uncharacteristic of Birtwistle. Works with which he is unhappy are usually simply withdrawn (*3 Sonatas for 9*

Instruments, *Monodrama*, *Medusa*), though his string work written for Paul Sacher, *Still Movement*, and *Slow Frieze*, written for the pianist Joanna MacGregor, are at present (1999) pending revision. The reasons for the revision of *Gawain* were, I suspect, more pragmatic (and most definitely *not* a response to certain critics' views that the Seasons Masque was too long): the work simply needed to be shorter to avoid incurring expensive overtime payments on performance nights for the staff of the Royal Opera House. Birtwistle regards the original and revised versions as having equal status. It should also be noted here that *Gawain's Journey*, the twenty-five-minute orchestral suite drawn from the opera (in which vocal lines are transferred to instruments), was not primarily the work of Birtwistle but of his long-time friend, collaborator and conductor of both versions of *Gawain*, Elgar Howarth.

7 *Episodion V* – 'On Stasis in Progress': Line, Melody, Tonality

1 Rhian Samuel, 'Birtwistle's *Gawain*: an essay and a diary', *Cambridge Opera Journal*, 4/2 (1992), p. 163. Birtwistle's declaration is discussed on p. 167 of Samuel's article.

2 Ibid., p. 173

3 Raymond Williams, *Keywords: a Vocabulary of Culture and Society* (London: Fontana, 1976), p. 205

4 Birtwistle's note on *The Triumph of Time*, reproduced in Hall, *Harrison Birtwistle*, p. 175

5 Arnold Whittall, 'Modernist aesthetics, modernist music: some analytical perspectives', in *Music Theory in Concept and Practice*, ed. James M. Baker, David W. Beach and Jonathan W. Bernard (Rochester NY: University of Rochester Press, 1997), pp. 176, 175

6 Paul Griffiths, *Modern Music and After: Directions Since 1945* (Oxford: Clarendon Press, 1995), p. 219

7 Günter Grass, *From the Diary of a Snail*, tr. Ralph Manheim (London: Minerva, 1997; first published in German in 1972), pp. 310, 298

8 Ibid., p. 294

9 See Samuel, 'Birtwistle's *Gawain*', p. 167

10 Quoted in Paul Griffiths, 'Three virtuoso trumpet concertos', liner note to accompany the work's CD recording (Philips Classics, 1991), 432 075-2

11 Birtwistle in conversation with Paul Griffiths, in *New Sounds, New Personalities*, p. 188
12 *Harrison Birtwistle*, p. 84
13 See Margaret A. Sullivan, *Bruegel's Peasants* (Cambridge: Cambridge University Press, 1994), p. 133
14 Notes made by Birtwistle prior to composing *Secret Theatre*, London Sinfonietta 'Response' Programme Book (1987), p. 19
15 *Harrison Birtwistle*, p. 84
16 'Birtwistle's *Gawain*', p. 167
17 In conversation with the author, in 'The Idea of Kong', first broadcast on BBC Radio 3, 24 June 1995
18 'Birtwistle's *Gawain*', p. 166
19 Stephen Walsh, *The Music of Stravinsky*, pp. 140–1
20 Birtwistle discussing *Exody* on *Proms News*, first broadcast on BBC Radio 3, 30 August 1998
21 In 'The Idea of Kong'
22 A claim he reiterated in his Colston Lecture at the Department of Music, University of Bristol, 3 November 1998
23 Stephen Walsh, *The Music of Stravinsky*, p. 141, quoting Igor Stravinsky and Robert Craft, *Conversations with Igor Stravinsky* (London: Faber and Faber, 1959), p. 17
24 Igor Stravinsky, *Poetics of Music in the Form of Six Lessons*, p. 36
25 Birtwistle in conversation with Griffiths, *New Sounds, New Personalities*, p. 188
26 Arnold Whittall, 'Comparatively complex: Birtwistle, Maxwell Davies and modernist analysis', *Music Analysis*, 13/2–3 (1994), pp. 152, 151
27 He claims that the first film he saw, probably during the War, at the Accrington Hippodrome, was Eisenstein's *Alexander Nevsky*. The film's violent images left a strong impression, such that when he saw it again much later in life he found he could remember the entire film. (Birtwistle in private conversation with the author, 25 August 1998.)
28 Edward T. Cone, 'Stravinsky: the progress of a method', pp. 18–26
29 See Hall, *Harrison Birtwistle*, p. 145
30 Samuel, 'Birtwistle's *Gawain*', p. 173
31 Cone, 'Stravinsky: the progress of a method', p. 20
32 In a non-broadcast part of the interview with the author for 'The Idea of Kong'
33 Paul Klee, *Pedagogical Sketchbook*, p. 33

34 For further details, see Zinovieff's libretto (p. 34, *et passim*) as presented for the recording of *The Mask of Orpheus* (London: NMC, 1997), NMC D050
35 In 'The Idea of Kong'
36 Arnold Whittall discusses 'Urlar' in relation to issues in *Melencolia I* in 'Modernist aesthetics, modernist music'
37 Samuel, 'Birtwistle's *Gawain*', p. 167
38 See Richard Taruskin, *Stravinsky and the Russian Traditions*, p. 1489
39 Ibid., p. 1487
40 *Harrison Birtwistle*, p. 20

8 *Exodos* – Futures

1 Virgil, *The Georgics*, p. 140
2 I visited the composer at his home in Mere, Wiltshire, on 13 March 1999, in order to discuss the opera. I am very grateful to him for allowing me access to his work in progress.
3 Birtwistle quoted in Michael Hall, *Harrison Birtwistle in Recent Years* (London: Robson, 1998)
4 Ibid., pp. 152–3
5 Ibid., p. 153
6 *Tempo*, 207 (December 1998), music supplement, pp. 4–5
7 Birtwistle in conversation with Stephen Pruslin, Michael Tippett Centre, Bath, 20 January 1999

Chronological Catologue of Works

Unless otherwise stated, all works from Refrains and Choruses *to* The Second Mrs Kong *are published by Universal Edition (London) Ltd, with the exception of* An Interrupted Endless Melody, *which is published by Boosey and Hawkes Music Publishers Ltd; all works since* The Cry of Anubis *are published by Boosey and Hawkes Music Publishers Ltd.*

c.1950

Oockooing Bird, for solo piano; unpublished; copy of score in possession of Stephen Pruslin. The score is prefaced with the words:

Once I saw an Oockooing bird
so white
o God so white

1957

Refrains and Choruses, for flute, oboe, clarinet, horn and bassoon; Portia Wind Ensemble, Cheltenham, 11 July 1959

1958

Three Sonatas for Nine Instruments; withdrawn after first rehearsal; score unpublished, now housed in Paul Sacher Stiftung, Basel

1959

Monody for Corpus Christi, for soprano, flute, horn and violin (texts: Old English carol, 'The faucon hath borne my make away'; James, John and Robert Wedderburn (sixteenth century), 'O my deare hert, young Jesu sweit'); New Music Ensemble, John Carewe (cond), London, 5 April 1960

1960

Précis, for solo piano; John Ogdon, Dartington, August 1960

1961

The World is Discovered (six instrumental movements after Heinrich Isaak), for 12 players (1960–1); Portia Wind Ensemble, London, 6 March 1961

1962

Entr'actes, for flute, viola and harp; members of Bournemouth Symphony Orchestra, Wardour Castle, Autumn 1962. Later incorporated as the first part of *Entr'actes and Sappho Fragments* (see below) and now unavailable separately

1963

Chorales for Orchestra (1960–3); New Philharmonia Orchestra, Edward Downes (cond), London, 14 February 1967
Narration: A Description of the Passing of a Year, for chorus (text: anon., *Sir Gawain and the Green Knight*, translated by Brian Stone); John Alldis Choir, John Alldis (cond), London, 14 February 1964
Music for Sleep, for children's voices, piano and percussion; pupils of Knighton House and Port Regis Schools, composer (cond), Bryanston, winter 1963; published by *Musical Times* and *Music in Education* (March 1964)

1964

Three Movements with Fanfares, for chamber orchestra; English Chamber Orchestra, John Pritchard (cond), London, 8 July 1964
Entr'actes and Sappho Fragments, for soprano, flute, oboe, violin, viola, harp and percussion (text: Sappho, taken from *The Greek Anthology, with an English Translation*); Virtuoso Ensemble of London, Mary Thomas (sop), John Carewe (cond), Cheltenham, 11 July 1964

1965

Ring a Dumb Carillon, a 'dramatic scena' for soprano, clarinet and percussion (text: Christopher Logue, 'On a matter of prophecy', from *Wand and Quadrant*) (1964–5); Noelle Barker (sop), Alan Hacker (cl), Christopher Seaman (perc), London, 19 March 1965

Carmen Paschale, motet for chorus (SATB) and organ (text: Sedulus Scottus) (1964–5); Purcell Singers, Imogen Holst (cond), Aldeburgh, 17 June 1965

Tragoedia, for wind quintet (doubling claves), string quartet and harp; Melos Ensemble, Lawrence Foster (cond), Wardour Castle, 20 August 1965

Verses, for clarinet and piano; Alan Hacker (cl) and Stephen Pruslin (pno), London, October 1965

1966

The Mark of the Goat, a 'dramatic cantata' in 4 scenes for actors, singers, two choruses, three melody instruments, three players at one piano, and large and small percussion ensembles (text by Alan Crang); first broadcast BBC Schools Programmes, Spring 1966

The Visions of Francesco Petrarca, an 'allegory' for baritone, mime ensemble, chamber ensemble and school orchestra (text: seven sonnets by Petrarch, translated by Edmund Spenser) (1965–6); Robin Black (cond), York, 15 June 1966; withdrawn

1967

Punch and Judy, a 'tragical comedy or comical tragedy' in one act (libretto by Stephen Pruslin) (1966–7); English Opera Group, David Atherton (cond), Aldeburgh, 8 June 1968

Chorale from a Toy-Shop, for 5 players (various possible realizations); commissioned by and first published in *Tempo*, No. 81 (1967) in honour of Stravinsky's 85th birthday

Monodrama, for soprano, speaker, flute, clarinet, violin, cello and 2 percussion (text by Stephen Pruslin); Pierrot Players, Mary Thomas (sop), composer (cond), London, 30 May 1967; withdrawn

Three Lessons in a Frame, for solo piano, flute, clarinet, violin, cello and percussion; Pierrot Players, Stephen Pruslin (pno), Peter Maxwell Davies (cond), Cheltenham, 17 July 1967; withdrawn

1968

Nomos, for 4 amplified wind instruments and orchestra (1967–8); BBC Symphony Orchestra, Colin Davis (cond), London, 23 August 1968

Linoi, for (1) clarinet and piano; Alan Hacker (cl) and Stephen Pruslin (pno), London, 11 October 1968; (2) clarinet, piano, tape (realized by Peter Zinovieff) and dancer; London, 22 April 1969; (3) clarinet, piano and cello

Four Interludes for a Tragedy, for basset clarinet and tape (realized by Peter Zinovieff); first performance without tape, Alan Hacker, London, 18 October 1968; with tape, London, 10 February 1969

1969

Verses for Ensembles, for 5 woodwind, 5 brass and 3 percussion (1968–9); London Sinfonietta, David Atherton (cond), London, 12 February 1969

Some Petals from my Twickenham Herbarium, for piccolo, clarinet, viola, cello, piano and bells; Pierrot Players, composer (cond), London, 22 April 1969

Down by The Greenwood Side, a 'dramatic pastoral' in one act (text by Michael Nyman, after English Mummers' Play and the 'Ballad of the Cruel Mother') (1968–9); Music Theatre Ensemble, David Atherton (cond), Brighton, 8 May 1969

Cantata, for soprano, flute, clarinet, violin, cello, piano/celesta and glockenspiel/bongo (text: tombstone inscriptions, Sappho and *The Greek Anthology*); Pierrot Players, Mary Thomas (sop), composer (cond), London, 12 June 1969

Ut Heremita Solus (after Ockeghem), for flute, clarinet, violin, cello, piano, glockenspiel; Pierrot Players, composer (cond), London, 12 June 1969

Hoquetus David (after Machaut), for flute, clarinet, violin, cello, glockenspiel, bells; Pierrot Players, composer (cond), Sheffield, 22 October 1969

Medusa, for flute/picc, clarinet/sax, violin/viola, cello, piano/celesta, percussion, 2 tapes and 'shozyg'; Pierrot Players, composer (cond),

Sheffield, 22 October, 1969; withdrawn. A second extended version was first performed in London, 3 March 1970

Eight Lessons for Keyboards; Stephen Pruslin (pno/cel), London, 13 January 1970; unpublished

1970

Signals, for clarinet and tape; Alan Hacker (cl), Edinburgh, 25 August 1970; unpublished

Dinah and Nick's Love Song, for 3 melody instruments and harp; first public performance, Matrix, Sheffield, 26 October 1972

Nenia: the Death of Orpheus, a 'dramatic scene' for soprano, 3 bass clarinets/clarinet, piano/prepared piano and crotales (text by Peter Zinovieff); Matrix, Jane Manning (sop), London, 20 November 1970

1971

Meridian, for mezzo-soprano, 6 soprano voices, horn, cello and 11 players (text: Christopher Logue, 'The image of love', from *Wand and Quadrant*; Thomas Wyatt, 'Blame not my lute' and 'My lute awake') (1970–1); London Sinfonietta, London Sinfonietta Chorus, David Atherton (cond), London, 26 February 1971

Prologue, for tenor, bassoon, horn, 2 trumpets, trombone, violin and double bass (text: Aeschylus, Watchman's speech from *Agamemnon*, translated by Philip Vellacott); London Sinfonietta, Philip Langridge (ten), composer (cond), London, 18 April 1971

An Imaginary Landscape, for brass, 8 double basses and percussion; BBC Symphony Orchestra, Pierre Boulez (cond), London, 2 June 1971

The Fields of Sorrow, for 2 sopranos, chorus (SATB) and 16 players (text: Decimus Ausonius) (rev. 1972); Dartington, 7 August 1971

Tombeau in memoriam Igor Stravinsky, for flute, clarinet, harp and string quartet; London Sinfonietta, Elgar Howarth (cond), London, 17 June 1972

1972

Chronometer, for 2 x 4-track tape (realized by Peter Zinovieff) (1971–2); London, 24 April 1972

The Triumph of Time, for orchestra (1971–2); Royal Philharmonic

Orchestra, Lawrence Foster (cond), London, 1 June 1972
Epilogue, for baritone, horn, 4 trombones, 6 tam-tams (text: Shakespeare, 'Full fathom five', from *The Tempest*); London Sinfonietta, Michael Rippon (bar), composer (cond), Southwark, 23 April 1972
La Plage: Eight Arias of Remembrance, for soprano, 3 clarinets, piano and marimba (text after Alain Robbe-Grillet, *La Plage*); Matrix, Jane Manning (sop), Sheffield, 26 October 1972

1973

Grimethorpe Aria, for brass band; Grimethorpe Colliery Band, composer (cond), Harrogate, 15 August 1973
Chanson de geste, for amplified sustaining instruments and tape (Peter Zinovieff); Fernando Grillo (double bass), Perugia, July 1973; withdrawn

1975

Five Chorale Preludes (after J. S. Bach), for soprano, clarinet, basset horn and bass clarinet; Matrix, Jane Manning (sop), London, 15 September 1975

1976

Melencolia I, for solo clarinet, harp and 2 string orchestras; Scottish National Orchestra, Alan Hacker (cl), Alexander Gibson (cond), Glasgow, 18 September 1976
For O, for O, the Hobby-Horse is Forgot, for 6 percussionists; Les Percussions de Strasbourg, Tokyo, 10 February 1978

1977

Silbury Air, for 15 players; London Sinfonietta, Elgar Howarth (cond), London, 9 March 1977
Pulse Field (Frames, Pulses and Interruptions), ballet for 6 dancers and 9 players; Ballet Rambert, Snape, 25 June 1977
Bow Down, music theatre for 5 actors and 4 musicians (text by Tony Harrison, after versions of the 'Ballad of the Two Sisters'); members of the National Theatre, London, 5 July 1977

Carmen Arcadiae Mechanicae Perpetuum, for 14 players; London Sinfonietta, composer (cond), London, 24 January 1978

1979

... *agm* ... for 16 voices (SATB) and 3 instrumental ensembles (text: Sappho, Fayum fragments) (1978–9); Ensemble InterContemporain, John Alldis Choir, Pierre Boulez (cond), Paris, 9 April 1979
Choral Fragments from ... agm ... for 16 voices; John Alldis Choir, John Alldis (cond), London, 4 April 1979; withdrawn

1980

Mercure – Poses Plastiques (after Satie's ballet), for 14 players; London Sinfonietta, Elgar Howarth (cond), London, 4 April 1980
On the Sheer Threshold of the Night, for soprano, counter-tenor, tenor, bass and chorus of 12 voices (SATB) (text: Boethius, 'Stupet tergeminus novo', from *De Consolatione Philosophiae*); John Alldis Choir, John Alldis (cond), Hessischer Rundfunk, Frankfurt, May 1980
Clarinet Quintet, for clarinet and string quartet; The Music Party, Alan Hacker (cl), Huddersfield, 21 November 1981

1981

Pulse Sampler, for oboe and claves; Melinda Maxwell (ob), John Harrod (claves), Huddersfield, 20 November 1981

1983

The Mask of Orpheus, a 'lyrical tragedy' in 3 acts (libretto by Peter Zinovieff) (1973–5, 1981–3); English National Opera, London, 21 May 1986
Duets for Storab, for 2 flutes; Endymion Ensemble, London, 25 March 1984

1. 'Urlar'
2. 'Stark pastoral'
3. 'Fanfare with birds'
4. 'White pastoral'
5. 'From the church of lies'
6. 'Crumluath'

Deowa, for soprano and clarinet (text based on the phonemes of the title); Jane Manning (sop), Alan Hacker (cl), London, 29 March 1983

1984

Yan Tan Tethera, a 'mechanical pastoral' in one act (libretto by Tony Harrison) (1983–4); Opera Factory/London Sinfonietta, Elgar Howarth (cond), London, 7 August 1986
Still Movement, for 13 solo strings; Polish Chamber Orchestra, Jerzy Maksymiuk (cond), London, 20 July 1984
Secret Theatre, for 14 players; London Sinfonietta, David Atherton (cond), London, 18 October 1984
Songs by Myself, for soprano, flute/alto flute, piano, vibraphone, violin, viola, cello and double bass (texts by the composer); London Sinfonietta, Penelope Walmsley-Clarke (sop), composer (cond), London, 18 October, 1984
Berceuse de Jeanne, for piano
Words Overheard, for soprano, flute, oboe, bassoon and strings (text by the composer); Scottish Chamber Orchestrea, Penelope Walmsley-Clarke (sop), composer (cond), Glasgow, 17 November 1985

1986

Earth Dances, for orchestra (1985–6); BBC Symphony Orchestra, Peter Eötvös (cond), London, 14 March 1986

1987

Hector's Dawn, for piano
Endless Parade, for solo trumpet, vibraphone and string orchestra (1986–7); Collegium Musicum, Håkan Hardenberger (tpt), Zurich, 1 May 1987
Fanfare for Will, for brass ensemble; BBC Philharmonic Orchestra, composer (cond), London, 10 July 1987
Les Hoquets du Gardien de la Lune (after Machaut's *Hoquetus David*), for orchestra; English Northern Philharmonia, Elgar Howarth (cond), London, 6 September 1987; unpublished

1988

Four Songs of Autumn, for soprano and string quartet (text: Bunya Yasuhide, 'The grasses and trees'; anonymous poems from Japanese Kokinshu, translated by Geoffrey Bownas and Anthony Thwaite) (1987–8); London Sinfonietta, Sarah Leonard (sop), London, 24 January 1988
An die Musik, for soprano and 10 players (text: Rainer Maria Rilke); London Sinfonietta, Elizabeth Laurence (sop), composer (cond), London, 4 May 1988
Machaut à ma Manière (after Machaut, *O livoris feritas*, *Hoquetus David*, and an 'Amen' from the *Messe de Notre Dame*), for orchestra; Hamburg Philharmonic Orchestra, Gerd Albrecht (cond), Hamburg, 10 March 1990

1989

Salford Toccata, for brass band; Salford College Brass Band, Elgar Howarth (cond), Salford, 12 April 1989
The Wine Merchant Robin of Mere, for male voice and piano (text by the composer); Geoffrey Dolton (bar), John Leneham (pno), BBC Radio 3, 26 December 1989; published in *Yapp '89* (Yapp Brothers, Mere, Wiltshire)

1990

Ritual Fragment, for 14 players; London Sinfonietta, London, 6 May 1990

1991

Gawain, an opera in 2 acts (libretto by David Harsent, after anon., *Sir Gawain and the Green Knight*) (1989–91, rev. 1994); Royal Opera House, Covent Garden, Elgar Howarth (cond), London, 30 May 1991
Four Poems by Jaan Kaplinski, for soprano and 13 players (text: Jaan Kaplinski, translated from the Estonian by Sam Hamill and Jaan Kaplinski); London Sinfonietta, Sarah Leonard (sop), composer (cond), Snape, 19 June 1991
Gawain's Journey, for orchestra (arranged from *Gawain* by Elgar Howarth); English Northern Philharmonia, Elgar Howarth (cond), Vienna, 21 October 1991

An Interrupted Endless Melody, for oboe and piano; Nicholas Daniel (ob), Julius Drake (pno), London, 7 November 1991

1992

Antiphonies, for solo piano and orchestra; Philharmonia Orchestra, Joanna MacGregor (pno), Pierre Boulez (cond), Paris, 5 May 1993
Five Distances for Five Instruments, for flute, oboe, clarinet, horn, bassoon; Ensemble InterContemporain, London, 7 May 1993

1994

The Second Mrs Kong, an opera in 2 acts (libretto by Russell Hoban) (1993–4); Glyndebourne Touring Opera, Elgar Howarth (cond), Glyndebourne, 24 October 1994
Fanfare for Glyndebourne, for brass ensemble and timpani; London Philharmonic Orchestra, Andrew Davis (cond), Glyndebourne, 28 May 1994; unpublished
The Cry of Anubis, for solo tuba and orchestra; London Philharmonic Orchestra, Owen Slade (tuba), Elgar Howarth (cond), London, 16 January 1995

1995

Hoquetus Petrus, for 2 flutes/picc and piccolo trumpet; members of Chicago Symphony Orchestra, Chicago, 30 March 1995
Panic, for alto saxophone solo, drummer and orchestra of woodwind, brass and percussion; BBC Symphony Orchestra, John Harle (sax), Paul Clarvis (drums), Andrew Davis (cond), London, 16 September 1995
Slow Frieze, for solo piano and 13 players; London Sinfonietta, Joanna MacGregor (pno), Markus Stenz (cond), London, 26 April 1996

1996

9 Settings of Celan, for soprano, 2 clarinets, viola, cello, double bass (text: Paul Celan, translated by Michael Hamburger; English and German versions) (1989–96); first complete performance, Witten, 28 April 1996 (as part of *Pulse Shadows*)

Thread suns (1995); Klangforum Wien, Witten, 28 April 1996
White and Light (1989); Composers Ensemble, Brighton, 13 May 1989
Psalm (1996); Klangforum Wien, Witten, 28 April 1996
With Letter and Clock (1994); Composers Ensemble, London, 21 November 1994
An Eye, open (1996); Ensemble InterContemporain, Basel, 27 April 1996
Todtnauberg (1995); BBC Radio 3, 10 December 1995
Tenebrae (1992); Composers Ensemble, London, 18 September 1992
Night (1992); Composers Ensemble, London, 18 September 1992
Give the Word (1996); Klangforum Wien, Witten, 28 April 1996

9 Movements for String Quartet (4 Friezes and 5 Fantasias) (1991–6); first complete performance, Witten, 28 April 1996 (as part of *Pulse Shadows*)
Freize 1 (1991); Arditti String Quartet, Vienna, 18 November 1991
Fantasias 2 and 4 (1993); Arditti String Quartet, Antwerp, 8 November 1993
Fantasias 1, 3 and *5*; *Friezes 2–4* (1995–6); Arditti String Quartet, Witten, 28 April 1996

Pulse Shadows (interleaving of *9 Settings of Celan* and *9 Movements for String Quartet*); first complete performance, Witten, 28 April 1996

Bach Measures (after J. S. Bach: *Orgelbüchlein*), for 15 players; London Sinfonietta, Diego Masson (cond),London, 4 May 1996

1997

Exody '23:59:59', for orchestra (1996–7); Chicago Symphony Orchestra, Daniel Barenboim (cond), Chicago, 5 February 1998

1998

Harrison's Clocks, for solo piano (1997–8); first performance (4 movements only), Joanna MacGregor, Manchester, 19 April 1998; first complete performance, Joanna MacGregor, Cheltenham, 13 July 1998

Three Niedecker Verses, for soprano and cello (text: Lorine Niedecker, 'My Friend Tree'); commissioned by and first published in *Tempo*, No. 207 (1998) in honour of Elliott Carter's 90th birthday

The Woman and the Hare, for soprano, narrator and ensemble (text: David

Harsent); Nash Ensemble, composer (cond), London, 9 March 1999
The Silk House Tattoo, for 2 trumpets and percussion; Lake Placid, 19 May 1999
Placid Mobile, for 36 muted trumpets; London, 26 March 1999

1999

Love Cries (arranged from *The Second Mrs Kong* by Michael Berkeley) (1998–9); BBC Symphony Orchestra, Martyn Brabbins (cond), London, 29 April 1999
The Last Supper (libretto by Robin Blaser) (1998–9); Staatsoper, Berlin, 18 April 2000

National Theatre Productions

Hamlet (1975)
Tamburlaine (1976)
Volpone (1977)
Oresteia (1981)
The Trojan War Will Not Take Place (1983)
Coriolanus (1984)
Cymbeline (1988)
The Tempest (1988)
A Winter's Tale (1988)

(with Dominic Muldowney:)
Julius Caesar (1977)
Herod (1978)
The Cherry Orchard (1978)
As You Like It (1979)

Film Score

The Offence (1973), dir. Sidney Lumet

Discography

Many of the recordings listed below have been deleted. A listing here does not necessarily imply that the recording is currently available.

. . . agm . . .
Erato STU 71543 (LP) (1984); John Alldis Choir, Ensemble InterContemporain, Pierre Boulez (cond)

Antiphonies
Collins Classics 14142 (CD) (1994); Joanna MacGregor (pno), Radio Filharmonisch Orkest, Michael Gielen (cond)

Carmen Arcadiae Mechanicae Perpetuum
Etcetera KTC 1052 (CD) (1987); London Sinfonietta, Elgar Howarth (cond)

Chronometer
Argo ZRG 790 (LP) (1975); tape (realized by Peter Zinovieff)

Clarinet Quintet
Clarinet Classics CC019 (CD) (1998); Roger Heaton (cl), Kreutzer String Quartet

Earth Dances
Collins Classics 20012 (CD) (1991); BBC Symphony Orchestra, Peter Eötvös (cond)
Argo 452 104-2 (CD) (1996); Cleveland Orchestra, Christoph von Dohnányi (cond)

Endless Parade
Philips 432 075-2 (CD) (1991); Håkan Hardenberger (tpt), Paul Patrick (vib), BBC Philharmonic Orchestra, Elgar Howarth (cond)

The Fields of Sorrow
Decca HEAD 7 (LP) (1974); Jane Manning (sop), London Sinfonietta, David Atherton (cond)

Five Distances for Five Instruments
Deutsche Grammophon 439 910-2 (CD) (1995); Ensemble InterContemporain

For O, for O, the Hobby-Horse is Forgot
Etcetera KTC 1130 (CD) (1992); Percussion Group, The Hague

Four Interludes for a Tragedy
L'Oiseau-Lyre DSLO 17 (LP) (1977); Alan Hacker (cl), tape (realized by Peter Zinovieff)

Gawain (1994 revised version)
Collins Classics 70412 (CD) (1996); Royal Opera Chorus, Orchestra of the Royal Opera House, soloists, Elgar Howarth (cond)

Gawain's Journey
Collins Classics 13872 (CD) (1993); Philharmonia Orchestra, Elgar Howarth (cond)

Grimethorpe Aria
Decca HEAD 14 (LP) (1976); Grimethorpe Colliery Band, Besses o' th' Barn Band, Elgar Howarth (cond)

An Imaginary Landscape
Collins Classics 14142 (CD) (1994); BBC Symphony Orchestra, Paul Daniel (cond)

Linoi
Clarinet Classics CC019 (CD) (1998); Roger Heaton (cl), Stephen Pruslin (pno)

The Mask of Orpheus
NMC D050 (CD) (1997); BBC Symphony Orchestra, BBC Singers, soloists, Andrew Davis and Martyn Brabbins (conds)

Melencolia I
NMC D009 (CD) (1993); Anthony Pay (cl), Helen Tunstall (hp), London Sinfonietta, Oliver Knussen (cond)

Meridian
NMC D009 (CD) (1993); Mary King (sop), Michael Thompson (hn), Christopher van Kampen (vc), London Sinfonietta, London Sinfonietta Voices, Oliver Knussen (cond)

Nenia: the Death of Orpheus
Decca HEAD 7 (LP) (1974); Jane Manning (sop), The Matrix, Alan Hacker (cond)
cpo 999 360-2 (CD) (1995); Rosemary Hardy (sop), Musikfabrik NRW, Johannes Kalitzke (cond)

Nomos
Collins Classics 14142 (CD) (1994); BBC Symphony Orchestra, Paul Daniel (cond)

Oockooing Bird
Clarinet Classics CC019 (CD) (1998); Stephen Pruslin (pno)

Panic
Argo 452 104-2 (CD) (1996); John Harle (sax), Paul Clarvis (drum kit), BBC Symphony Orchestra, Andrew Davis (cond)

Précis
HMV ALP 2098/ASD 645 (LP) (1965); John Ogdon (pno)
Clarinet Classics CC019 (CD) (1998); Stephen Pruslin (pno)

Pulse Sampler
NMC D045 (CD) (1996); Melinda Maxwell (ob), Richard Benjafield (claves)

Punch and Judy
Decca HEAD 24/25 (LP) (1980); London Sinfonietta, soloists, David Atherton (cond); reissued on **Etcetera KTC 2014** (CD)

Refrains and Choruses
Philips SAL 3669 (LP) (1966); Danzi Wind Quintet
Etcetera KTC 1130 (CD) (1992); Netherlands Wind Ensemble

Ring a Dumb Carillon
Mainstream MS 5001 (LP); Mary Thomas (sop), Alan Hacker (cl), Barry Quinn (perc)

Ritual Fragment
NMC D009 (CD) (1993); London Sinfonietta
cpo 999 360-2 (CD) (1995); Musikfabrik NRW

Secret Theatre
Etcetera KTC 1052 (CD) (1987); London Sinfonietta, Elgar Howarth (cond)
Deutsche Grammophon 439 910-2 (CD) (1995); Ensemble InterContemporain, Pierre Boulez (cond)
cpo 999 360-2 (CD) (1995); Musikfabrik NRW, Johannes Kalitzke (cond)

Silbury Air
Etcetera KTC 1052 (CD) (1987); London Sinfonietta, Elgar Howarth (cond)

Three Settings of Celan ('White and Light', 'Night', 'Tenebrae')
Deutsche Grammophon 439 910-2 (CD) (1995); Christine Whittlesey (sop), Ensemble InterContemporain, Pierre Boulez (cond)
see also 'White and Light'

Tragoedia
HMV ASD 2333 (LP); Melos Ensemble, Lawrence Foster (cond); reissued on **Argo ZRG 759** (LP)
Deutsche Grammophon 439 910-2 (CD) (1995); Ensemble InterContemporain, Pierre Boulez (cond)

The Triumph of Time
Argo ZRG 790 (LP) (1975); BBC Symphony Orchestra, Pierre Boulez (cond)
Collins Classics 13872 (CD) (1993); Philharmonia Orchestra, Elgar Howarth (cond)

Verses
Clarinet Classics CC019 (CD) (1998); Roger Heaton (cl), Stephen Pruslin (pno)

Verses for Ensembles
Decca HEAD 7 (LP) (1974); London Sinfonietta, David Atherton (cond)
Etcetera KTC 1130 (CD) (1992); Netherlands Wind Ensemble, Percussion Group, The Hague, James Wood (cond)

'White and Light'
NMC D003 (CD) (1992); Mary Wiegold (sop), Composers Ensemble, Dominic Muldowney (cond)
see also Three Settings of Celan

Bibliography

Principal Writings on Birtwistle

Adlington, Robert, '*Antiphonies*', *Music Review*, 53/1 (1992), pp. 71–3

– 'Harrison Birtwistle's recent music', *Tempo*, 196 (April 1996), pp. 2–8

– *The Music of Harrison Birtwistle* (Cambridge: Cambridge University Press, 2000)

Birtwistle, Harrison, in conversation with Ross Lorraine, 'Territorial rites 1', *Musical Times*, 138/10 (October 1997), pp. 4–8

– in conversation with Ross Lorraine, 'Territorial rites 2', *Musical Times*, 138/11 (November 1997), pp. 12–16

Bowen, Meirion, 'Harrison Birtwistle', in *British Music Now*, ed. Lewis Foreman (London: Elik, 1975), pp. 60–70

Bruce, David, 'Challenging the system', *Musical Times*, 137/4 (April 1996), pp. 11–16

Chanan, Michael, 'Birtwistle's *Down by the Greenwood Side*', *Tempo*, 89 (1969), pp. 19–21

Clements, Andrew, 'Harrison Birtwistle: a progress report at 50', *Musical Times*, 125/3 (March 1984), pp. 136–9

– '*The Mask of Orpheus*', *Opera*, 37/7 (July 1986), pp. 851–7

– '*Yan Tan Tethera*', *Opera*, 37/10 (October 1986), pp. 1199–1202

Cross, Jonathan, 'Analytical issues in Birtwistle's *Four Songs of Autumn*', in M. Finnissy and R. Wright, eds, *New Music '89* (Oxford: Oxford University Press, 1989), pp. 16–23

– 'Lines and circles: on Birtwistle's *Punch and Judy* and *Secret Theatre*', *Music Analysis*, 13/2–3 (1994), pp. 203–25

– 'The challenge of modern music: Birtwistle's *Refrains and Choruses*', in A. Pople, ed., *Theory, Analysis and Meaning in Music* (Cambridge: Cambridge University Press, 1994), pp. 184–94

– 'The action never stops, it only changes' [on *The Second Mrs Kong*], *Musical Times*, 135/11 (November 1994), pp. 698–703

– 'Birtwistle's secret theatres', in C. Ayrey and M. Everist, eds, *Analytical Strategies and Musical Interpretation* (Cambridge: Cambridge University Press, 1996), pp. 207–25

Crosse, Gordon, 'Birtwistle's "Punch and Judy"', *Tempo*, 85 (1968), pp. 24–6

Ford, Andrew, 'The reticence of intuition – Sir Harrison Birtwistle', in *Composer to Composer: Conversations about Contemporary Music* (London: Quartet Books, 1993), pp. 52–9

Griffiths, Paul, 'Harrison Birtwistle', in *New Sounds, New Personalities: British Composers of the 1980s* (London: Faber Music/Faber and Faber, 1985), pp. 186–94

Hall, Michael, 'Birtwistle in good measure', *Contact*, 26 (1983), pp. 34–6

– *Harrison Birtwistle* (London: Robson, 1984)

– 'The sanctity of the context: Birtwistle's recent music', *Musical Times*, 129/1 (January 1988), pp. 14–16

– 'Birtwistle's "Pulse Shadows"', *Tempo*, 204 (1998), pp. 12–13

– *Harrison Birtwistle in Recent Years* (London: Robson, 1998)

Howarth, Elgar, '*The Mask of Orpheus*', *Opera*, 37/5 (May 1986), pp. 492–5

Moore, Gillian, *Harrison Birtwistle* (London: Channel 4 Television, 1987)

Morgan, Tom, 'Birtwistle's *The Mask of Orpheus*', in M. Finnissy and R. Wright, eds, *New Music '87* (Oxford: Oxford University Press, 1987), pp. 76–8

Nyman, Michael, 'Two new works by Birtwistle', *Tempo*, 88 (1969), pp. 47–50

Samuel, Rhian, 'Birtwistle's *Gawain*: an essay and a diary', *Cambridge Opera Journal*, 4/2 (1992), pp. 163–78

– 'Time remembered: Birtwistle's "The Second Mrs Kong"', *Opera*, 45/10 (1994), pp. 1153–8

Samuels, Robert, '*The Mask of Orpheus*', *Tempo*, 158 (September 1986), pp. 41–4

Taylor, Michael, 'Birtwistle's first *The Triumph of Time*', *Mitteilung der Paul Sacher Stiftung*, 8 (March 1995), pp. 17–21

– 'Harrison Birtwistle: *Endless Parade*', in F. Meyer, ed., *Settling New Scores: Music Manuscripts from the Paul Sacher Foundation* (Mainz: Schott, 1998), pp. 41–3

Warnaby, John, 'Secret Theatre', *Tempo*, 152 (March 1985), pp. 25–7

– 'The theatre of nature: Birtwistle's "Earth Dances"', *Tempo*, 157 (June 1986), pp. 43–4

– 'Having his way with Machaut: Harrison Birtwistle's "Machaut à Ma Manière"', *Tempo*, 173 (June 1990), pp. 68–70

Whittall, Arnold, 'The geometry of comedy', *Musical Times*, 134/1 (January 1993), pp. 17–19

– 'Comparatively complex: Birtwistle, Maxwell Davies and modernist analysis', *Music Analysis*, 13/2–3 (1994), pp. 139–59
– 'Modernist aesthetics, modernist music: some analytical perspectives', in James M. Baker, David W. Beach and Jonathan W. Bernard, eds, *Music Theory in Concept and Practice* (Rochester, NY: University of Rochester Press, 1997), pp. 157–80
– 'The mechanisms of lament: Harrison Birtwistle's "Pulse Shadows"', *Music and Letters*, 80/1 (1999), pp. 86–102
Wintle, Christopher, 'A fine and private place', *Musical Times*, 137/11 (November 1996), pp. 5–8
Wright, David: 'Clicks, clocks and claques' [Birtwistle at 60], *Musical Times*, 135/7 (July 1994), pp. 426–31

Other Writings

Adorno, Theodor, *Philosophy of Modern Music*, tr. Anne G. Mitchell and Wesley V. Blomster (London: Seabury Press, 1973)
Albright, Daniel, *Stravinsky: the Music Box and the Nightingale* (New York: Gordon and Breach, 1989)
Aristotle, 'On the Art of Poetry', in *Classical Literary Criticism*, tr. T. S. Dorsch (Harmondsworth: Penguin, 1965)
Artaud, Antonin, *The Theatre and its Double*, tr. V. Corti (London: Calder, 1993)
Beckett, Samuel, *Waiting for Godot* (London: Faber and Faber, 2nd edn, 1965)
Becks-Malorny, Ulrike, *Paul Cézanne 1839–1906: Pioneer of Modernism* (Cologne: Taschen, 1995)
Bernard, Jonathan, *The Music of Edgard Varèse* (New Haven: Yale University Press, 1987)
Blaser, Robin, *The Holy Forest* (Toronto: Coach House Press, 1993)
Brecht, Bertolt, *The Threepenny Opera*, tr. and ed. R. Manheim and J. Willett (London: Methuen, 1979)
Brook, Peter, *The Empty Space* (London: Pelican, 1972; 1st pub. McGibbon and Kee, 1968)
Carpenter, Humphrey, *Benjamin Britten: a Biography* (London: Faber and Faber, 1992)
Carter, Elliott, *The Writings of Elliott Carter*, ed. Else and Kurt Stone (Bloomington: Indiana University Press, 1977)
Cave, Terence, *Recognitions: a Study in Poetics* (Oxford: Clarendon Press, 1988)

Chew, Geoffrey, 'Pastoral', in S. Sadie, ed., *New Grove Dictionary of Opera*, Vol. 3 (London: Macmillan, 1992)

– 'Pastoral and neoclassicism: a reinterpretation of Auden's and Stravinsky's *Rake's Progress*', *Cambridge Opera Journal*, 5/3 (1993), pp. 239–63

Cone, Edward T., 'Stravinsky: the progress of a method', *Perspectives of New Music*, 1/1 (1962), pp. 18–26

Cross, Jonathan, *The Stravinsky Legacy* (Cambridge: Cambridge University Press, 1998)

Drever, James, *The Penguin Dictionary of Psychology* (Harmondsworth: Penguin, rev. 1964)

Empson, William, *Some Versions of Pastoral* (Harmondsworth: Penguin, 1966; 1st pub. 1935)

Esslin, Martin, *The Theatre of the Absurd* (Harmondsworth: Penguin, 3rd edn, 1980)

Fordham, Frieda, *An Introduction to Jung's Psychology* (Harmondsworth: Penguin, 3rd edn, 1966)

Forte, Allen, *The Structure of Atonal Music* (New Haven: Yale University Press, 1973)

Goehr, Alexander, *Finding the Key: Selected Writings of Alexander Goehr*, ed. D. Puffett (London: Faber and Faber, 1998)

Golding, John, 'Cubism', in *Concepts of Modern Art: from Fauvism to Postmodernism* (London: Thames and Hudson, 3rd edn, 1994)

Grass, Günter, *From the Diary of a Snail*, tr. Ralph Manheim (London: Minerva, 1997; 1st pub. in German, 1972)

Graves, Robert, *Collected Poems 1975* (London: Cassell, 1975)

Griffiths, Paul, *New Sounds, New Personalities: British Composers of the 1980s* (London: Faber Music/Faber and Faber, 1985)

– *Modern Music and After: Directions Since 1945* (Oxford: Clarendon Press, 1995)

Harrison, Tony, *Theatre Works 1973–1985* (Harmondsworth: Penguin, 1986)

Hoban, Russell, *The Medusa Frequency* (London: Picador, 1988; 1st pub. 1987)

– *The Moment Under the Moment* (London: Picador, 1993)

Klee, Paul, *Pedagogical Sketchbook*, tr. and intr. Sibyl Moholy-Nagy (London: Faber and Faber, 1953)

Kramer, Jonathan, 'Discontinuity and proportion in the music of Stravinsky', in Jann Pasler, ed., *Confronting Stravinsky: Man, Musician, and Modernist* (Berkeley: University of California Press, 1986), pp. 174–94

Lambert, Constant, *Music Ho! a Study of Music in Decline* (London: Faber, 1934)

Lawrence, D. H., *Sons and Lovers* (Harmondsworth: Penguin, 1981; 1st pub. 1913)

Lévi-Strauss, Claude, *Structural Anthropology*, tr. C. Jacobson (Harmondsworth: Penguin, 1968)

Lynton, Norbert, *Klee* (London: Hamlyn, 2nd edn, 1975)

Medina, Joyce, *Cézanne and Modernism: the Poetics of Painting* (Albany, NY: State University of New York Press, 1995)

Nietzsche, Friedrich, *The Birth of Tragedy*, tr. W. Kaufmann (New York: Vintage, 1967)

Paddison, Max, *Adorno, Modernism and Mass Culture: Essays on Critical Theory and Music* (London: Kahn and Averill, 1996)

Panofsky, Erwin, *The Life and Art of Albrecht Dürer* (Princeton, NJ: Princeton University Press, 4th edn, 1955)

– '*Et in Arcadia Ego*: Poussin and the Elegiac Tradition', in *Meaning in the Visual Arts* (Harmondsworth: Peregrine, 1970)

Pevsner, Niklaus, *The Englishness of English Art* (Harmondsworth: Penguin/Peregrine, 1964; 1st pub. 1956)

Schwarz, Elliott and Childs, Barney, eds., *Contemporary Composers on Contemporary Music* (New York: Holt, Reinhart and Winston, 1967)

Sobel, Dava, *Longitude* (London: Fourth Estate, 1996)

Spiller, Jürg, ed., *Paul Klee Notebooks. Vol. 1: The Thinking Eye*, tr. R. Manheim (London: Perry Lund, 1961)

Stravinsky, Igor, *Poetics of Music in the Form of Six Lessons*, tr. Arthur Knodel and Ingolf Dahl (Cambridge, MA: Harvard University Press, 1942; 5th printing 1979)

– *An Autobiography (1903–1934)* (London: Marion Boyars, 1975)

Stravinsky, Igor and Craft, Robert, *Conversations with Igor Stravinsky* (London: Faber and Faber, 1959)

– *Dialogues* (London: Faber Music/Faber and Faber, 1982)

– *Expositions and Developments* (London: Faber Music/Faber and Faber, 1981)

Sullivan, Margaret A., *Bruegel's Peasants* (Cambridge: Cambridge University Press, 1994)

Taruskin, Richard, *Stravinsky and the Russian Traditions: a Biography of the Works Through Mavra* (Oxford: Oxford University Press, 1996)

Thompson, D'Arcy Wentworth, *On Growth and Form* (Cambridge:

Cambridge University Press, abridged edn, 1961; 1st pub. 1917)

Tippett, Michael, *Those Twentieth Century Blues: An Autobiography* (London: Hutchinson, 1991)

van den Toorn, Pieter C., *The Music of Igor Stravinsky* (New Haven: Yale University Press, 1983)

Virgil, *The Pastoral Poems*, tr. E. V. Rieu (Harmondsworth: Penguin, 1949)

– *The Georgics*, tr. L. P. Wilkinson (Harmondsworth: Penguin, 1982)

Walsh, Stephen, *The Music of Stravinsky* (Oxford: Clarendon Press, 1993)

– *Stravinsky: Oedipus Rex* (Cambridge: Cambridge University Press, 1993)

Watkins, Glenn, *Pyramids at the Louvre: Music, Culture, and Collage from Stravinsky to the Postmodernists* (Cambridge, MA: Belknap Press, 1994)

White, Eric Walter, *Stravinsky: the Composer and his Works* (London: Faber and Faber, 2nd edn, 1979)

Whittall, Arnold, 'Webern and atonality: the path from the old aesthetic', *Musical Times*, 124/12 (December 1983), pp. 733–7

Williams, Raymond, *Keywords: a Vocabulary of Culture and Society* (London: Fontana, 1976)

Wörner, Karl H., *Stockhausen: Life and Work* , tr., ed. and intr. Bill Hopkins (Berkeley: University of California Press, pb edn, 1976)

Index

Numbers in italics indicate musical examples; those in bold are Figures.